Praise

www.Aspatore.com

Aspatore Books, a Thomson business, is the largest and most exclusive publisher of C-Level executives (CEO, CFO, CTO, CMO, partner) from the world's most respected companies and law firms. Aspatore annually publishes a select group of C-Level executives from the Global 1,000, top 250 law firms (partners and chairs), and other leading companies of all sizes. C-Level Business Intelligence™, as conceptualized and developed by Aspatore Books, provides professionals of all levels with proven business intelligence from industry insiders—direct and unfiltered insight from those who know it best— as opposed to third-party accounts offered by unknown authors and analysts. Aspatore Books is committed to publishing an innovative line of business and legal books, those which lay forth principles and offer insights that, when employed, can have a direct financial impact on the reader's business objectives, whatever they may be. In essence, Aspatore publishes critical tools—need-to-read as opposed to nice-to-read books—for all business professionals.

Inside the Minds

The critically acclaimed *Inside the Minds* series provides readers of all levels with proven business intelligence from C-Level executives (CEO, CFO, CTO, CMO, partner) from the world's most respected companies. Each chapter is comparable to a white paper or essay and is a future-oriented look at where an industry/profession/topic is heading and the most important issues for future success. Each author has been carefully chosen through an exhaustive selection process by the *Inside the Minds* editorial board to write a chapter for this book. *Inside the Minds* was conceived in order to give readers actual insights into the leading minds of business executives worldwide. Because so few books or other publications are actually written by executives in industry, *Inside the Minds* presents an unprecedented look at various industries and professions never before available.

INSIDE THE MINDS

Environmental Law Deal Strategies

*Leading Lawyers on Identifying Environmental
Liabilities, Structuring Transactions, and
Developing a Negotiation Strategy*

Mat # 40705186

ISBN 978-1-59622-868-9
Library of Congress Control Number: 2007942411

For corrections, updates, comments, or any other inquiries, please e-mail aspatoreeditorial@thomson.com.

First Printing, 2007
10 9 8 7 6 5 4 3 2 1

Environmental Law Deal Strategies

Leading Lawyers on Identifying Environmental Liabilities, Structuring Transactions, and Developing a Negotiation Strategy

CONTENTS

Establishing and Achieving Client Goals

Sharon R. Newlon

Member

Dickinson Wright PLLC

As a lawyer, the first task is to ask about and understand your clients' business and personal goals. As an environmental lawyer, you must understand and explain to your clients how their projects interface with environmental media (i.e., water, land, air) and the laws and liabilities surrounding those media. Then you work together to address the environmental issues in a manner designed to comply with applicable laws while maximizing achievement of your clients' goals.

A good portion of any environmental lawyer's work is that of an interpreter. A technical degree can be a real plus in this aspect of the work. We gather, analyze, and explain information from and to a number of participants in any deal—client environmental and management representatives, environmental consultants, environmental regulators, business attorneys, lenders and investors, and other interested parties. In addition to the overriding importance of listening to clients throughout any deal, we also focus on making sure our clients will be satisfied with the deal not only at the time of closing, but in the years following as the long-term impacts of the transaction become more evident.

Environmental Issues

Environmental lawyers are involved with a variety of issues including short- and long-term liabilities associated with the acquisition and divestiture of property and businesses; environmental compliance, both in terms of proactive environmental management (e.g., obtaining permits) and reactive environmental management (e.g., responding to claims); and working with other environmental professionals when needed on a project.

Many people divide environmental law into transactional, litigation, and compliance work. Transactional environmental law encompasses the identification and negotiation of environmental liabilities associated with acquisitions and divestitures, as well as the management of issues related to development, such as wetlands permitting and brownfield funding. Counseling on the environmental risks associated with lending, foreclosure, bankruptcy, and estate planning would also be considered transactional environmental work. Environmental litigation work includes individual damage claims, class action work, commercial litigation among companies, government claims, and claims brought in administrative law courts.

Environmental litigation can range from claims between neighbors relating to water rights to multi-party neighborhood class action cases relating to the contamination of drinking water or the deposition of lead from a former smelter's smoke stack. Environmental compliance work can include responding to governmental claims associated with permits and business operations, environmental auditing and management, general environmental permitting, and remediation work. These areas overlap and intersect with each other, and with other legal areas such as employee training and Occupational Safety and Health Administration compliance.

Others divide environmental law into different regulatory programs and environmental media. This may be particularly true for those whose practice is primarily in environmental compliance and administrative law. Environmental compliance law is largely based on highly technical environmental programs and regulations. Some areas, such as air permitting, are sufficiently complex that an environmental attorney may specialize primarily in that area. Some environmental attorneys who work in the western states, where water is scarcer, may have practices that focus exclusively on water contamination and water rights issues. Some attorneys specialize in Superfund cleanup work, while others specialize in Superfund litigation. Other, narrower specialty areas in environmental law may include crisis management, homeland security, natural resource damages, and environmental insurance.

Financial Implications

Many of the financial implications of environmental law are associated with avoiding environmental costs. In some instances, environmental law implications can be positive to a client's bottom line. In the context of environmental deals, the environmental lawyer's ability to identify and quantify environmental risks can help clients decide if a proposed purchase price is fair. The environmental lawyer can suggest and prepare documents that allocate these risks and set aside funding to address them. For instance, when one client was selling a former industrial property for redevelopment as housing, we obtained an agreement from the buyer not only to indemnify the seller for environmental liabilities, but also to clean the property to residential standards and refrain from selling the property until the cleanup was complete. Not only was the liability for existing conditions shifted, but also the agreement ultimately provided for that liability to be extinguished, through the requirement of active remediation. (A redacted version of that agreement language is attached as Appendix A.) A proper allocation of risk in a transaction can provide significant financial benefits to the client.

By appropriately identifying the client's potential liabilities, a lawyer can advise a client on the effect of various allocations of risk. The identification of the liabilities requires not only an understanding of the environmental conditions at the property, but also the environmental laws of the jurisdiction. For example, in states where cleanup liability is based on ownership of property (status-based liability), a new owner's agreement to indemnify the prior owner for cleanup costs may be less significant financially, because the new owner would be assuming that liability in any event through operation of law. In a state where liability is causation-based, a new owner who indemnifies a prior owner is potentially taking on new liabilities it would not otherwise have.

The financial implications of environmental impacts in a transaction can also be controlled or limited by establishing an appropriate cleanup standard at the time of the transaction. If a property has been and will continue to be used for industrial purposes, a seller that agrees to maintain some environmental liability can limit that liability to the level of cleanup necessary for industrial properties. Steps can also be taken in the context of a transaction to limit potential future exposures to impacted media, thus reducing future cleanup costs. For example, if groundwater on-site is impacted above drinking water standards but below other potentially applicable cleanup standards, the parties can agree to impose a deed restriction on the property that prohibits the use of groundwater for drinking water purposes.[1] The anticipated costs of addressing environmental risks can also be controlled to some extent by attaching time limits to any environmental obligations, such as an indemnity only for historic conditions identified within one year of the closing. In addition to limiting the environmental risk, this type of provision may make it easier to identify which party is at fault.

---

[1] Note that while some states recognize the enforceability of environmental deed restrictions whenever they are imposed, other states have held that they may not be enforceable unless they are recorded in the context of a transfer of the property.

The presence of environmental impacts can actually make properties more attractive and financially viable than undeveloped properties if the impacted properties qualify for brownfield funding incentives. Brownfield funding can provide technical assistance and loan and grant money from government entities to defray many costs associated with redevelopment, such as environmental assessment, demolition, and cleanup work. In many states, brownfield development can also lead to long-term tax exemptions and credits. Brownfield development also provides financial benefits to the participating governments by redeveloping properties that might otherwise be abandoned, creating jobs and generating new and increased property and income taxes. Brownfield redevelopment also makes use of existing infrastructure and benefits the environment by limiting the potential expansion of industrial impacts to greenfield properties.

In the general area of environmental compliance, legal assistance in identifying those factors in a client's operation that trigger regulation and the potential benefits of modifying or limiting those factors can also benefit a client financially. Examples include advising a client to move its outside storage inside to eliminate the need for an industrial storm water permit, the costs associated with it, and the regulatory flag it may create. Another example, often cited, is to suggest that a client may avoid certain reporting and spill planning requirements by reducing on-site chemical inventory to levels below the thresholds of certain environmental regulatory programs.

In certain instances, an environmental lawyer can help a client identify ways to market products or services, a direct financial benefit to the client. We were able to do this in a matter involving the regulation of zinc hydroxide waste as a hazardous waste in Michigan. Our client recycled this material and depended on feedstock from its suppliers, who generated the waste from their manufacturing processes. During a response to a notice of violation, we informed the client that the characterization of this material as waste depended on the end product the client incorporated it into after recycling. The client had been incorporating it into a fertilizer, which the state considered to be land application, so the state regulated the raw material as hazardous waste. However, the client could also incorporate it into an animal feed product, which would not be considered land application and therefore the raw material would not be considered hazardous waste. The client realized this could relieve the suppliers from ever having to treat the material as hazardous waste, eliminating special storage, inspection, training, and disposal requirements. By obtaining a letter from the state confirming this interpretation, we were able to put the client in a position to market the reduced regulation of the waste zinc hydroxide to its suppliers, to build its feedstock. Significant financial savings and benefits accrued.

Common Mistakes

Record Keeping

Although this chapter focuses primarily on transactional environmental law, no list of common mistakes in environmental law would be complete without a reference to the most common mistake, record keeping. Record keeping is both the easiest way for clients to run into difficulty and the quickest violations for an agency to identify. These violations may take the form of missing inspection or monitoring reports, incomplete documentation of employee training, and inaccurate documentation of repairs made to pollution control equipment. Companies may be liable not only for failing to properly implement environmental requirements, but also for failing to properly oversee the work of others hired to do so. In recent cases, the Environmental Protection Agency has sought penalties from companies that have failed to properly oversee contractors hired to perform independent monitoring work. A good environmental management system that incorporates a regular review of record keeping requirements can greatly assist a company in avoiding these most common mistakes.

Waiting to Conduct Environmental Due Diligence

Often, companies involved in real estate and corporate transactions leave the environmental issues to the end of the transaction, because the parties want to confirm that the deal is likely to go through before they spend the money and resources necessary to conduct environmental due diligence. Proper environmental due diligence takes time, and the older and more industrialized the property or company being acquired, the more detailed and time-consuming the due diligence. Phase I environmental assessments can generally take anywhere from one week to one month to complete. Phase II assessments often require at least three weeks to perform and may take significantly longer. In a merger, the surviving company generally assumes all of the historic liabilities of the acquired company, including liabilities associated with former company holdings and historic off-site disposal. In such cases, due diligence should include a review of all formerly owned and leased properties and a review of known locations for off-site disposal. Parties that do not leave sufficient time for an appropriate level of due diligence may push themselves into a poor negotiating position where risk allocation is based more on guesswork than on useful information. Additionally, certain incentive programs, such as brownfield development incentives, may require prior approvals and significant lead time. Clients who do not adequately plan may lose their eligibility for these valuable development incentives.

Assuming Environmental Law Is Universal

Another common mistake that can have severe consequences is assuming environmental laws are generally the same from state to state. Clients operating from a different state often make this erroneous assumption. For example, some states require that any known impacts above state standards be reported by the property owner, while other states do not. In one matter, we found that our client's property was included on a state list of sites impacted with hazardous materials and we submitted a Freedom of Information Act request to identify the basis for the listing. The basis turned out to be documents submitted by the client under the mistaken belief that any evidence of a release to the environment had to be disclosed. In fact, similar to the federal release reporting requirements under the Comprehensive Environmental Response, Compensation, and Liability Act of 1980, the state only required twenty-four-hour releases of a set amount of hazardous substances to be reported. Unfortunately, there was no way to take back the information, and the property would remain listed until it was cleaned up to the state's satisfaction. Without the listing, the property would still have been impacted, but an independent cleanup could have satisfied new owners and their lenders. Most historic releases do not require reporting.

Some states have due diligence requirements that can provide liability exemptions. However, if the statutory time limits are not met, the exemptions may be lost (and the time limits vary from before the closing date to within a certain time afterward). Other states have private party disclosure requirements that, if not followed, can lead to a loss of liability exemption. Clients should involve local environmental professionals to avoid these pitfalls if possible.

Ignoring Environmental Compliance Issues

Other mistakes in acquisitions include focusing only on the environmental condition of property while ignoring the current compliance and environmental issues when deciding how to structure the acquisition and determining what environmental risks are posed by the transaction. In the acquisition of an ongoing operation, environmental compliance issues may present more immediate risk of liability than property condition issues. For example, if a company lacks the necessary permits or is chronically out of compliance with its existing permits, a significant enforcement action may be just around the corner. In addition to significant penalties, enforcement actions can curtail or shut down processes and may require significant capital expenditures in new equipment to meet the permit limits. Lawyers can also advise clients to be on the lookout for regulatory red flags that may indicate increased agency interest in a property, including regulation under programs that involve frequent inspections. With respect to the structure of an acquisition, in an asset purchase, historic environmental liabilities can often be severed from the new owner. In contrast, with a merger, the surviving company generally assumes all of the historic liabilities of the acquired company. Potential environmental liabilities do not often drive the structure of an acquisition, but they should be considered if the transaction is otherwise flexible.

Looking Only to the Present

Finally, clients sometimes focus only on the environmental issues as they appear at the time of the transaction, rather than also looking to future implications. For example, the immediate goal may be to sell a property for as much money as possible, but that may have long-term implications if an indemnity has to be given as an incentive. On the other hand, if the immediate goal is to buy a property as cheaply as possible, not only in terms of the price but also in terms of the transactional costs, that may lead to increased environmental risks and costs in the future. In a lending transaction, the immediate goal may be to obtain a new customer for the bank, and the value of the real property may be just part of the collateral. With lender and prospective purchaser liability exemptions, the lender might feel protected against future cleanup liabilities and may feel more comfortable putting off its complete due diligence unless and until foreclosure becomes necessary. However, before making the loan, the lender needs to consider whether the property will be marketable to others if the borrower is unable to pay back the loan.

In states where due diligence can provide a liability exemption, a purchaser may ignore the fact that environmental conditions may make the property more difficult to sell in the future. This liability may be especially true under the recent federal bona fide prospective purchaser exemption. While the new owner may be exempt from cleanup liability per se, the owner may also be responsible for due care obligations such as preventing unreasonable exposures to people and the environment, preventing exacerbation of existing conditions, and performing some source control. Because no regulations have yet been promulgated to better explain these responsibilities, the practical implications of these due care requirements is yet unknown. This issue highlights another reason why sellers and purchasers need to look to the future in allocating environmental risks—environmental laws are constantly changing.

Looking to the Future

The future implications of current environmental conditions come in many forms. In addition to due care responsibilities (discussed above), parties must consider how future environmental duties will be implemented. For example, a seller that retains environmental cleanup obligations will also want to retain some access rights to perform them. The purchaser will want some assurances that those access rights will not affect its ongoing use of the property. The seller will want to limit its obligations to the current use and configuration of the property and take full advantage of any deed restrictions that could reduce cleanup costs. The buyer will want to maintain the greatest amount of flexibility in future property use and limit any obligations to maintain long-term use restrictions. In a recent matter, we represented the seller of a property that included foundations for several former buildings. The seller retained some liability for known environmental conditions, so we added language to limit the cleanup obligation to not only the current industrial use, but also to the current configuration of the property. Although the purchaser intended to use the property as a parking lot, it argued against that limitation, wanting the seller to be responsible if the purchaser removed foundations and discovered impacts underneath. The seller held fast, in part because a cleanup order the seller was operating under had identified the foundation of one building as part of the remedy.

Purchasers will also want to consider future development plans. As in the example, some underground environmental impacts may not be an issue for the current use of a property. However, future development, particularly actions that may require excavation into contaminated media, may create additional issues ranging from employee exposure to specialized soil disposal to the risk of exacerbating existing site impacts. When a purchaser intends to modify the property use, particularly if the modification will require invasive work, environmental lawyers generally recommend that the proposed expansion area be included in any Phase II sampling performed as part of the purchaser's due diligence.

Beyond environmental contamination concerns, purchasers must also be aware of any anticipated development that might involve interface with sensitive environmental areas or receptors, such as wetlands, flood plains, or endangered species. Lawyers must identify these issues early, as they may significantly affect the development value of a property.

Adding Value

Environmental lawyers add value for their clients in a variety of ways and in numerous situations. To help clients avoid last-minute environmental issues, most lawyers maintain working relationships with real estate and corporate attorneys so they can serve as part of the initial deal team. Environmental lawyers assist clients in reviewing their business goals for the transaction, including immediate and future plans for a property, to help identify the appropriate level of due diligence for the transaction. They advise them of any applicable regulatory due diligence requirements and discuss regulatory and business-driven deadlines for completing that work. They then assist clients in identifying, hiring, and directing the work of environmental professionals with experience in the geographic area and uses of the property. If a compliance audit is appropriate, environmental lawyers arrange for that work as well.

Whether representing sellers, purchasers, or lenders, environmental lawyers explore the client's future plans and obligations with respect to a property and advise them accordingly. When seller clients choose to maintain environmental liabilities, lawyers define their obligations as narrowly as possible, provide for access, and maintain their rights to impose reasonable restrictions on property use to facilitate cleanup. For purchasers, lawyers define sellers' obligations broadly, maintain as much flexibility in the future use of the property as possible, and assist the purchaser in identifying future plans for the property that may intersect with cleanup work or sensitive environmental receptors. Although these activities may be in the future, anticipating them will provide a sounder basis for allocating environmental risks in the transaction. In general, environmental lawyers help their clients focus on issues (not just risks, but implementation) beyond the closing. This approach is beneficial for both the client's interests and our continuing relationship.

Defining Success

Success is primarily dependent upon developing and maintaining a good understanding of a client's personal and business goals, for both the short and long term. To develop that understanding, regular communication, especially listening, is critical. When an attorney and client have a mutual understanding of the client's goals, it is easier for the attorney to analyze and present environmental data and risks in a manner that puts them in the context of those goals.

Staying on Top

To keep on top of the constantly changing environmental laws and regulations, most environmental lawyers review daily environmental updates on relevant case law, legislation, and regulatory issues from a number of published sources, both state-specific and federal. Most also participate actively in the appropriate state bar's environmental law section, both as a speaker and audience member. For instance, this past year I served on a work group convened by the state's environmental law agency to review the existing state environmental cleanup law and propose recommendations for its improvement.

I have also participated in peer review of proposed regulations and in update programs for client and trade groups. I have found that preparing client and trade group updates is an excellent way to digest new environmental developments.

I have also developed an excellent network of contacts throughout the environmental arena, consisting of other environmental attorneys, environmental consultants, government personnel, and, of course, client contacts. The communications back and forth along that network are some of the most beneficial to all aspects of my professional development. Participation in state and federal bar activities is an excellent way to develop and cultivate relationships with other environmental attorneys. Working together on programs and other projects can enhance an attorney's reputation for quality work that can lead to referrals and other professional opportunities. While incoming referrals are always welcome, the ability to refer a client to competent counsel in another jurisdiction is always appreciated. Most environmental consultants are happy to develop relationships with attorneys, as they see them as potential clients. The most successful of these relationships occur where the referrals are mutual. Consultants can be an excellent source for education on technical issues, and we have often paired up to present the legal and technical sides of new environmental issues to our combined client bases. Having a broad range of consultant contacts can help an environmental attorney identify the one most likely to help the client achieve its goals. Government contacts may seem more difficult when they arise primarily during adversarial proceedings. However, honesty and fair dealing will earn respect even in an adversarial setting, and opportunities exist for non-adversarial communications in the context of peer review, work groups, and bar activities.

Working with Clients

The first step to working with a client is always speaking with client representatives to identify the personal and business goals. By understanding the client's goals, an environmental lawyer can better analyze and present environmental information in light of those goals. Without that understanding, it would be difficult to assess the client's immediate and long-term needs, risk position, and negotiation flexibility.

Initially, environmental work on transactional matters is often assigned by real estate or corporate attorneys. To begin, I ask clients about some of the basic deal information, such as the structure of the transaction, negotiating position, and the risk aversion of the client. In a lending transaction, I also ask about the role of property as collateral in a transaction. In both cases, I ask about the anticipated timing of the transaction and the factors driving the timing. It is also important to determine whether the client anticipates any brownfield or other incentive funding for the transaction, as these may require significant lead time.

In a non-transactional matter, such as a response to a notice of violation from a government agency, I ask client representatives directly about the operations involved in the violation, how they are prepared to address the violation, and what result they hope to achieve. Often, client representatives hope to address the violation without penalty, and this is a worthy goal. However, sometimes the goal is also to develop internal support for an environmental management system.

Federal Laws

In transactional matters, state and federal cleanup laws and regulations are generally the primary laws that govern what due diligence is performed and how environmental risks are allocated. At the federal level, those laws often would include the Comprehensive Environmental Response, Compensation, and Liability Act of 1980 (CERCLA) and the Resource Conservation and Recovery Act of 1976 (RCRA). If the transaction is a merger or an assert purchase where existing operations will continue, other environmental permitting and compliance laws may also play a role. Also, if the transaction involves brownfield redevelopment, state and federal brownfield incentive legislation applies.

Under the CERCLA, a new owner or operator may qualify for one of three defenses: the innocent purchaser defense, the bona fide prospective purchaser defense, or the contiguous property owner defense. Each of these defenses requires a new owner or operator to complete pre-closing due diligence, which consists of making "all appropriate inquiries" into the past use of the subject property and adjacent properties to determine whether it is likely that a release of hazardous substances has occurred on or about the property. The due diligence also assists the new owner or operator in identifying the due care obligations that may be applicable under the CERCLA. If the acquisition is a merger or involves affiliated parties, the new owner or operator may not qualify for any of the CERCLA defenses, but the due diligence may still be critical in the risk identification and allocation process.

If the property is an RCRA current or former permitted or interim status hazardous waste treatment, storage, and disposal facility, the CERCLA defenses may not apply. In that case, the environmental cleanup or corrective action liability attaches to the property, and a new owner or operator is liable for performing the corrective action. (If a former owner signed an RCRA corrective action consent order with the U.S. Environmental Protection Agency or a state, the former owner may continue to be liable for that work, but the liability may be joint.) Underground petroleum storage tanks are also regulated at the federal level under the RCRA (Subtitle D). The liabilities for tanks will depend on their status at the time of the transaction (i.e., in use, closed, removed).

Brownfield legislation affects the availability of federal, state, and local funding to provide incentives for redevelopment of impacted properties. The brownfield laws establish incentives available to governments and developers for certain qualified activities and investments. Other potentially relevant environmental laws include those associated with environmental compliance obligations and those associated with the interface of land and water resources, such as wetlands and floodplain laws.

State Laws

The effect of state hazardous waste and underground storage tank laws would be similar to the effect of the RCRA, as states generally operate their programs under the delegated authority of the RCRA. General state cleanup programs, however, may differ substantially from the CERCLA. Some states, similar to the CERCLA, offer exemptions from liability if certain pre-purchase due diligence is conducted. Some state programs are causation-based, where only the party that caused an impact is responsible for its cleanup. Some states only use a status-based liability program. Others offer combinations of these liability schemes. Michigan, for example, has a mixed liability program. Historic property owners and new owners or operators who have prepared and submitted to the state a baseline environmental assessment enjoy a causation-based liability scheme. New owners or operators who fail to timely prepare and submit the baseline assessment report (and are not otherwise exempt) are strictly liable for all existing site conditions.

States with Liability Exemptions Based on Due Diligence

In states where due diligence is necessary to qualify for exemptions from cleanup liability, that due diligence may require Phase II environmental sampling. A purchaser could expect to perform invasive due diligence whenever it is likely that a release of hazardous substances may have occurred. The purchaser will want to obtain access for sampling in the initial agreement between the parties. These liability exemptions are generally an advantage to both the seller and purchaser in the transaction. In these states, the seller may refuse to provide any environmental indemnity on the basis that the purchaser is adequately protected by the state's liability exemptions. In some cases, when representing a seller, we have drafted language requiring the purchaser to qualify for the statutory exemption, to limit the possibility that the state would pursue the new owner and the new owner would pursue the seller. If the purchaser did not obtain the statutory exemption, it was required to indemnify the purchaser. (See Appendix B.)

States with Causation-Based Liability

In states where liability is causation-based, the level of due diligence depends on the risk allocation between the parties and the proposed future use of the property. If the purchaser is not taking on any seller liability and is not intending to use any materials similar to those that have affected the property in the past, it may be less critical to perform Phase II sampling. (However, it may still be useful, as the information developed may affect the price and resale potential of the property.) If the purchaser is planning to conduct similar operations, establishing baseline conditions may be critical to both parties. The due diligence can help distinguish existing impacts from future operations, and it can assist both parties in determining whether to enter into a contractual arrangement that allocates liabilities in a different way than the statute would.

States with causation-based environmental programs can present more simplified negotiations, as a party may assume only the liability imposed by the statute. However, in practice, especially where similar operations have been conducted at a property by a succession of different owners, causation-based liability schemes may present significant problems of proof in a lawsuit. Therefore, baseline due diligence can be critical. The contract language may reflect the causation scheme of the statute.

States with Strict Liability

In other states, liability may be strict, status-based liability without any exemptions available to new owners and operators. Environmental due diligence is essential for a potential purchaser to understand the liabilities it would assume if it purchased a company or its property. However, in such cases, a new owner, operator, and seller may wish to perform a Phase I assessment but refrain from Phase II sampling, so as not to trigger any affirmative cleanup liabilities. In these states, a purchaser may be more willing than in other jurisdictions to provide a release (and indemnity) to the seller where the purchaser would assume the seller's liability by operation of law in any event.

Although strict, status-based liability presents the greatest risks to a purchaser, it may be the simplest in terms of due diligence and risk allocation. Because the new owner is liable to the government and third parties for all site impacts, its interest in due diligence may be limited (particularly if it is not a factor in pricing). However, because the seller is liable only for impacts existing prior to the transfer, the seller may have the most incentive to establish a baseline. Because liability is strict, purchasers often seek indemnity protection from sellers for preexisting conditions. Because the seller's liability is also strict, the seller may be willing to provide this protection or adjust the purchase price accordingly.

A state's environmental liability scheme may be a factor in the selection of a site for development. For example, the availability of liability exemptions may be attractive. However, issues such as brownfield redevelopment incentive programs and other economic incentives tend to be more influential.

Structuring the Deal

The deal would be dependent first on the personal and business goals of the client, including the client's leverage and the level of risk the client is willing to assume. If the deal is a merger, the seller will often cease to exist after the transaction, so allocation of risk is often managed through price concessions. However, where the merger involves payment for the stock of those who managed the company, escrow agreements are sometimes negotiated to hold back a portion of the stock purchase price from the directors to address certain liabilities. If the deal is an asset purchase and the seller will continue to exist as a solvent entity, indemnities may be more appropriate. The purchaser's proposed use of the property can also influence the structure of the environmental terms of the deal. If the purchaser intends to use a former commercial or industrial property for residential development, it may be appropriate to have the purchaser assume any costs associated with cleaning the property to residential standards.

The client's personal and business goals ultimately drive the deal. Beyond that, the client's leverage is critical in negotiating advantageous risk allocation provisions. As in most deals, a client who is willing to walk away from a deal has a stronger negotiating position. On the other hand, if a property or business opportunity is critical to a client, the client may be willing to accept more risk to move the deal forward. In certain cases, this perspective may lead to a focus on short-term resolutions at the expense of long-term implementation.

The level of risk the client is willing to accept is a key factor in structuring a transaction. Some clients want to take all steps necessary to eliminate or limit to the extent possible any environmental risks. These clients may insist on qualifying for liability exemptions, obtaining indemnities from the other party, and even obtaining prospective purchaser agreements or pre- or post-closing "no further action" letters from government agencies. Some risk-averse sellers will terminate transactions rather than grant rights to a purchaser to conduct Phase II sampling that might confirm site impacts.

If the client is willing to assume some risk, that client enjoys greater flexibility in negotiations and/or due diligence. Environmental risks can be allocated between the parties through price concessions, indemnities, escrow agreements, or by leaving the parties with their respective liabilities under law. The level of due diligence can be increased or decreased to mirror the level of uncertainty and thus risk the purchaser and/or seller are willing to assume in the transaction. For example, if a seller is willing to provide some indemnity, the purchaser may be satisfied with a reduced level of due diligence. Conversely, if the purchaser is willing to provide an indemnity or complete release, the seller may agree to price concessions. Escrow agreements may be useful to fund short-term liabilities or cleanup obligations. However, they may not be appropriate for long-term environmental remediation projects unless there is a mechanism to add funds to maintain certain funding levels if the remedial costs increase.

Negotiation Topics

The issues clients are willing to negotiate on vary from transaction to transaction. In some cases, purchase price is negotiable, but generally only when significant environmental issues are discovered during due diligence and the seller is unwilling to maintain long-term liabilities for environmental issues at the property. The period for performing due diligence, its scope, and its funding are often negotiable. While these terms may be set at the beginning of a transaction, they are frequently modified during the transaction where it serves the goals of both parties. For example, a limited due diligence period may be expanded to provide for additional testing that assists the parties in better defining the environmental risks that may be posed by an issue discovered at the property.

Environmental lawyers generally negotiate the environmental representations and warranties, particularly as to whether they are limited to the seller's knowledge, limited in time, or limited in the duration of any survival. For example, a representation that a company is in compliance with environmental laws may be limited to the seller's (company officers') knowledge, as some items of non-compliance are minor and difficult to identify in the absence of a state inspection. The compliance representation may also extend only to the period of two years prior to the closing, to limit the amount of backwards due diligence necessary to identify issues that have been resolved. The compliance representation may terminate at closing. Exceptions to environmental representations are often reflected on a disclosure schedule to the agreement. The parties may negotiate whether the disclosure schedule can merely reference existing environmental reports or whether the seller must specifically identify issues that are exceptions to the representations. This concern is particularly an issue when the representations are limited to matters that constitute a material adverse effect on the value of the assets. In such cases, the purchaser wants the seller to opine as to whether an identified liability may have a material adverse effect.

Finally, the ultimate allocation of the environmental risk is always negotiated, as the allocation is generally specific to the transaction. When the allocation consists of a seller indemnity, the survival of that obligation is often limited. This is especially true where the indemnity covers potentially unknown conditions, and the purchaser is given a period of time to identify them. This type of limitation may encourage the purchaser to update its environmental due diligence prior to the expiration of the indemnity period. However, it also provides a seller with a smaller risk that it will be asked to address conditions exacerbated by the purchaser's use of the property. Where a seller agrees to perform certain response activities, the description of those activities and their completion is negotiated. Escrow terms are also negotiated.

Lending transactions often involve execution of an environmental certificate and an environmental indemnification agreement. The provisions of these agreements are rarely negotiable for several reasons. First, the lender may have developed generic environmental documents to use in all transactions. The documents were likely generated by a committee, and the lender may be comfortable with their language. For the sake of treating its customers equally, and not deviating from a committee-approved document, the lender may be hesitant to accept any revisions to the documents. Additionally, if the lender does not have a relationship to the property but for the borrower's request for financing, the lender will likely seek to avoid all liability, imposing it on the borrower even where the law would not have imposed the liability on the borrower. For example, a lender may require a borrower to clean up all impacts at a site even where the borrower qualifies for a liability exemption. The lender would impose such an obligation to protect the value of its collateral.

Identifying Negotiation Goals

When negotiating, an environmental lawyer must have a thorough understanding of the client's goals to maximize the positive effects of the transaction for a client. Developing and communicating the most complete information on the factors that affect the client's risks is also critical. Those factors include understanding the past, current, and future uses of the property and how they may affect the property's condition and its anticipated use. They also include a thorough understanding of the state and federal laws and regulations that affect the seller's and purchaser's potential liability for environmental impacts at and from the property and, where applicable, their respective liabilities for potential environmental non-compliance. Additionally, it is critical to understand the opposing party's ability to accept environmental risks that may be imposed on it during the negotiations. An indemnity obligation without sufficient funding to support it may be worthless.

To achieve this understanding, most environmental lawyers begin by discussing with their clients the desired goals, timing, leverage, risk position, and long-term plans with respect to a property or company. Then they would engage an environmental consultant to gather information about the past and current uses of the property and perform a compliance audit. Then the lawyer would review the applicable laws and the information developed by the consultant in light of those laws. A review of the structure of the transaction would assist in identifying the seller's or purchaser's ability to manage environmental risks.

The greater the base of information on potential environmental risks, the more likely the client will be able to negotiate to a position it can live with over the long term. When risks are well understood, they can be accounted for in risk allocation between the parties. Lack of information increases the level of risk and may put a client in a position of gambling on the eventual outcome of the risk allocation. Confirming whether an opposing party has adequate resources to manage its potential environmental risks early in the transaction, and understanding the consequences of its failure to do so, can assist a client in developing a realistic and sound risk management plan.

Negotiation Style

Different lawyers have different styles of negotiation, depending on the issue under discussion. In an environmental transaction, I prefer to negotiate in a cooperative fashion. Generally, transactions are positive for both sides, because the parties are working toward a common goal. Additionally, my clients prefer that I act as a facilitator to a transaction, not a roadblock. This approach does not prevent me from taking strong positions at the direction of and to the benefit of my client. It merely avoids competition for competition's sake. Adopting a cooperative demeanor can also reduce the amount of time necessary to resolve negotiations on environmental transactions.

In the early stages of government enforcement matters, I tend to adopt a problem-solving demeanor in negotiations. It can be important to maintain a cordial relationship with regulators who have the long-term responsibility of overseeing a client's operations. If the matter escalates, or in matters of private party litigation, depending on the client's goals and directions, negotiations can become more competitive.

Cooperative negotiations are beneficial for a number of reasons. First and foremost, they generally get the job done. Second, they can reduce costs over more competitive negotiations. Third, they tend to foster positive relationships among the parties. When both parties to a transaction are satisfied and see each other as a collaborator rather than a competitor, it is more likely that future disputes may also be resolved cooperatively. The parties, and counsel, may look for other business opportunities together. Finally, cooperative negotiations generally lead to positions that recognize and seek to minimize risk for both parties. If reasonable positions are taken, it is easier to present them to a client for approval, especially where they see compromises on both sides of the transaction. In general, the benefits to a client of a cooperative negotiating style are more important than the perception of a competitive advantage, as long as the client is satisfied with the end product.

Cooperation is not always the best approach, however. One negative attribute is that the cooperative style does not work as well with a totally risk-averse client, as the client may impose inflexible negotiating positions. It can be difficult to ask for concessions if your client is unwilling to give any in return. Nonetheless, the client's goals dictate all aspects of the negotiations. Another potentially negative attribute occurs when a lawyer is negotiates with a person or opposing party who adopts a competitive negotiating strategy. If the party is clawing for every point, and the other party is willing to compromise on certain provisions, there may be a perceived advantage to the competitive party.

In general, if an opposing party is overly competitive, it will warrant a response from even a cooperative negotiator. If it does not disadvantage the client, I may become more inflexible on issues important to the other side. Additionally, there are ways to apply pressure without direct confrontation (e.g., the client may decide to raise business issues directly with the other side, rather than go through its counsel). If the competitive negotiator discourages the opposing party from doing business with the company in the future, it has not benefited its client.

A client that views a transaction as a cooperative negotiation with a balancing of risks will facilitate the resolution of the terms of an agreement. If the client has certain specific goals (e.g., to limit the duration of any indemnity agreement), it may be possible to negotiate that important provision while appearing to compromise on a less important provision. A party that is totally averse to risk will make a transaction difficult, and in some cases impossible.

I prefer to discuss back-up positions with a client when going into negotiations with another party. Some clients, however, prefer not to provide those options until they know the other party has rejected their preferred position. This approach can increase the time necessary for negotiations, but it may address a client's desire to be more actively involved in the negotiations without actually participating in direct communication.

Protecting the Client

Aside from understanding the client's goals and negotiating specific provisions, environmental lawyers typically take several steps to protect a client in environmental law transactions. When engaging environmental consultants to perform due diligence, for instance, the work is generally contracted through counsel to preserve the attorney work product privilege. Draft reports are not finalized without counsel approval. The terms of the consultant's contract are negotiated, particularly in the areas of indemnity and liability limitation. When providing environmental documents to the opposing party, lawyers often require confidentiality agreements to prevent the other party from disclosing the documents or their contents without our prior written consent. These agreements generally require the opposing party to return all copies of the documents if the transaction does not close. In some cases, the seller may not want to be made aware of negative environmental findings. In such cases, we have included provisions suggesting that copies of the purchaser's due diligence reports are not to be provided to the seller until after the closing. Some provisions go further and state that if the purchaser terminates the agreement based on the findings of its due diligence, it will destroy any environmental reports it generates. This approach may prevent affirmative reporting or cleanup obligations from being triggered under state law.

Lawyers can also protect their clients by negotiating a good position but reserving the client's right to approve or disapprove the terms. This approach is appropriate even where a client has already approved a given position. It enables the client to reconsider the negotiated document as a whole before committing to individual revisions.

Protecting a client's interest requires an understanding of the opposing party and its status following the transaction, as this may affect the way a deal is structured. If the deal is a merger, the opposite party will become part of the new company, which affects the allocation of risks and may suggest managing the schedule for payment of stock purchased by the company's managers. If the seller is a small company with limited assets, or if it intends to distribute the proceeds of the sale and dissolve immediately after the transaction, lawyers would not recommend an indemnity to protect the purchaser from historic liabilities, as no assets may be available when the indemnity is triggered. If the opposing party is a purchaser willing to accept a significant share of the environmental risks contractually, but without sufficient assets to do so practically, the seller may take additional steps to limit its liabilities. In some cases, this approach could include addressing known environmental risks in advance of closing or maintaining the right to do so post-closing.

Lawyers strategize for their clients by understanding their client's personal and business goals as well as those of the opponent. Knowing the opponent's ultimate goals assists an attorney in presenting its position to the opponent in a way intended to help the opponent meet its own goals. To be successful, an environmental deal should be sensitive to both parties' goals.

Dealing with Hostility

If a transaction is hostile and that hostility comes primarily from the opposing party, it is often best to work through the opposing party's counsel, assuming a relationship of trust exists between them. If the hostility comes from the opponent's counsel, it can be beneficial to encourage a client to negotiate the basic deal directly with the opponent. This approach has been successful in limiting the areas open for negotiation with a hostile counsel. I often try to neutralize emotional reactions by maintaining a business-like demeanor throughout the negotiations and asking the hostile party for its input on the resolution of a given issue. Sometimes hostile personalities merely want to create controversy and negative emotions. It may be easy for them to attack or challenge an opponent's suggestions. Asking them to provide a resolution can limit their ability to criticize the process and its outcome. Unreasonable positions, however, must be challenged firmly, but with a focus on the issue at hand, not the person or emotions involved.

It is generally counterproductive to meet hostility with hostility. It may feel good at the time, but it is rarely helpful in assisting a client meet its goals. If feeling powerful is a goal of the opponent, that can be managed while negotiating a deal that is otherwise advantageous to a client. Sometimes it is better to accept hostility. Hostility for its own sake may cause an opponent to ignore some of its other goals in the transaction. That approach can cut both ways, however, and it may not be prudent to take full advantage of that situation if the client anticipates future business dealings with the opponent.

Benchmarking Strategies

The benchmark of whether a strategy is appropriate is always whether it helps the client achieve its long- and short-term personal and business goals. Minimizing the client's level of environmental risk is generally one of the client's primary goals, so a strategy that identifies and minimizes the level of environmental risk borne by the client is a proper strategy. Sometimes the time necessary to identify and quantify environmental risks in detail may conflict with other client goals, such as meeting a certain schedule for closing the transaction. In those cases, a proper strategy is one that enables the client to balance the risks against the competing client goals. If the client's personal and business goals are met, the attorney has been successful in the transaction and is likely to be used by the client in future matters or referred by the client to others in need of similar assistance.

Occasionally a client is dissatisfied with the results of an environmental deal where the attorney felt the negotiations were successful. This situation may occur where the attorney failed to understand the client's expectations and correct them, as appropriate. Examples of this can arise in the context of negotiating a settlement agreement with a governmental agency to resolve alleged violations. The attorney may consider the matter a success if the negotiated penalty is below a certain threshold the client has indicated it can bear. Nonetheless, the client may be dissatisfied with the result, feeling that the alleged violation was questionable or that the government should have accepted correction of the violation as the remedy. Often in these circumstances, if the client is truly dissatisfied with the attorney's performance, it is because the attorney did not adequately prepare the client for the probable results of the settlement negotiations. It is imperative for an environmental attorney to monitor trends in enforcement, to properly advise clients facing enforcement issues. In other circumstances, the client may have backed itself into a poorer position by not engaging an attorney until after enforcement has escalated on a notice of violation. It is a responsibility of the environmental attorney to refocus the client on the likely resolution moving forward from the time the attorney was involved. During or following the negotiations, the environmental attorney can suggest alternative ways to manage a notice of violation, should one arise in the future. Managing client expectations is key.

Walking Away

Rarely does an environmental attorney walk away from the negotiation table. Using that strategy too often undermines an attorney's credibility in future negotiations. However, when the client's needs dictate a certain outcome, walking away may be the only option. For example, if the seller wants to limit its cleanup obligations to remedies consistent with the current configuration of a property, it might be appropriate to walk away if the purchaser insists that the seller should be liable even if the property configuration or use changes. In one matter we negotiated, because a foundation in place at a property was already a component of the seller's remedy, we walked away from the table when the purchaser insisted on being able to remove it and have the seller pay for any additional remediation. In that matter, the purchaser later came back and agreed to the seller's proposed language. Despite the time and money that had been expended on the transaction, the client was prepared to market the property to another purchaser if necessary.

More often, the client may walk away from an established closing date that may have significance to the opposing party if issues have not been adequately resolved. This step often puts sufficient pressure on the opposing party to lead to a compromised position on the outstanding issues. Unfortunately, if the closing date is critical to the business needs of the opposing party, the approach can result in termination of the deal. For example, if a purchaser needs to be in some just-in-time manufacturing space to meet the needs of its customers, it may not be flexible in moving the closing date. This leverage can be used by the seller in negotiations. However, the seller may not wish to press this advantage fully if it hopes to do continuing business with the purchaser.

Because the main driving force of any environmental attorney is the satisfaction of client goals, my attitude toward opposing parties is not often a significant factor in striking the deal. However, if I have the impression that the opposing party is more flexible or less demanding in general, I may take advantage of that in negotiations as long as it does not conflict with a client goal. To meet client needs, it is sometimes necessary to educate the opponent, particularly if the opponent is practicing outside its normal jurisdiction. In doing so, I provide a complete explanation of my understanding of the relevant law or information (recommending that they confirm it) and offer a rationale for my position. If the opposing party is reasonable and flexible in its negotiations, I will also be reasonable within the limits of my client's goals.

Risks in Environmental Law

Two primary risks are involved in all deals involving environmental law. One risk is that unknown environmental conditions will be discovered. The second risk is that environmental laws, including liability schemes and cleanup standards, will change over time.

The most important strategy in dealing with environmental risks is not to ignore these risks just because they are not quantified at the time of the deal. The liability for these risks should be allocated between the parties in the context of the deal. Their allocation generally follows the risk allocation for known conditions. For example, where a seller provides an indemnity for five years after the closing date, that indemnity will generally cover newly discovered historic impacts and changes in law that occur during that five-year period, but the purchaser will assume the risks for changes occurring after that five-year period has lapsed. Sellers seeking to avoid these liabilities with an "as is" clause must also include a full release provision, as courts have decided an "as is" provision only allocates liabilities under current laws, but that release also allocates liabilities arising from changes in law.

The presence of both risks provides a purchaser with further incentives for seeking to qualify for liability exemptions available under state and federal laws. Those exemptions generally protect new owners from unknown as well as known risks.

It is more difficult to address the risks associated with changes in law, particularly if those changes affect the overall liability scheme. However, an environmental attorney should monitor trends in environmental law development and identify to the client those that may affect the client's allocation of risks. For example, the Environmental Protection Agency has been considering a significant reduction in indoor air exposure cleanup levels for certain common solvent impacts such as trichloroethylene. If trichloroethylene impacts are present at a property in levels below the current standard but above the potential new standard, attorneys for the purchaser and seller should both advise their clients of the potential effect of the proposed change in law on the parties' allocation of risks. Ultimately, though, decisions of taking on risks are up to the client.

Changing Strategy

Sometimes an environmental attorney must change strategy mid-negotiation. In such a situation, where the change in strategy is significant and may not be well received by the other side, I try to identify some aspect of the opponent's goals that has not been addressed and explore whether the client's requested change can be presented in a manner intended to address the opponent's goals as well.

With respect to the client, I explore the rationale for the change. If the change goes against recommendations we have discussed, to address some other personal and business goals of the client, we review the rationale for the initial recommendations, and I assist the client in developing an alternate strategy and in understanding the potential implications of the change in strategy. I also document the decision-making for the file.

Changing an environmental strategy in the heart of a deal can result in loss of credibility and confidence. However, if the change is necessary to bring both parties to a level of risk allocation they can accept, changing the strategy may lead to ultimately executing the deal. Because the client's goals are the primary driver of any strategy, if a change in strategy will better achieve the client's goals, and the client has been fully apprised of the pros and cons associated with the change, the change should be made.

Sharon R. Newlon is a member in the Detroit office of Dickinson Wright PLLC, where she has practiced in the environmental practice group since 1988. Her practice spans the gamut of state and federal environmental laws, and includes a specialty in hazardous waste, brownfield redevelopment, and transactional support issues.

Ms. Newlon has lectured on numerous environmental law topics, including the environmental aspects of property purchase and lending, federal and state hazardous waste management laws, brownfield redevelopment, baseline environmental assessments, and site remediation. She has served as an environmental law lecturer for Michigan's Institute for Continuing Legal Education, for the State Bar Association's environmental law section, and for the Southwest Michigan chapter of the Air and Waste Management Association. In 2006–2007, she served on the Michigan Department of Environmental Quality's Part 201 work group to review Michigan's environmental remediation and redevelopment laws. She co-authored the 1988–1990 Environmental Law Survey for the Wayne State University Law Review, *and she has written articles for various publications, including* Michigan Lawyers Weekly. *She enjoys presenting materials at the Cranbrook Institute/AAUW Explorathon to high school and junior high girls considering careers in math and science, and she has served as a judge for the American Chemical Society at the Detroit Science Fair.*

Ms. Newlon is a graduate of the University of Notre Dame Law School (J.D., magna cum laude) and the University of Detroit (B.S. in chemistry, magna cum laude). She is a member of the Detroit and Michigan Bar Associations, and she has served on the Michigan Bar Association's environmental law section's council, program committee, and ethics committee.

Dedication: *To my husband Mark and our son Brian, my support and my constant inspiration.*

Helping Clients
Make Informed Decisions

Michael J. Quinn

Partner

Seyfarth Shaw LLP

In my practice in environmental law, I advise clients in the acquisition, redevelopment, and sale of environmentally impacted property. My specific tasks include negotiating the scope of environmental investigations; explaining the legal consequences of the results of those investigations; negotiating the allocation of liability between buyers and sellers, and negotiating the responsibility for remediation; securing indemnities from sellers and "no further action" letters or similar assurances from state or other governmental environmental agencies; and securing environmental insurance.

I work with environmental consultants as well as the client's staff to identify material environmental issues and then provide the client with reasonable assurance that any residual environmental risk is not significant. This may be accomplished through undertakings or indemnities from the seller, no further action or similar closure assurances from governmental environmental officials, and insurance. When representing sellers, my task is to make sure that, following closing, the seller will have no further liability for environmental issues at the property.

The Main Issues: Five Key Areas of Environmental Law

The main areas of environmental law I handle in my practice are as follows:

1. In real estate acquisitions, to identify significant environmental risks present at the property.
2. In corporate acquisitions, to identify significant environmental risks associated with the seller's operations (both past and present), as well as significant environmental risks present at any properties to be acquired along with the purchased entity.
3. To negotiate the scope of environmental review among the seller, buyer, and environmental consultant. Sellers may want to limit review, and buyers' ability to investigate may be constrained by time and cost issues. Industry standard environmental assessments divide responsibility between consultant and client, and it is critical to make sure each step in the review is appropriately assigned. In this process, consultants also try to limit their liability for errors or missed issues.

4. To advise clients on ways to minimize liability through "no further action" letters and/or prospective purchaser agreements, or shift liability through environmental insurance and/or indemnities from sellers, for example.

5. To identify significant issues such as historic contamination of the site; past, current, and proposed uses of the property and the environmental significance of each; presence of wetlands or other sensitive uses; significance of groundwater; and allocation of liability among the buyer, seller, and third parties.

Approaching an Environmental Law Case

There are two ways to analyze an environmental law case. First, in a real estate acquisition, we might examine the historical use of the property and the potential for soil and groundwater contamination. Once any issues are identified, we examine what must be done, such as the remediation that must be performed to secure a "no further action" letter or other closure documentation from regulatory authorities. Then we look at what can be done in terms of cleanup levels necessary for the intended use of the property. For example, a seller may only be willing to remediate historic contamination at a site to a level that will permit commercial or industrial reuse of the property. The buyer, however, may plan for more sensitive uses—medical, residential, recreational, and so on. Someone will have to pay the extra cost to perform any additional cleanup necessary to permit the more sensitive uses. This might be accomplished by adjustments to the purchase price, or by allocation of cleanup responsibilities. The seller might secure a "no further action" letter permitting commercial/industrial uses, following which the buyer submits a subsequent application to allow more sensitive uses.

The second way to approach a case is to look at the medium into which a pollutant might be introduced, whether air, water, or ground. From there, it is possible to examine the past and present uses and the current condition of the property to determine whether any of these media have been contaminated. If so, one must determine the legal implications for the seller, buyer, or third parties. For example, are there wetlands on or near the property in question? Have they been impacted by past or current uses of the property? Will they be impacted by the buyer's anticipated use? If they will be impacted, what are the regulatory issues? Can the impacts be mitigated? Which regulatory officials—Army Corps of Engineers, state environmental agencies, or local agencies—have jurisdiction over the wetlands and will decide what can be done? One goes through a similar analysis for air, surface water, groundwater, and soil issues. A truly comprehensive examination of a property or acquisition would undertake both of these analyses.

Identifying and Accomplishing Key Tasks

Once the key tasks have been identified, the next step is to discuss with the client the specifics of each of the various tasks. This discussion should include the time and cost necessary to perform these tasks, the possible people who could perform them (whether outside consultants, the client's personnel, or me), and the consequences of not performing one or more of these tasks. There is tremendous pressure in the market today to reduce the time allowed for due diligence, and some property owners are reluctant to permit wide-ranging investigations. For example, sellers are justifiably reluctant to permit fishing expeditions. It is important to recognize that there may not be time to perform every investigation one might want to perform, given unlimited time and money. I work with consultants to provide clients with a range of options: the minimum amount of investigation necessary, without which it would be foolish to proceed; the optimum investigation given time and budget constraints; and finally, the ideal model without such constraints. We then advise the client as to what they are getting and what they might be missing with each such option.

When looking at substantive issues of air, water, and ground, we quickly try to determine which issues are significant for this transaction. For example, if the buyer's contemplated use does not entail air discharges, the seller's past air pollution is probably of no consequence in a real estate acquisition. On the other hand, in a corporate transaction in which the buyer may be responsible for the seller's past conduct, air issues may be important even if the buyer will have no present air discharges. Again, given time and budget constraints, we simply cannot examine every issue from scratch. The purpose of initial investigations and a Phase I environmental assessment is to identify those issues that need further investigation, as well as those issues that do not require further investigation. Once the investigation is complete, I advise clients on the legal consequences of the conclusions of that investigation, the options available to avoid or minimize the negative consequences, and then work with them to achieve the desired result.

The Financial Impact

The major financial implication of environmental law is that a property owner can be compelled to clean up an environmental problem they had no role in creating. Discovering an environmental problem after a piece of property has been bought can frustrate the purchaser's intended use and may leave the new owner exposed to lawsuits for personal injury or property damage. My role is to help clients achieve their goals while minimizing environmental risk.

To give an example, I advised one client on the acquisition of several properties that were former defense-related plants. Most were heavily contaminated. The seller had cleaned up the surface of the properties to the extent that they could be reused for non-sensitive uses such as industrial, warehouse distribution, or office use. I negotiated undertakings with the seller to continue cleanup post-closing and to set remediation targets, both as conditions of closing and post-closing. I also coordinated contacts with lead environmental agencies to determine their requirements, and prepared and coordinated presentations to underwriters to secure environmental insurance. This was a big win for the client because these impacted properties were the only property available in that market for the client's intended use. We also preserved the possibility to redevelop some of these properties for more sensitive uses, which will be an added bonus for the client.

The Danger Zone: Underestimating Environmental Issues

The single most damaging mistake people make in this area of law is to belittle the issue. A buyer has no responsibility for the environmental condition of a piece of property until they buy it, at which point responsibility may be unavoidable. Of course, buyers don't want to spend the time or money. "I'm only building a shopping center! What are the environmental problems with that?" Well, if the property used to have a dry cleaner, gas station, photo processor, or a number of other retail uses, there can be a number of environmental issues that could frustrate the buyer's expectations. In the context of an office building, for example, does it have asbestos? Did it ever have asbestos? Is the HVAC or plumbing system contributing to a mold issue? Was it ever heated with oil? Are there tanks in the basement?

This is not a problem limited to buyers. Two of the worst environmental messes in which I have been involved both had the same cause: A seller who probably was capable of managing the problem allowed the property to get into the hands of a buyer who was not capable of managing the problem, and in fact made it immeasurably worse. Once it became apparent that the buyer had mismanaged the problem, regulatory authorities (in one case) and private parties (in the other) sued to compel the former owner, the seller, to solve the problem. Because under the relevant environmental laws the seller was at least arguably liable, the sellers in both cases ended up settling the cases and either assumed control of and responsibility for the cleanup (in one case) or contributed substantially to the cost of cleanup (in the other).

We provide the most value for clients by first identifying the situations before the client is on the hook. This is the principal purpose of pre-acquisition investigations. If you know about a problem, you can plan for it. For example, existing soil contamination or underground tanks might be addressed at marginal costs as part of development of a site. On the other hand, discovering a problem in the middle of construction can lead to delays, demobilization and remobilization costs, damage suits by workers, defaults under loan agreements, and other unpleasant consequences. If the problem is sufficiently serious, you can walk away from a deal unless, of course, it is already closed.

We also plan with clients, both buyers and sellers, to address and allocate identified environmental risks. What, if anything, should the seller do before or after closing? Who between buyer or seller should secure a "no further action" letter or similar closure assurance from the relevant environmental authorities? Can remediation activities be coordinated with the buyer's development activities? If there is residual environmental contamination on the site, and the seller is willing to offer an indemnity, is the seller good for it? Will the seller be good for it ten years from now? If I am representing the seller, what are the appropriate limits, in terms of time or type of claim, to such indemnities? Can the risk be shifted to a third party like an environmental insurer?

Staying on Top of the Game

Over the years, I have striven to educate clients on the various environmental issues likely to affect their business, either through representation on particular matters or through presentations or written communications. Most of the people I represent are relatively risk-averse, at least with respect to environmental risk, and so they are willing to listen to a discussion of the potential issues and the steps necessary to identify the significant ones. In most acquisitions, there are industry standard protocols that determine the scope of investigation. We start with these protocols and determine whether any issues outside the standard scope might be present at the property in question—wetland, asbestos, or mold, for example—and design a specific protocol for the property to be investigated.

Success is simply defined as achieving the client's objective, whether it is acquisition of a property or corporate entity, while at the same time minimizing environmental exposure. To keep my edge and stay successful in this practice, I have taught as an adjunct professor at a local law school, teaching an environmental law course. Furthermore, I try to write at least a few articles a year for business publications dealing with current environmental issues, and I do a lot of homework. This is an area of law that is constantly evolving, and it is critical to stay on top of a lot of material, such as legal publications, business publications, and newspapers. The most recent example is, of course, possible regulations related to climate change and the regulation of carbon in the atmosphere. Managing the massive amount of information that is out there will help a lawyer achieve the client's goals more efficiently and effectively.

Deal Strategies

When taking on a new environmental case, the first step in determining an appropriate strategy is to discuss the client's goals and, with those goals in mind, identify available information regarding the condition of the property or business entity to be acquired or sold. This initial information focuses the remainder of the investigation. Through a discussion with the client, one can gather whatever information they have at their disposal, which in a sale transaction may be sufficient. In a purchase transaction, however, one must also include due diligence deliveries and representations and warranties from the seller.

The Legal Environment: Critical Laws

In most business and real estate transactions, the most important law to consider is the state Superfund law. Most states control most voluntary cleanup programs, which will commonly be used to minimize liability going forward. In other cases, however, a property may be subject to the federal Resource Conservation and Recovery Act (RCRA), which governs hazardous waste and presents more challenges.

The federal Comprehensive Environmental Response, Compensation, and Liability Act and its state equivalents impose liability for releases of hazardous substances on three parties: the owner of the property at the time of such release, the party that caused the release, and most importantly for our purposes, the current owner of the property on which the release occurred, even if the current owner had nothing to do with the release. With the exception of businesses that discharge pollutants into the air or water or generate hazardous waste, this is the law that affects most businesses and property owners. There are several defenses to liability under this act, but most of these defenses must be established before the property is acquired. Securing these defenses is one of the driving forces behind pre-acquisition environmental investigations.

Furthermore, state brownfield laws encourage the redevelopment and reuse of property by establishing mechanisms for owners or others to limit or extinguish their liability for past contamination of property, either by cleaning it up or by demonstrating that any residual contamination poses no significant impact to human health or the environment. State brownfield laws permit owners to determine the cleanup standard that will apply to their property, based on the current and intended future use of the property and the use, if any, of the groundwater underneath the property. Once parties know what must be done to return a property to reuse, parties can determine how much the necessary cleanup will cost, or the impact on the value of the property of any restrictions imposed on future uses. These costs can then be factored into the purchase price of the property, or otherwise allocated in the transaction. In the absence of the certainty provided by these state laws, parties could not determine what cleanup standards might apply (there are always multiple choices) and thus could not determine the expected cost of any remediation. For that reason, contaminated properties simply did not move in the market. These brownfields help both sellers and buyers identify the appropriate remediation strategy, either active or passive remediation or restrictions on future uses, or a combination of each of these; factor the costs into the transaction; and resolve their liability for historic contamination of the site.

The RCRA is a more restrictive law that, in general, will require a more thorough investigation of a property. The law will also limit the options available to owners in addressing any contamination found at the site. The added complexity of RCRA obligations will, in many cases, kill a deal. In one recent transaction, the seller intended to address existing contamination post-closing in phases, but in terms of the problem to be addressed— shallow soils, deep soils, groundwater—and in terms of different geographic areas of the property. The seller would secure no further action for each phase, as completed, and get off its indemnity obligations to the buyer for that phase. When the buyer and its representatives met with state officials, however, we were informed that the property was regulated under the RCRA, which does not contemplate closure in phases—there would be no closure assurances from the state until all cleanup work at the site was completed, which will probably not occur for decades. This affected the seller because it couldn't get off its indemnity obligations, but it also impacted the buyer because the buyer would not receive a "no further action" letter for the foreseeable future, which limits its ability to finance the property and may prevent certain contemplated uses of the site. We spent the next six months renegotiating the purchase contract.

Environmental Law at the State Level

Environmental issues at most properties are regulated by state environmental officials, since the federal government generally focuses only on the most heavily contaminated sites, which presently have negative market value and so are not involved in most business transactions. The practice of environmental law does not vary greatly from state to state, however, as state environmental agencies in major markets generally approach issues in similar ways. Of course, some focus more than others on particular issues, such as vapor intrusion into buildings. Other states, notably New York, have been slow to adopt brownfield voluntary cleanup laws. However, the basic framework is similar among the various states, with only one major exception: New Jersey, whose Industrial Sites Recovery Act is essentially unique. As a result, New Jersey tends to get involved in transactions more deeply than other states

In practicing across state lines, it is interesting to see the different approaches to a problem. For example, Texas has a statute allowing for the creation of "municipal source designations," by which a municipality can, by ordinance or resolution, restrict the use of specific properties and prohibit the use of groundwater. This in turn will simplify the process of securing closure through the state's voluntary cleanup program. Illinois achieves the same end by a series of "memoranda of understanding" between the state and local governments. As mentioned above, New York was until very recently a difficult state in that it did not offer brownfield voluntary cleanup benefits. These state-by-state differences, however, do not greatly affect the overall principles of environmental legal practice.

Formulating Strategy

The strategy and structure of a deal will depend greatly on the circumstances of the individual case. In a purchase transaction, for instance, what is the client's proposed use of the property? Is it a "sensitive use"? If residual contamination will remain on the site, is the seller willing to provide an indemnity, and if so, are they good for it? What is the client's risk tolerance? These key questions create a foundation for moving forward with the case.

When working with an environmental law client, the strategy will be most affected by the amount of information available and the time allocated for due diligence. The seller's willingness to make representations and warranties about the property and provide indemnities for continuing issues is also highly influential. In essence, these factors are interrelated. If the seller is unwilling to provide representations, warranties, or indemnities, the buyer must have the additional time and be willing to spend the money to do a more comprehensive investigation. If the seller is unwilling to provide the time to conduct extensive due diligence, the buyer should insist on, at a minimum, representations and warranties about the scope of document deliveries and the condition of the property so the investigation that is conducted can be properly focused. If the seller is unwilling to do either, the buyer should understand that it is jumping blind, and perhaps the purchase price should reflect the unknown risk the buyer is assuming.

Negotiations and Deal Structure

When negotiating with an opposing party in an environmental matter, it is usually easiest to negotiate disclosure of information and document production. Most sellers are also willing to make some limited representations and warranties about the property to be acquired. On the other hand, sellers are most reluctant to negotiate post-closing liability. Most sellers want to be done with a property after closing and do not want a purchaser to chase them after closing in an attempt to force the seller to cough up the purchase price. The best strategy is to get as much information from each side on the table as soon as possible. This can be accomplished by:

1. Due diligence disclosures and document production
2. Use of a good consultant and an investigation of adequate scope
3. Representations and warranties from the seller regarding the condition of the property and its enforcement history
4. Contacts with relevant environmental agencies
5. Indemnities from the seller

Of course, in some deals, not all of these approaches will work. For example, in buying property out of foreclosure, lenders typically will not give any representations and warranties, and in general may not have much information. In other transactions, the seller may be unwilling to provide information. Using multiple approaches should typically produce as much relevant information as possible. If not, we can at least make sure the client understands they are jumping blind.

When it comes to negotiation style, everyone has a style that works best for them. Some people are better at knocking the other side back on their heels, while others are better at presenting a more affable front. I prefer to begin a transaction in a cooperative fashion and continue with that approach as long as it works. When we all believe we are trying to address a common problem and achieve common goals—specifically, to close the transaction while minimizing everyone's risk—we are more likely to achieve the goal while minimizing transaction costs.

Working with the Environmental Law Client: The Risk Factor

The principle issue affecting our legal strategy is the client's risk tolerance for environmental risk. Some clients have little risk tolerance in this area, while others have great tolerance for risk. The client's position on the time frame and financial investment necessary for due diligence can also affect how we proceed. Generally, if a client has low risk tolerance for environmental risk, we will try to use more of the techniques listed above, including due diligence disclosures, representations and warranties from the seller, indemnities, insurance, and so on. If the client is unconcerned about environmental risk, we may not push so strongly to get all of these aspects into the deal.

Of course, nothing offers complete protection. The statutory defenses to liability in the federal Superfund and its state law equivalents offer only limited defenses and may require significant post-closing expenditures by the property owner to maintain the defenses. The other investigative tools—Phase I assessments, due diligence, representations and warranties from the seller, and insurance and indemnities—do not offer complete protection, but should reduce the risk to the point where other risks are more significant. Ultimately, the amount of risk that is acceptable in any deal is not up to me, or indeed any lawyer, to decide. In my experience, lawyers are more risk-averse than their clients. It is my job to explain the risks and their consequences to the client, but they have to make the ultimate decision as to whether the risks are acceptable. Sometimes, if asked, I will offer my opinion as to whether I would go forward with the deal were it my money at stake, but while some clients appreciate that input, most are perfectly capable of making their own decision.

The most difficult factor of any environmental law deal is handling all the information we simply do not know about a piece of property or entity to be acquired. No matter how many precautions and legal protections are in place, risk is always a significant factor in this business. The best strategy for success is simply to ensure, as much as humanly possible, that the client understands the risks they face and makes a conscious, informed decision regarding those risks. The last thing a lawyer wants to hear from a client is, "You didn't tell me this could happen!"

Michael J. Quinn is a partner in the Chicago office of Seyfarth Shaw LLP. In more than twenty years of legal service, he has advised institutional investors, investments advisers, developers, and corporate clients regarding environmental issues affecting significant real estate investments. He offers extensive experience in environmental issues with respect to acquisitions and dispositions of real estate, land use, the cleanup of hazardous substances under federal and state Superfunds, and environmental litigation. He also assists clients in the closure of hazardous waste disposal facilities under the Resource Conservation and Recovery Act.

In addition to advising clients on environmental issues in real estate transactions, Mr. Quinn has extensive experience in conventional real estate acquisitions and dispositions, including the purchase and sale of existing projects, creation of development ventures, and project financing.

Mr. Quinn earned his B.A. from Marquette University, his M.U.P. from the University of Wisconsin, and his J.D., cum laude, from the University of Wisconsin Law School.

Dedication: *To my wife, Elizabeth Gracie, and daughter, Maureen Quinn.*

Key Questions for Addressing Environmental Issues in a Transaction

Pamela K. Elkow

Partner

Robinson & Cole LLP

When I am first hired to represent a client on a deal, I start by asking questions. With apologies to any journalists who may be reading this, and to bring some sense of order to the inevitable messiness of due diligence and deal-making, I have organized these questions using the useful, if somewhat hackneyed, "Who, what, when, where, why, and how?" Once I have answers to those questions, I am in a much better position to advise the client on the best way to get the deal done, or, as is occasionally necessary, to avoid the deal altogether. In this chapter, I set out the types of questions I ask the client or the corporate or real estate counsel with whom I am working—the "who, what, when, where, and why"—and certain deal strategies that can get the deal done—the "how."

First and foremost, my role in a transaction is as a member of the team. I think of myself as a deal lawyer who happens to practice environmental law. My role is not to throw up roadblocks and protect the client to the point that they cannot engage in their core business, whatever that might be. My role is to find out the facts, make sure the client understands the facts and the risk associated with them, and negotiate a deal that is favorable to my client.

"Who?" Identifying the Client's Needs

Who is the client? Are they the buyer or seller? Is it a real estate developer or investor? Or a large institutional client selling off unused assets? Will they be redeveloping the property, or using it for its current purposes? If there is an embryonic structure to the deal, has it been decided who will be assuming the environmental risk—buyer or seller? Is the entity assuming the risk a viable entity, or are they a special purpose entity that has no assets other than the underlying real property? Are there institutional investors involved who have different risk profiles or takeovers than the client?

Clearly, the first question is the most important—do I represent the buyer or seller? The answer to that question completely changes how I negotiate the agreement. For example, if I represent the seller, I try to limit the representations and warranties, maybe to the point of making no representations or warranties, while I try to make them as expansive as possible when representing the buyer. However, I find that no matter whom I represent, it is important to find out how much is known about the site and to have that information provided as early as possible. Most environmental issues are manageable if the buyer is willing to take on at least minimal risk, but information shared at the last minute will at least put off the closing date, and at worst kill a deal.

Is the client a developer who finds that it is worthwhile to take some risks because it is counting on the returns? Or is the client a large, publicly traded company with deep pockets and regulatory reporting obligations? A large company selling property is much more likely to want to control the environmental issues at a site, even post-closing, as past experience has shown that contractual protections alone will not isolate the company from the past. Institutional clients will often have fully investigated a site, and if remediation is required, will either perform it prior to selling or will conduct the remediation itself, post-closing, so as to ensure it is done properly. They will further want to control the future uses of the property to limit future liability. If that work takes place post-closing, the contract must provide that the new owner will allow for limitations on future use.

In contrast, the smaller real estate development or investment company may forego investigations, relying on insurance, indemnities, or escrows in the event that something is later discovered at the property.

"What?" The Nature of the Transaction

What is the client buying or selling? Is this strictly a real estate transaction, or is it a corporate transaction involving an ongoing business? If it is a corporate transaction, is it a stock deal or an asset deal? Will the client be staying in its current location or moving the business? If it is a real estate transaction, is the client buying the real estate, leasing, or investing? What are the environmental conditions? Do we know, or do we have to investigate? Will the seller allow an investigation?

Real estate transactions are simpler. We are generally just concerned about the environmental conditions at the property, although there are some operational issues that arise as well. When talking about the environmental conditions of a property, we are really asking, have there been spills or releases of hazardous materials at the property, or was the property used for the disposal of hazardous materials? The operational issues are similar to those a property assessment would uncover and provide information necessary to allow the new owner to manage the property properly. Is there a septic system, or does the waste go to the city sewer? Septic systems can be the site of releases of hazardous materials. How is the building heated? If it is heated by oil, are the tanks underground and have they leaked? These are all questions that are readily answered by standard environmental due diligence, known as a Phase I environmental site assessment.[1] Other questions to ask, which may not be answered by a standard Phase I, include: Is there asbestos in the building, and if so, is it in good condition? Does the building have lead-based paint, which is an issue in residential properties and can be an issue for commercial properties if there will be building renovation or demolition resulting in construction debris? Again, the purpose of asking the questions is twofold: first, to allocate responsibility for correcting any deficiencies, and second, to provide the new owner with the information necessary for managing the property going forward.

Corporate transactions are more complex. If the corporate deal includes the acquisition of real estate, one has to ask all the questions discussed above. But a corporate deal also requires an understanding of the business and the other environmental requirements that may apply to the business. What permits are required to conduct the business? Are they about to expire? Have there been past violations of the permits, or of any other applicable environmental law? How does the company store its raw materials and waste materials? Where does the company send its waste material? Have there been any complaints from employees or neighbors about the operations at the facility?

In a corporate transaction, it is critical to know whether it will be a stock purchase or an asset purchase. If one is acquiring the stock of a corporation, one is acquiring all the assets and liabilities, including the

---

[1] ASTM has standardized the Phase I environmental site assessment, found at ASTM Standard E1527-05. While the ASTM standard could be a subject of its own chapter, for purposes of this chapter, it is important to know that the purpose of the ASTM Phase I environmental site assessment is to meet the definition of "all appropriate inquiry" set forth in the federal Superfund statute, thereby allowing a purchaser of property to prove it has met "all appropriate inquiry" and therefore can claim to be either an innocent purchaser or a bona fide prospective purchaser, avoiding Superfund liability. Unless requested by the user of the Phase I, it does not include information on permitting, on asbestos or lead-based paint, or the applicability of any state statutes.

environmental liabilities. So if the corporation has been named as a potentially responsible party at a Superfund site as a result of historic waste disposal practices, the acquiring entity will acquire that liability as well. This is true even if the company has not yet been named as a potentially responsible party, because the corporation continues to exist and to have the liability. Similarly, liability for failure to have a permit will continue after the acquisition of the stock of the company.

Under traditional corporate law, an asset transaction is different. A buyer acquires only those assets or liabilities it agrees to acquire. However, in many if not all states, courts have adopted a variety of theories whereby those who acquire assets have been held responsible for the past sins of "the business." Successor liability has and will continue to be the subject of court cases, articles, and treatises, but for the purposes of this discussion, it is enough to understand that if one is buying "the business," even if through an asset transaction, the buyer should assume it has the potential to be held liable for the business's past actions. What this means is that the due diligence is just as important as in a stock transaction, and it is even more critical to lay out in as much detail as possible those liabilities the buyer is assuming and those the seller is retaining.

"When?" Building an Appropriate Time Frame

When is the closing? Ok, when is the closing really? How long is the due diligence period? Can it be extended for any reason? When can the buyer get out of the deal for environmental reasons? When can the seller?

In my experience, particularly in corporate transactions, environmental issues are not front burner issues in the transaction—and, unless they are critical to the core business, appropriately so. However, it has also been my experience that not addressing environmental issues until the last minute results in needlessly elevating the importance of issues that were likely resolvable, had the parties had time to learn more about the issues and appropriately evaluate the risks entailed.

Any purchase and sale agreement should set out the parameters of the due diligence period, how long it will be, whether it can be extended and why, and whether and how the buyer can terminate based on the results. When representing the buyer, I want to make sure the buyer can terminate the agreement "for any reason or no reason at all." If I am representing the seller, I may try to curtail that option—such as allowing termination only when the anticipated costs of remediation exceed a certain amount. I could curtail that option further by requiring the buyer to move forward if the seller is willing to take on liability over a certain amount.

What is often neglected in negotiating such termination provisions is the ability of the seller to terminate an agreement based on due diligence. If the parties have agreed that the seller will be responsible for the environmental conditions, and the due diligence reveals a previously unknown condition or that the cost of remediation would be significant, when representing a seller, I will want the seller to be able to terminate as well. Without such a contingency, a seller could be stuck with the cost of remediation if the buyer goes ahead with the deal.

Due diligence provisions should also address the scope of the due diligence. Will the seller allow invasive testing, such as sampling of soil or groundwater, often referred to as Phase II assessments? Many sellers have investigated their properties and do not want any additional sampling, on the chance that unexpected conditions are discovered. Yet investigations protect the buyer from the unknown. Therefore, if a seller will not allow invasive sampling, I ask for representations that the buyer has been provided all the information known about the environmental conditions at the property, and there are no other adverse conditions. I will also ask for an indemnity for breaches of such a representation and for any liability because of environmental conditions.

Sellers who allow the buyer to conduct Phase II sampling must decide whether they want the results (sometimes ignorance is bliss) or simply want to know whether the deal is going forward. If they are provided the results, I recommend requiring the consultant performing the work to allow the seller to rely on the results. This allows the seller to pursue the consultant for errors, under the contract, just as the buyer would be able to do. Whether they obtain the information or not, sellers should insist on a confidentiality provision, which requires the buyer to keep its information confidential unless otherwise required by law.

Other terms of access, which can either be set forth in the purchase agreement, if it will be signed before due diligence actually starts, or in a separate access agreement, include: notice of the timing and scope of investigation, restoration of the property after the investigation, responsibility of the party conducting the investigation to properly dispose of soil or groundwater generated as a result, insurance and/or indemnity for incidents that occur during the investigation, and confidentiality, as discussed above.

"Where?" Location, Location, Location

Where is the property or company? Different states have certain specific requirements triggered upon sales of businesses or real property, as well as different remediation programs to address contamination. In addition, state law will govern the requirement, if any, to report the environmental conditions discovered during the due diligence period to the appropriate agency. State law will also govern the types of permits required for a particular business or use.

Many states require sellers to notify either buyers or the state agency of the environmental conditions at the property at the time of a conveyance. Each state has its own applicability provisions, as well as specific reporting requirements. It behooves parties to a transaction to make sure they understand the framework within which they are operating, to avoid running afoul of such laws. Local counsel is an obvious resource for such information. Local environmental consultants, who are often conducting the due diligence on behalf of the buyer, are also a good resource.

Similarly, states differ greatly when it comes to the required reporting of environmental conditions discovered during due diligence. Requirements such as these are the reason many sellers do not want buyers to conduct any invasive sampling of a property. The results may trigger reporting to an agency and the subsequent enforcement action for the remediation of the conditions.

Some states require any person with knowledge of a "release" to report it to the state agency, while others only require reporting by the person responsible for the release. Some states require the reporting of the detection of contamination over certain published criteria. Again, it is important to understand the obligations of reporting before beginning due diligence.

On a more positive note, many states have voluntary remediation programs that allow "innocent" purchasers to conduct remediation and receive a covenant not to sue from the state agency. Such programs can increase the value of the property and eliminate the buyer's concern that it will become liable for environmental conditions on the property simply by being within the chain of title.

"Why?" Defining Client Goals

Why are we here? Why is the client interested in buying or selling the property? What is the client's goal in the transaction? If the client is a real estate investor or developer, is this a long-term investment or will the property be flipped in the near future? Will there be redevelopment or additions to the building? If this is a corporate transaction, are the economics of the overall deal such that the potential costs of the environmental liabilities or issues are not significant? Will the business continue to be conducted from the current location, or will it be moved or consolidated to another location in the near future?

Real estate investors have different strategies. Some purchase underperforming properties that need work, fix them up, and resell them. Others are more interested in the value presented by the current tenants, and their return is the cash flow of the property, rather than the increase in value generated by renovating or improving the property. If the client falls into the first category, we need to understand the potential impact of the environmental conditions at the property on that strategy. Will the environmental conditions result in significant increased costs to renovate the property, or even prevent it altogether? If the client is more like the latter, we need to know who the tenants are and what they might have done to the property.

Obvious potential environmental impediments to renovation are asbestos-containing materials and lead-based paint. Not so obvious impediments include contaminated building materials resulting from past use of the property. Buildings built before 1981 should generally be assumed to contain asbestos-containing materials and lead-based paint. Asbestos-containing materials are regulated by certain federal laws and regulations, specifically the Clean Air Act and the Occupational Safety and Health Administration's asbestos regulations, as well as state law. In general, asbestos in good condition need not be removed from a building, unless the building will be demolished or the structural members containing or on which the asbestos is located will be removed. However, friable asbestos-containing material (that is, asbestos that is not in good condition) must be removed.

Lead-based paint is generally only an issue for residential properties. The concern is the impact of elevated levels of lead in a child's blood. But lead-based paint can also render construction debris hazardous, depending on the concentrations of lead in the debris. It is generally a good idea to know where and how much lead paint is present to better understand the impact or regulatory status of the waste material.

Similarly, if a building is to be demolished, the potential impact of past uses of the building on the make-up of the construction debris must be determined. For example, transformers that leaked PCB-containing oil result in concrete that may need to be treated as a regulated waste and properly disposed of under the federal Toxic Substances Control Act. PCBs have also been found in paint, particularly in areas subjected to high heat, and the disposal of building materials with such paint may be regulated.

If the value of the property is in the occupants or tenants, the buyer should learn something about the tenants, specifically whether there is anything they have done or are doing that affects the environmental conditions at the property. Does the business handle hazardous materials? Are they being managed properly? Have there been releases? A commercial strip center with a dry cleaner presents a very different risk proposition to a buyer than one without. If the property is industrial in nature, perhaps with a single tenant, is it compliant with all applicable environmental laws? Many environmental laws apply to the "owner" and "operator," and a good buyer or landlord would be well served ensuring that the tenant is complying with applicable laws.

A good Phase I site assessment will involve learning more about the regulatory history of the tenants. It should also include a walk-through of all tenant spaces, to ensure that there are not sloppy housekeeping practices or obvious violations that will become an issue later. The best way to ensure that such issues are the tenant's, and not the landlord's, is a strong environmental section in the lease. Buyers need to review the leases from the point of view of the environmental obligations, as contractual obligations are likely to be stronger and a contract claim is often easier to substantiate than a common law negligence claim or a statutory cost recovery claim, if one is even available.

A lease may be an even more valuable tool when the investor is buying property that was previously sold in a sale-leaseback transaction. In the original sale-leaseback, the buyer had the representations and warranties and any covenants or obligations set forth in the sales agreement, and the ongoing obligations of the lease. When that buyer sells the property again, unless the sales agreement is assignable, the new buyer will only have the protections of the lease, or any new lease it may negotiate. This may be an opportunity to obtain some protections that were not obtained during the sale of the property.

"How?" Creative Strategies, Successful Deals

How can we protect the client? How can we address the environmental issues? How do we get a deal done? These are not mutually exclusive goals. The key is creativity. Set forth below are a few strategies I have used to get a deal done, even when it did not seem possible. These strategies fall into a few categories: due diligence, representations and warranties, covenants, cost allocations, and indemnifications.

For a buyer, the first tool is due diligence. Knowledge is power, and the person who knows more can negotiate a better deal. This means the seller should also know as much as possible about the site before selling it, so parties are on a level playing field when the negotiations begin. The buyer should look at records, have a Phase I site assessment performed even if there is no lender involved, and allow time for a Phase II site assessment if it proves necessary. If there will be renovation or demolition in the near future, consider having an asbestos survey performed. Some of this may be done pre-contract, but much of it will be done after the contract is signed, during the due diligence period. Therefore, the parties may have already negotiated the allocations of responsibilities and costs. Negotiating in the absence of information can be difficult (for example, with no remediation cost estimate, how do we factor that into the project cost?), but agreements can be structured to make allowances for that. The key is creativity and understanding the parties' objectives.

The seller may hesitate to let a buyer conduct an investigation, because it does not want to obtain unfavorable environmental information and the deal to be terminated for environmental reasons. The buyer does not want to step into an unknown liability. The parties could agree that the buyer can do the investigation, but unless the estimated cost of remediation is more than an agreed-upon amount, the buyer must go forward, and if it is over that amount, the seller has the option of paying the excess over the agreed-upon amount. This serves both parties' objectives—a firmer deal and a fixed exposure.

Due diligence also plays a role in allocating responsibility for site conditions, with the line being drawn at the closing date. It is not uncommon for the parties to divide responsibilities as follows: The seller indemnifies for pre-closing conditions, and the buyer indemnifies for post-closing conditions. If there is no baseline as to the environmental conditions on the property, and the entities are engaged in the same business using the same materials, it is often difficult to know whether a particular condition is a pre-closing or post-closing condition.

Indemnifications can also make or break a deal. As my clients hear from me all the time, an indemnification is only as good as the entity giving it. This is why large institution clients do not like selling property with environmental legacies to developers in return for a transfer of environmental liability—most often the buyer is a single-purpose entity with no assets other than the contaminated property. A solution may be a corporate guaranty, which has more substance. Another solution may be environmental insurance, either cost-cap or third-party liability insurance, which backstops the single-purpose entity's indemnification.

For the sale of a business, is the buyer interested, but highly concerned about being in the chain of title of the underlying property? Perhaps it is a business at which there were historically sloppy business practices, for which the buyer does not want to be responsible? Would a sale of the business assets, but a lease of the real property, satisfy both sides? Restructuring the deal may make it happen.

Does the seller want to avoid the responsibility for the environmental remediation solely for logistical reasons—the facility has shut down, the headquarters are located out of state, but it would just be difficult to get the work done. Does the buyer like the idea of doing the remediation because it has control, can ensure that the remedial work does not interfere with the business, but does not want to have paid the cost? Discounts are useful, but there are concerns. What if the estimate is wrong? The seller loses if the estimate is high, and the buyer loses if it is low. Escrows can avoid this issue. Putting the remediation costs estimate into an escrow allows the buyer to draw down on the escrow to pay the costs, but if there are funds remaining, the seller receives them.

The Bottom Line

There are as many ways of addressing environmental issues in a transaction as there are environmental issues. The key to any of these solutions is in understanding the client, its risk tolerance, and its business objectives. It is also important to understand the other side's goals and motivations, as they will need to buy into any solution as well. Once the client's needs are understood, creativity is necessary for coming up with a solution that can accomplish the client's objectives. Lastly, it is important to remember that occasionally the best way to satisfy the client's objectives is to kill the deal.

Pamela K. Elkow's environmental practice focuses on the voluntary remediation and redevelopment of brownfields; transactional environmental issues; compliance counseling; federal, state, and municipal permitting; and federal and state enforcement. She also works with clients on occupational health and safety issues, in both compliance and enforcement scenarios. Her clients include major corporations, municipalities, and other governmental entities. Ms. Elkow has been involved in a variety of brownfield redevelopment projects for both municipal and private-sector clients. She has also been involved as environmental counsel on a wide variety of transactions, negotiating environmental provisions of purchase and sale agreements, obtaining and reviewing environmental due diligence, and advising clients on post-closing remediation.

Ms. Elkow is a founder and member of the executive committee of the Connecticut Society of Women Environmental Professionals, an organization for women involved or interested in environmental law, science, business, and policy. She served as co-chair from 1999 through 2003. She is also a member of the executive committee of the Connecticut chapter of the National Brownfields Association. She has spoken and written on a wide variety of environmental issues to diverse audiences. She is a member of the American Bar Association's section on environment, energy, and resources and is a vice chair of its environmental technology and brownfields committee.

Ms. Elkow received her B.A., cum laude, from Colgate University. She received her J.D., with honors, from George Washington University, where she was a member of the Law Review. *She was a recipient of a Connecticut Bar Association 2006 Pro Bono Award. She is admitted to practice in Connecticut, New York, and the District of Columbia.*

Weighing All the Costs and Opportunities

Andrew D. Otis

Counsel

Curtis, Mallet-Prevost, Colt & Mosle LLP

The Skills of an Environmental Lawyer

My day-to-day practice as an environmental lawyer can be divided into three categories. First, I identify and analyze environmental risks and opportunities in transactions, which involves undertaking due diligence as well as retaining and supervising environmental engineering professionals. Furthermore, I identify and quantify risks and liabilities to help the parties determine how environmental assets should be allocated in the transaction. I help achieve and implement agreements through drafting documents, such as provisions of purchase and sale agreements and environmental indemnity agreements. Secondly, I supervise the remediation of contaminated assets and interact with the government on enforcement matters. Finally, I lead transactions that reduce greenhouse gas emissions in countries overseas to generate credits under the Kyoto Protocol. In my work, the greatest benefit I can offer my clients is the ability to identify, describe, and facilitate understanding of the potential liabilities and assets under the environmental regulatory structure of both the U.S. and foreign countries and relate those assets and liabilities to my client's overall business objectives.

Adding Value for the Environmental Law Client

The time at which I am brought into a transaction can vary greatly, but I am most effective when I am brought in as early as possible, when the client is still just considering a transaction either on the buy side or the sell side. When I am brought in early, I can help the client strategize about the structure of the transaction and the method of due diligence that should be used or allowed. I can also help the client think about price, both in selling and buying. On the sell side, I organize the data that will be provided, and on the buy side, I organize the due diligence that will be performed.

If I am working with a buyer, I add direct financial value by gathering as much information as the seller, or in some cases gathering even additional information that can be used to argue for a lower price. If I am working with a seller, I perform information analysis and prepare assets for sale in such a way that I reduce uncertainty, which in turn reduces the risk premium the buyer will demand. To the extent that there are unknown environmental liabilities, buyers tend to ask for a premium to deal with those unknown factors. However, by quantifying the environmental liabilities to the extent possible, one can reduce or even eliminate these premiums.

Troubled Times: Avoiding Client Mistakes

One of the most common mistakes on the sell side of a transaction is the seller's failure to understand the environmental conditions of the facilities. I occasionally hear my colleagues mention clients who claimed their property was clean and had no known problems, only to discover the site is completely contaminated and may require millions of dollars and several years to remediate. I always recommend that my clients know their site well when they are preparing for a sale.

Likewise, it is critical to perform extensive due diligence on the buyer's side. To the extent possible, make sure all the data is analyzed thoroughly. It is always cheaper to invest in a Phase I environmental site assessment than to find out the asset is worth $2 or $3 million less than anticipated because of undiscovered contamination.

Finally, I always urge my clients to reveal as much as possible about the environmental conditions of a site. It is never fruitful to hide the ball, because the information will eventually be discovered and come back to haunt you. It is not necessary to shy away from contaminated assets when both sides are open about the conditions. Obtaining contaminated sites at a discount, cleaning them up in an efficient manner, and reaping the value of a relatively clean site can be highly lucrative. In fact, many of my clients have begun to include this as part of their overall business strategy.

Fostering a Successful Working Relationship

As part of my personal approach, I strive to relate the environmental condition of the facility in question to my client's business goals. Environmental strategy should be part of and support the overall business strategy, and transactions should be structured such that my client can achieve a business advantage using environmental information or issues. This may mean either a price reduction on the buy side or a firm price on the sell side. I always try to help my clients understand what their risks and potential gains are, and then help them achieve those gains.

When a client has incorporated the environmental components into their overall business strategy, as opposed to thinking about the environment as a box that needs to be checked, I consider my work a success. I want to help my clients think about environmental issues when they think about the price of an asset, how long they will hold onto it, and how it fits into their overall set of assets. Clients should always consider their overall strategy in buying or selling a site.

I often find that clients require some education regarding environmental law, and once we have educated them, they can actively use environmental issues as part of their overall business strategy. I am always surprised at the variation in risk tolerance that exists in the marketplace. I have represented clients that have had contaminated assets to sell, and the response of different buyers regarding that contamination has been remarkably varied. Just because one buyer does not want to take on a contaminated asset does not meant no one will. Likewise, just because one buyer demands a large premium or price reduction does not mean another will not be willing to negotiate. Once clients understand there is real strategy behind the environmental considerations of a business, they will be able to use that strategy to achieve their goals more quickly and efficiently.

Lastly, in fostering a good working relationship with the client, it is critical to stay on top of one's knowledge of environmental law. I subscribe to four or five publications I review on a weekly basis, keeping me up to date on the general state of environmental policy and the changing rules of each program. I also try to participate in an annual environmental transaction roundtable, where environmental professionals who regularly participate in transactions can get together to exchange ideas and discuss the direction of the field. Additionally, I try to maintain an informal network of environmental lawyers with whom I speak on a regular though unstructured basis. This helps me get a sense of where people are coming from across the field. Each transaction brings up a new set of regulatory issues, and it is crucial to stay on top of developments to handle transactions appropriately.

Integrating the Environment into Business Structure

The proper way to integrate environmental matters into the overall structure of a company will depend on the parties and strategies involved. Will there be an entity that exists on the seller's side after the transaction? What will the buying party do with the assets? The tools I use the most are traditional indemnifications and escrows, price reductions, and separate environmental agreements. Approximately one out of every five clients has explored some sort of environmental insurance, but I have never been involved in a transaction where the client actually purchased such insurance due to the cost. However, I have seen transactions in which the client's target was covered by environmental insurance, which was used to address both known and suspected contamination. While I explore the issue of insurance two or three times yearly, keeping up on market terms and conditions, it is not typically a viable option for my clients.

Approaching the Initial Meeting

When first meeting with a client about environmental issues in a transaction, I inquire as to the structure of the transaction. The first question is to determine whether it is an asset deal versus a stock deal. From there, we discuss how long the client intends to hold onto the assets, whether they intend to operate the assets, whether they intend to integrate the assets with other assets, and their projected time frame for the transaction and for holding the assets.

In an asset deal, there are a great many more options for parceling or allocating liability. In a stock deal, the options are minimized by the fact that the buyer is assuming the liabilities of the seller. If I know whether the client will be operating the assets, how long they will hold onto them, and whether they will try to integrate those assets into other aspects of their operations, it helps me design the due diligence to answer the most important questions regarding any liabilities and ongoing compliance issues. Furthermore, I can answer the question of whether the assets will be operated in a way that is consistent with the client's environmental health and safety policies. From there, we can discuss the integration and time frame issues moving forward.

Lastly, it is important to talk about whether the target is a public or private company. If it is a private company, due diligence is relatively easy and straightforward. In a public company, however, there are a number of constraints on the way due diligence must be performed, as well as the message that performing due diligence sends.

In the first meeting, it may become apparent that a client has unrealistic goals for the transaction. For example, I find that only about 40 percent of clients have a realistic expectation for the time frame of a transaction. Those of us who work in the legal and environmental community are service professionals, so we do what we can to accommodate the time frames of our clients. Schedules can certainly be adjusted based on the resources available, and I will recommend working with a particular environmental consultant to clients who are operating on a particularly compressed time frame. However, clients must be aware that working on a compressed time frame can add additional costs. Furthermore, certain activities will require a certain amount of time, no matter how much money or resources the client can afford. I try to be as clear with my clients as early as possible about the reasonable time frames for these activities.

The Influence of Location

In the United States, laws in various jurisdictions do not have a great influence on strategy. Some jurisdictions in the United States have property transfer laws, including Connecticut and New Jersey, as a pre-condition to the transfer of title. These procedures can present a critical path constraint that must absolutely be dealt with to close the transaction, and which can push to resolve environmental contamination issues and assign responsibility. However, these special considerations are more an exception than a rule.

Outside the United States, location can have a much greater impact on strategy. In Western Europe, the regimes are fairly clear, and while European emissions reduction or remediation requirements tend to be negotiated to a greater degree than in the United States, there is at least some level of certainty as to the ultimate requirements. In Latin America, China, and other developing nations, there is much less environmental legal and regulatory infrastructure. While fewer regulatory requirements may at first appear to result in fewer responsibilities, in reality it can in fact be a burden, as it creates more uncertainty. In these circumstances, I urge the parties to be very specific about who will do what and when, creating an agreement between themselves regarding what tasks need to be undertaken as the transaction moves forward. Transactions in developing areas, therefore, can require more creativity.

There are two big challenges that affect international environmental transactions. The biggest is the general lack of regulatory structure, as this leads to greater uncertainty about potential liabilities. Most areas around the world have very general legal statements forbidding the pollution of the environment, without having any real regulatory underpinnings to describe what constitutes a violation. Therefore, specific emissions and remediation requirements are left to the discretion of enforcement authorities. Because the rule of law may or may not be operative and government officials unconstrained by law can always change requirements, sometimes for reasons unrelated to the environmental impact of a given facility or practice, this uncertainty can create additional problems.

Secondly, culture and language can present two significant barriers to transactions. For instance, I am currently working on documents from the Ukraine that have two separate and different English translations. It is one thing to translate a document into English, but it is another thing entirely to have that document mean the same thing in English as in its original language. This is especially salient in dealing with countries in which the rule of law is not as prevalent as in the United States and there may be different expectations of what an agreement can and should achieve. Even differences between common law and civil law jurisdictions can create different expectations regarding legal requirements and the role of regulatory authorities.

Environmental Negotiations: Structure, Challenges, and Attitudes

There are certain points within an environmental negotiation that tend to be negotiated more often or openly than others are. For instance, there is always a negotiation surrounding who will be responsible for addressing known and suspected contamination. Usually, negotiations also proceed over who will actually perform the work, who will pay the costs, and who will interact with the government. Keeping all three of those responsibilities with the same party usually properly aligns incentives, since a party who is responsible for paying the costs without overseeing the operations may feel that the other party is gold-plating the remediation or improving the facility at their expense. Furthermore, the entity that will maintain the assets after remediation is completed will usually want to be the entity that takes the lead in speaking with the government. However, parties may have legitimate reasons for separating these responsibilities. Environmental law is an interesting field in that it forces parties who would not otherwise interact post-closing to find a way to cooperate.

Negotiations on any deal point can vary from collegial to less collegial. However, if ongoing negotiations, ongoing responsibility, or joint operations will be required after closing, both parties have a vested interest in maintaining as much goodwill during the negotiations as possible. I occasionally see irresolvable issues pushed off to post-closing, but it is unrealistic to expect that parties who cannot reach an agreement prior to closing will succeed in doing so after closing. This can ultimately result in a breakdown of negotiations and, potentially, litigation. Because it is almost always more expensive to litigate a disagreement over remediation or compliance activity than it is simply to perform the activity, these are critical points to resolve before the negotiations end. There are, however, clients that will use post-closure indemnification as a tool to adjust the ultimate purchase price in a transaction, address issues unresolved prior to closing, or manage ongoing compliance or remediation obligations. Although it can be possible to recoup the cost of compliance and remediation investments through post-closure indemnification litigation, such strategies include all of the costs and risks of litigation generally.

I generally approach negotiations with a problem-solving, cooperative attitude. While I have been involved in competitive negotiations, I find that a cooperative approach is far more productive for both sides. Still, there are certain points that will be difficult to bridge, no matter how congenial the environment may be, and my ultimate goal is to protect my client's best interests. The most difficult points to negotiate are the post-closing cooperative actions, where both parties want to maintain a stake in dealing with the environmental issues. Conditions of uncertainty also make negotiations difficult, as there is no common understanding of the problem at hand. Lastly, the client's attitude can influence the negotiations quite a bit, and I strive to help the client understand what is necessary to achieve the best outcome in a negotiation, thus minimizing circumstances in which the client's attitude acts as a barrier to their own best interests.

Lawyer as Advocate: Working on the Client's Behalf

There are certain steps I can take to protect a client during negotiations. First, I can act as the bearer of bad news to the other side, if appropriate. I can also act as the one who stakes out a particular technical position and pushes for it, only to be pulled back by the client at the end to resolve an issue. In addition, if the two parties are having difficulty communicating, I can attempt to facilitate communication. Finally, I protect my client by being the first to receive technical information, thus saving the client a great deal of time analyzing data that can be more effectively summarized in a brief statement.

During the negotiations themselves, my role on behalf of the client is dependent upon the client's own expectations of me. Some clients want the lawyer to lead the negotiation and bring back a solution that works for them. Other clients want to be highly involved or even in charge of the negotiation, in which case I act as a support. I am flexible in either situation, as my goal is to achieve the best outcome for the client. This may require playing different roles depending on the dynamics of the negotiation.

In any case, I find it is very important to understand the dynamics of the negotiations outside the environmental area, which allows me to understand the role the environment plays in the negotiation. Of course, sometimes a client will determine it is not in their best interest for me to have access to that information. Again, these decisions are ultimately made by the client, and I am perfectly willing to act in whatever capacity they deem most useful.

The Flexibility Factor

It is always a challenge to work on a deal in which the opposing party is hostile. My best antidote to hostility is reasonableness, and in tense situations, I strive to maintain my composure as much as possible.

Occasionally, hostility needs to be met with hostility, although this decision must be made strategically as opposed to emotionally in the context of a negotiation.

In any negotiation, one must be willing to walk away from the table as a strategy. If an adversary is simply holding onto a position to test where the breaking point is, and I am reasonably certain that either the client will not deal under those circumstances or the deal will not be killed, I will consider advising my client to walk away. In some ways, taking this strategy can be like dealing with a child. The child pushes to try to find the boundary, and when that boundary is reached, there must be consequences.

Of course, there is a certain amount of flexibility in negotiation structure. I have had clients inform me of changes in risk tolerance midway through a deal, which to me indicates that the structure of the negotiation must be changed to adjust to the client's change in risk tolerance. If a client has a true change of heart and no longer wishes to pursue the deal, the question is how to terminate the negotiations while minimizing exposure to the other side's attempts to seek compensation.

One of the biggest mistakes an attorney can make in this area is to be focused on environmental issues to the exclusion of the overall business strategy, particularly for those of us dealing with specialty commercial transactions. Maintaining an overly narrow focus on one's specialty is like having the tail wag the dog. For me, the key is to use the environmental issue to contribute to the business strategy, rather than having the environmental issue drive the deal. An attorney overly focused on environmental issues can often make the mistake of pushing their clients to become locked into a particular outcome. Furthermore, they may get caught up in the specifics of drafting language in an agreement and lose sight of the client's overall objective for the transaction, which is never productive. Most of my clients recognize these pitfalls as much, if not more, than I do. They are quick to inform me if I am too focused on my specialty area. While there are cases in which I feel the client has not given due consideration to a certain point, clients have a general wariness about lawyers messing up agreements between parties through the drafting. I always strive to relate the drafting to my client's agreement, objectives, and understanding of the deal, explaining as clearly as possible why and how we have achieved their goals.

Advice for Environmental Law Practitioners and Clients

My best advice for another attorney in this area is to get to know the client, their business, and their objectives. While it is critical to know the law and the basic requirements thereof, it is impossible to know the laws of every jurisdiction completely. We are trained to understand and research legal issues, but there is no substitute for understanding the client, their goals, their risk tolerance, their business, and their expectations of each specific transaction. Most people will find that once they know the client, it is easier to make environmental issues part of the client's business plan. This gives the client another tool they can use to achieve their business objectives, allowing them to solve their issues in a more creative and productive manner.

On the client side, I have seen a recent trend toward increasing risk tolerance for contaminated assets. Today, looking at contaminated assets is no longer limited to specialty developers. A great many companies are looking to buy, clean up, and capitalize on contaminated assets. However, there are some issues related to this trend that are cause for client concern. One is the reopening by regulatory authorities of what were once considered remediated sites in order to address natural resource damage, which creates uncertainty about future remediation requirements. Clients become justifiably nervous about this issue, as they cannot account for the unknown costs and risks involved.

Of course, not all environmental issues are bad. Personally, I would like to see more clients considering the potential costs and opportunities associated with climate change and carbon emissions. There is a great amount of business opportunity to be had in this area, which I believe is, for now, somewhat underappreciated in the business world.

Andrew D. Otis practices in the area of environmental law. He defends and represents clients in matters involving environmental laws, regulations, and policies as they relate to transactions, litigation, and enforcement actions. He has supervised due diligence investigations and negotiated contract provisions defining and allocating environmental risks and assets in multiple domestic and cross-border mergers and acquisitions, financings, and real estate developments. He advises clients on issues associated with greenhouse gas emission reduction projects, including drafting and negotiating emission reduction purchase agreements and financing documents. He also has experience in international arbitrations in which there were numerous claims of non-compliance with major U.S. and foreign environmental, health, and safety laws. He advises clients on compliance with a variety of environmental statutes and regulations, including the Clean Air Act and the Comprehensive Environmental Response, Compensation, and Liability Act.

Prior to joining the firm, Mr. Otis spent nine years at the U.S. Environmental Protection Agency, where he played a key policy advisory role in a number of areas, including global climate change, the use of market mechanisms as innovative policy tools, and hazardous air pollutant regulation. Among other activities, he coordinated contributions from the agency's policy office to President Clinton's 1992 "Climate Change Action Plan." He also served the "Enterprise for the Environment" multi-stakeholder project chaired by former agency administrator William Ruckelshaus.

Mr. Otis is co-chair of the international law and practice section committee on international environmental law of the New York State Bar Association. He has developed and taught classes in environmental policy and law at both Indiana University and Vassar College. He is admitted to practice in the state of New York. He earned his B.A. from the State University of New York, his M.P.A. from Indiana University, and his J.D., cum laude, from Indiana University.

From Red to Black
by Way of Green:
The Use of Risk Transfer
Strategies to Turn
Environmental Liability
into Opportunity

David H. Quigley

Partner

Akin Gump Strauss Hauer & Feld LLP

The Environmental Lawyer's Role

As an environmental lawyer working with clients in a transactional context, I focus on the identification and management of potential environmental liabilities. For example, in the past decade we have witnessed a dramatic increase in two types of transactions that involve industry, those associated with financial restructuring and those caught up in the rise of private equity. In both cases, a group of decision-makers not intimately familiar with the liabilities involved in specialty chemical companies, power plants, or auto parts manufacturers, for example, is inserted on top of existing management. The newcomers face a number of relatively unfamiliar liabilities, including those that stem from legacy environmental concerns, such as historic releases or poor past environmental management practices, such as failure to comply with Clean Air Act permitting requirements. Since both creditors and private equity owners need to account for these liabilities and the uncertainties associated therewith as they restructure their acquisitions (formally or informally), they need assistance in identifying the source and the solution. It is here that the environmental attorneys can offer creative assistance. It is our job to help clients identify those liabilities to manage, and those to manage to avoid. In the event of the latter, we also need to identify opportunities to transfer away the liabilities, either for a one-time fee or, better yet, for an incoming payment, as described in greater detail below.

Adding the Most Value for Clients

Traditionally, the approach to managing environmental liabilities—be they legacy or management-related—included putting some type of "box" around them. In other words, the primary tools available in the past to an environmental manager consisted of quantifying the liability, accounting for it, and putting it on a shelf where he or she could live with it while hopefully keeping it from growing. This box could be made from a variety of materials, but I would say three predominated: indemnity, insurance, and prayer. In the indemnity context, the private equity purchaser of the facilities and assets of an industrial company received an indemnity from the company against liability arising out of past releases and other events. While probably the most concrete of the three boxes, the indemnity is not without risk. First, as the new owner of the facility, the private equity entity incurs liability under the Comprehensive Environmental Response, Compensation, and Liability Act of 1980 (CERCLA) as an owner/operator, which is joint and several. While the indemnity intends to protect against this liability, the expense of pursuing relief is still an issue, and there are likely to be other concerns related to the interpretation of the scope of the indemnity (let alone deductibles, baskets, caps, and other limits on the recovery). The negotiation of a rock-solid indemnity is perhaps the area in the first box where an environmental attorney adds the greatest value. Of course, an indemnity is only as good as the company that makes it. If that company goes away, so does the indemnity.

Insurance policies also can play a role in "boxing" environmental liabilities. There are two types: those that cover all pollution liability moving forward, useful as a shield when the liability is unknown (but typically expensive), and the cost cap, for instances with known contamination with an expected remediation cost. If costs rise above that expected value, the insurance kicks in. These are not generally thought to be as protective as an indemnity. For example, an environmental risk manager once told me there are two types of environmental insurance claimants: those who have been denied coverage and those who will be. However, with the right endorsements, negotiated by the right environmental attorney and, as importantly, the right broker, the attorney should at least be able to obtain a scope of coverage with which everyone is comfortable. If nothing else, he or she should be able to identify the potential for liability not covered by the insurance, equally important in identifying what not to put in the box.

As a last resort, there is always prayer. Prayer becomes valuable when a new owner decides—either because of the commercial terms of a deal or the likelihood that an indemnitor will not survive tomorrow—that there is no viable backstop against environmental liability. At that point, the traditional response was to pray against what is referred to as a "trigger." In other words, sure, the potential for liability is there, but it is hoped that there is no triggering event that would cause a government to notice it now and make the company do something about it. Above all of the other value added by an environmental attorney in this section, this is where we can provide the most help. Our job is to decrease the number of potential issues in the prayer box, either through expanding the first two boxes to alleviate the new owner's concern or by transferring the prayer box away altogether, sending the issues inside along with it. I prefer to focus on the latter.

One such risk transfer involves an outside party "buying" your liability, although the word "buy" appears a slight misnomer (it remains possible, if not likely, that the seller actually pays the buyer). This can approximate an insurance policy, or more often, it takes the form of an "asset" transfer, where the liability forms the asset (spinning heads, and accountants, along the way). Take, for example, a private equity company's purchase of a specialty chemical company with ten operating facilities. In addition to management and legacy liabilities at those ten sites, the company also has ten former sites with fences around them that no longer operate. While the chemical company and the private equity firm view these legacy sites solely as liabilities into which they pour remediation money, a risk transferee (armed with remediation and redevelopment expertise) may see them as future malls, parks, or even houses. That transferee will "purchase" the site and assume its liability, remediate it in-house (at cost savings), and develop it or "flip" it to another party to develop. The private equity company gets the benefit of an indemnity and the cleanup of the site on another party's dime, and the transferee gets or shares in the redevelopment value. The negotiation of these transactions combines and multiplies the complexities involved in all three of the traditional boxes, so it is essential for an environmental attorney to have experience with all three boxes in helping a new owner through the process.

With respect to adding value proactively by averting potential liabilities, the risk transfer comprises a powerful weapon. As an environmental attorney, I can help ensure the completeness of an indemnity or the comprehensiveness of an insurance policy, both of which help keep your boxes neatly on the shelf and not growing. The risk transfer adds to that arsenal an ability to shrink the boxes, and in some cases find potential for positive value in what the client otherwise views as a net negative. If you can provide your clients with an unexpected source of value, your services pay for themselves (or at least feel that way).

The Different Components of Environmental Law

The different components of environmental law, in an oversimplified sense, include a regulatory compliance component, a transactional component, a litigation component, and perhaps a public policy component. Many great environmental attorneys would argue that a project component exists as well, likely correctly. However, for the purposes of discussing typical services provided by environmental attorneys, these three will do.

As an environmental lawyer, I work on behalf of my clients with respect to each of these components. In terms of regulatory compliance, a client typically calls to ask whether a proposed change in procedures complies with environmental law, and if not, how to remedy the violation before it occurs. These types of exploratory questions often help inform clients about the scope of what they are able to accomplish and the best way to go about executing a certain task or initiative. An example of this would be when a sales, marketing, or production opportunity has arisen through the sales arm of the company, and the legal arm wants to make sure the proposed activity does not run afoul of the regulatory framework in place. The company wants to know what it must do, the registrations it must obtain, and the limitations by which it must abide. We provide advice regarding these elements.

With respect to transactional assistance, the major legal/environmental issues for which clients generally seek the advice of outside counsel include negotiating the indemnity (and related) provisions of purchase agreements, insurance agreements, and risk transfer agreements that make up the above strategies. The negotiable provisions include definitions, indemnity, representations, and warranties. I would add that in this arena, there are several phases leading up to and following the actual negotiation in which we provide assistance. These areas include due diligence identifying recognized environmental liability and sources of potential environmental liability before the transaction, and post-transaction management of the liabilities identified and now purchased.

If my practice were a Venn diagram, the two bubbles for the transactional and regulatory counseling components would connect, with the intersection being the litigation component. During the post-transaction management of acquired liabilities, environmental attorneys assist clients in determining and negotiating with regulators the scope of any required investigation or remediation, using litigation to challenge that scope when it exceeds the regulators' authority. When the regulators do appropriately call for investigation and/or remediation activities, we can assist in recovering any costs the clients spend thereon, often through litigation interpreting and enforcing the agreements negotiated above. In brief, and by way of example, let us assume we assert an aggressive position limiting the soil investigation our clients must undertake at their new facility, recently purchased from a competitor. If a government or other third-party entity challenges that position, we may end up in litigation to confirm the legality of our actions. If our client agreed with the government, or if it seeks to perform investigation and remediation regardless of the government's position, we may be able to argue that the activities result from a false representation made by a seller (often in the form of undiscovered but historic contamination surfacing—literally, in some cases). We litigate to ensure that responsibility remains allocated appropriately and to recover costs expended in the investigation/remediation thereof.

Finally, with respect to public policy, if all of the above do not result in a favorable outcome for our clients, we work with the regulators and legislators to create a more equitable environment. For example, where the scope of investigation and remediation requested by the regulators appears to exceed their authority, we will work with them to clarify the scope or work with Congress to clarify the authority.

The Financial Implications of Environmental Law

The environmental risk transfer mechanism described below provides an excellent illustration of the financial implications of environmental law in two very different contexts. First, in the financial restructuring context, we represented the unsecured creditors of a metal/chemical company reorganizing under the bankruptcy code. As part of that reorganization, we helped identify and quantify the environmental liabilities associated with each facility. Based on additional environmental input, management then determined, because of the earning capacity of each facility, which facilities the reorganized entity would continue to operate and which it would look to sell.

We were able to add direct value during this sale process because we knew the extent of legacy liability remaining at the sites. We also knew that, while the facilities did not present the opportunity for profit as operated, they held value (in this case from scrap metal alone) that exceeded their environmental liabilities. While the company itself had no interest or capability in the scrap business, we worked with a liability transfer company, who could recognize greater scrap value and, more importantly, had a desire and capability to realize it. That transferee ultimately purchased the site, assumed the environmental liability, and provided the company with an indemnity therefore. We negotiated the terms of that indemnity, and more importantly, we were able to negotiate upward the liability transfer company's original offer because the due diligence we performed demonstrated that their projected environmental remediation cost exceeded reasonable estimates. The transaction ended up as a win/win scenario. Scrap value rose substantially and everyone involved made money off a site that no longer operated and weighed down an entire bankruptcy estate.

Similarly, we helped a private equity firm that had purchased the facilities of a specialty chemical company resolve some of the legacy environmental liabilities it inherited. First, we initiated, and favorably resolved, litigation applying the purchase agreement to recover the costs of ongoing remediation at one of the idled facilities. As an idled facility, the site offered little to no potential economic benefit to the private equity firm and faced millions of dollars in remediation costs. The litigation recovered a substantial portion of these costs, reducing the overall losses at the site. Indeed, we continue to work to transform the idled site into positive value for the private equity firm. The site, if clean, could serve a variety of light industrial, commercial, or even residential purposes. We currently are negotiating with environmental risk transfer companies and other potential liability purchasers to transfer the site for a potential net positive, in addition to the receipt of an indemnity for all known and unknown liability. Thus, we can create value at the idled legacy portions of an industrial company that a new purchaser may have written off as a net loss, or at best a net zero.

Common Client Mistakes with Respect to Environmental Law

The largest pitfall environmental attorneys generally face when working with clients in the transactional context is not getting the right information about the potential environmental liabilities. We call it giving due diligence its due. I think when companies ask their counsel (assuming they do), both legal and technical, to perform due diligence, often their only metric for measuring that diligence (if they are purchasing a company from a different industry, for example) comes down to what the materials reviewed said about the environmental liabilities. They may be too quick to evaluate the materials they receive from the target, often missing the larger issue of whether they received the right materials or even asked the right questions. An answer, even in the form of environmental due diligence materials, is only as good as the question asked.

It is of paramount importance to involve an experienced attorney early in the process. At my firm, for example, we develop industry and transaction-specific due diligence questionnaires building upon our past experiences with a particular industry or geographic area. We then carefully evaluate the initial response to those inquiries (unfortunately often akin to a form letter) to formulate a supplemental, more targeted, and if necessary more pointed supplemental due diligence request to gather the information necessary to evaluate the transaction. Clients need counsel and consultants who know the industry, know the applicable regulatory schemes, and hopefully, know how to anticipate any environmental concerns that might not be documented. At a minimum, an environmental attorney must ensure compliance with the relatively new appropriate inquiry standards to protect his or her client.

Promulgated on November 1, 2005, and effective one year later, the new "all appropriate inquiry" rule establishes the due diligence requirements that must be satisfied for a purchaser to avail itself of the innocent landowner protections of the CERCLA.[1] A party qualifies as an innocent landowner if, before acquiring the property, it did not know or have reason to know of any contamination thereon. Moreover, after taking possession of the

---

[1] The CERCLA imposes strict liability for removal or remediation activities at a contaminated facility on: the current owner or operator of the facility, the owner or operator of the facility at the time of the disposal of hazardous materials, and any party who arranged for the disposal of hazardous materials at the facility. See 42 U.S.C. §9607(a)(1)–(3). The act requires that a liable party either remove or remediate the contaminated materials itself, or reimburse third parties (including governmental entities) if those third parties step in to incur removal or remediation costs. See 42 U.S.C. §9607(a)(4).

property, the landowner must comply with all land use restrictions, take "reasonable steps" to prevent releases, and cooperate with regulators. See 42 U.S.C. §9601(35). Under the rule, the obligations of a party seeking the benefits of these defenses no longer end with the hiring of an environmental consultant to perform a Phase I assessment. The purchaser itself must (1) conduct a search of environmental cleanup liens affecting the site, (2) apply any specialized knowledge of the site and surrounding area to determine the likelihood of environmental impacts, and (3) assess the purchase price of the property in relation to the market and consider whether any diminished price suggests the possible existence of environmental contamination. The party must provide these results and conclusions to the environmental consultant preparing the site investigation report.[2]

Substantively, the "all appropriate inquiry" rule requires more from the consultants conducting the site assessment as well. The rule requires these environmental professionals to:

- Conduct an on-site investigation of the subject property and adjoining properties, the latter from the property line if access is not possible.
- Consider conditions indicative of a release of hazardous substances, and identify and resolve any significant data gaps that affect their ability to identify such conditions.
- Interview the current owner and occupants, past "major occupants," current and past site managers, past owners and operators, and neighboring landowners (if the property is abandoned).
- Review federal and state records, as well as those of tribal and local governments for a period as far back as the site contained structures.

In general, the consultant must complete these inquiries, or at least update them, within 180 days prior to the closing of the transaction.

---

[2] While the rule itself does not require this transfer of information, see 42 C.F.R. §312.25(b), a revised ASTM standard (E-1527-05) implementing the rule does.

How to Best Help Clients with Environmental Issues

Once the diligence is complete and the environmental liabilities have been identified, the focus shifts to what to do about it. While I certainly did not invent the liability transfer mechanism, we are now seeing the first wave of attorneys (and it is indeed a large wave) to grasp its full potential and recommend it to their clients. It may not yet be as prevalent as the use, or at least recommendation for use, ten years ago of environmental insurance (I think by now every corporate environmental manager has been directed to an environmental insurance policy by their attorneys or consultants at least once), but it is gaining traction quickly. Those of us who adopted the approach early and understand its nuances enjoy relating the liability transfer back to the environmental laws that spawned it, from the CERCLA to the various brownfield laws and voluntary cleanup programs sprouting from state to state. These programs typically "protect [a party] from having to conduct containment or cleanup…at a brownfield site if they meet the definition of a 'bona fide prospective purchaser' and the additional requirements in the statute." See, e.g., Virginia Department of Environmental Quality, Brownfields Land Renewal: Brownfields Manual 7 (2004). The bona fide prospective purchaser requirements often mirror the "all appropriate inquiries" standards laid out previously.

Achieving Success in the Role of Environmental Attorney

Success often is defined by how well an attorney works with his or her clients. In environmental law, counsel must work closely and openly with clients when developing an approach to identifying, managing, resolving, or disposing of environmental liability. In particular, the environmental attorney must be able to bridge the gap between the technical employees of the acquired or restructured company and the new management. The employees know the environmental liability and what it will take to remediate it. The management must box the liability, and must understand when and how to move the boxes when the remediation proffered by their employees and consultants does not fit within their business plans. Praying that the boxes will not grow does not always work. At times, remediation makes sense. At times, insurance makes sense. At times, prayer may even make sense. Any one of these options can lead to success under the right circumstances, but only if the attorney can understand the perspective of the technical people in the acquired company, the needs of the new management, and what constitutes the "right" circumstances. If he or she does not understand where the acquired company came from, where the management is going, and the background against which it all happens, it is not possible to truly achieve success.

Further, to achieve success in this field, it is important for attorneys to stay on top of their knowledge with respect to emerging and current issues in environmental law. While books are a great start, nothing replaces talking with the environmental management of a variety of companies from a variety of industries. I talk with my clients' environmental personnel every chance I get. Each person and company has their own way of documenting environmental concerns, cataloging and managing their legacy liabilities, and negotiating with regulators. More importantly, they are the people who have remediated the same or similar contamination you now face, so you can benefit greatly from the comparison between their projected costs and their actual liability. With all of this information in tow, it is possible to negotiate the indemnity for your current problem or determine when it makes sense to transfer that risk to someone else, knowing how much that risk may cost and to what degree of certainty. While this knowledge and interaction will not always enable an attorney to turn a negative into a positive, more often than not it will be possible either to reduce uncertainty or to turn the negative into a smaller negative.

The First Step in Determining the Type of Strategy to Follow

The first step in determining strategy in any environmental matter is understanding the long-term goals of the client. As counsel, I need to know how long the client intends to own/manage the asset and how much time I have to increase the value. This is a critical step, because this knowledge dictates the choice of boxes for the environmental liability. If the company intends to run the acquired entity indefinitely, they can stand to benefit from the redevelopment of the site, for example. I would rely upon the indemnity to fund the client's remediation, and then look to the client to redevelop the site once clean.

If my client has neither the time nor the energy to remediate, I am more likely to turn to a risk transfer firm to take the site off their hands. They can spend the time and money to remediate over the next few years. The client receives value for the site immediately (albeit smaller than if the company remediated and redeveloped the site itself) at the front end and can move on with the management of the going concern, unencumbered by the weight of the cleanup liability. I accomplish this step by really talking to my clients. While it sounds simple, it is amazing how few environmental attorneys talk to, or even meet, their clients. The corporate attorneys typically play this role, but in instances where environmental liabilities affect the bottom line, environmental attorneys should always be involved in the conversation.

The Laws That Govern the Way an Attorney Proceeds

While there is not one single law that governs the management of environmental matters (indeed, there are few environmental laws that do not come into play in any given transaction), the CERCLA does play a major role and serves as an excellent starting point.[3] The CERCLA sets out who the potentially responsible parties are at a site. Much of the language in an indemnity agreement, insurance policy, or liability transfer document emanates from the categories of responsible parties set out in CERCLA §107: the owner and operator of a facility; any person who at the time of disposal of any hazardous substance owned or operated any facility at which hazardous substances were disposed of; any person who arranged for the disposal of hazardous substances; and any person who accepts hazardous substances for transport or disposal.

In brief, the effect of this law is that it sets out who the government may order to investigate and remediate a contaminated facility and from whom those parties may seek contribution or cost recovery. While each state may have its own Superfund, or voluntary compliance program akin to those described above, most mirror (if not incorporate) the basic concepts of the CERCLA.

---

[3] While it is the better subject of a book than a chapter, other environmental laws typically at issue in a transaction, and for which due diligence must account, include the 1976 Resource Conservation and Recovery Act (waste management), the 1970 Clean Air Act (as amended in 1990), and of course 1969's National Environmental Policy Act (requiring federal agencies to incorporate environmental considerations in their decision-making).

Determining the Proper Way to Structure a Deal

As discussed above, when determining the proper structure for a deal, the tantamount concern comes back to the client's long-term plans, as well as the client's objectives, financial circumstances, and tolerance for risk. Secondarily, the degree of environmental contamination at the site and the uncertainty surrounding the cleanup costs play a role as well. A company and its counsel also must consider a variety of other factors, such as pending litigation, governmental response actions, and the future viability of the land.

The types of deals I have performed on behalf of private equity clients demonstrate the factors that must be considered when determining the ultimate deal structure. Typically, a private equity firm that purchases a corporation will acquire a variety of operating sites. Many of these sites are profitable and can more than cover their own environmental liabilities. Some, however, may remain idle at the time of acquisition, and either cost the firm money in remediation at the present time, forcing them to put it in the indemnity or cost cap insurance box, or risk costing the firm money in remediation later upon some sort of trigger (the prayer box). In this situation, there are two strategies a private equity firm can use to deal with the non-operating sites. The first strategy works if the firm has the know-how to conduct the remediation and the time and desire to do it. If so, the firm manages the environmental liabilities at the site, funds and conducts the environmental remediation, redevelops the site, and potentially sells it at a stepped-up value. Clients that pursue this option must be comfortable with the inherent risks of environmental remediation and likely have experience in the actual implementation of a remedy. The risks include higher-than-anticipated response costs, a slower-than-expected remediation process, the possibility of being sued, and the chance that the government may demand a more stringent cleanup remedy. General Electric's PCB experience and the looming battle over mercury remediation provide excellent illustrations of these risks.

To avoid these risks, or if a company does not possess the knowledge or desire to conduct a cleanup operation (which many private equity firms do not), the firm can transfer the environmentally contaminated sites to a firm that specializes in environmental remediation and redevelopment.

Following this second strategy produces several advantages for the private equity client. First, the client may obtain a significant up-front cash payment by selling the sites. Although they will not realize the same value as they would for a "clean" site or even a brownfield ready for redevelopment, the company receives some positive value, or at least makes a smaller payment. Secondly, these agreements typically include a full indemnity for the seller, under which the transferee assumes the risks delineated above with respect to increased response costs, heightened government cleanup requirements, and the risk of litigation. Eliminating these risks can provide peace of mind to the client and can free up managerial resources to focus on the primary business activities of the acquired company. Public companies can benefit from these transfers as well, which remove liabilities from balance sheets, clear up reserves, and avoid uncertainties over reporting requirements.

Each of these components must be accounted for in the structure of the deal, from the initial purchase agreement and its indemnities to the transfer agreement and its indemnities. The former protects the private equity firm or other purchaser should it decide to undertake remediation to position the site for redevelopment itself, and the latter offers protection in the event of a transfer to a third party to remediate the site. Either way, the indemnification must be structured to protect the seller from any future actions, administrative proceedings, claims, liabilities, losses, penalties, fines, and damages that may occur at the property. Additionally, in the case of a transferee, the purchaser must agree to fund and perform all future environmental remediation, including any environmental operations or maintenance activities that may be required by any federal, state, or local governmental agency. These provisions also release the seller from any potential liability under the CERCLA and transfer the risk of all future response actions onto the purchaser.

With respect to the factors that will influence the strategy, it ultimately boils down to the client's long-term plans, their tolerance for risk, and their capacity to manage environmental liabilities. Additionally, I need to identify the type of contamination present and the potential for expansion of the required investigation/remediation, either through the identification of additional contamination or the imposition of more stringent governmental requirements.

Negotiations in an Environmental Matter

In negotiating environmental matters, I find (somewhat surprisingly) that the numbers themselves often become the least controversial elements. Once the parties agree on the framework (in other words, on what liabilities are assumed, what risks of unknown contamination will transfer to the purchaser, and what scope of indemnity comes back and for how long) the numbers fall into place. Other commonly negotiated points include the allocation of third-party claims for personal injury and property damage, determining who maintains responsibility for natural resources damages, and structuring the form of and support for the indemnity (i.e., will it be backed by insurance or a trust/escrow account?).

I wish I could say this is because there is general agreement as to how much a certain contamination will cost to remediate and what the risk of government intervention is, but the reality is that these items become so much of an unknown in some cases that the parties avoid them, focusing instead on the items they can better evaluate. These latter items include the value of the property upon redevelopment, the amount for which the scrap material at the site can be sold, and other like matters. After that, everyone swaps their estimates of environmental costs. The environmental lawyer will do as much diligence as possible so he or she can support the client's estimate, and then it becomes a tug of war, one in which the side with better information almost always wins. Regardless, by that point, the attorneys already have allocated the number, and counsel just fills in the blank in the agreement when the negotiations are complete.

In contrast to the openly negotiated matters, I would say the aspects that are most often negotiated in a hostile manner include future use of the site. This almost always becomes an issue in dealing with non-operating legacy sites. The selling party has already placed their prayer box around a closed site, hoping that the best way to keep costs down is to keep the site idle. If my client, as purchaser, sees redevelopment value in the site, particularly for a higher use, the seller knows that will bring with it expensive remediation. If I am asking the other side to indemnify me for future costs, this will quickly become a sore subject. Sellers will argue that a trigger will never come, and they do not want to pay for newcomers forcing a triggering event through redevelopment. Buyers will argue that the contamination pre-dated their arrival, so the predecessor should pay.

Steps Taken to Protect Clients

There are a number of ways to protect clients when working on deals involving environmental law. First, the attorney can go outside of the deal and obtain insurance. Another method is to work within the deal to obtain an indemnity. Additionally, it is often possible to work to structure a deal to minimize the risk that your client will fall into one of the categories of responsible parties.

With respect to the indemnity obligation, it is important to recognize that an indemnity is only as good as the company that makes it. You will want to perform adequate research to ensure that sufficient assets lie within the indemnitor to cover its obligations.

A Typical Strategy for Use in Every Environmental Matter

The single most important strategy for any matter is simple: Get the best information. It is not possible to evaluate options for moving forward if you do not know what happens in the absence of any movement. Proper due diligence, which means going beyond simply reviewing whatever information the seller provides,[4] is the heart of every transaction involving industry. I liken the absence of doing appropriate due diligence in circumstances like these to ordering food at a new restaurant where you refuse to look at a menu or ask the waiter for suggestions. It is true that if you have been to enough similar restaurants, you may have an idea of the type of food available, but you probably do not know the pitfalls (for example, ordering sushi if the menu looks like that of a pancake house). As importantly, you are unlikely to know where to find unexpected sources of value.

---

[4] The biggest strategy mistake I have seen another attorney make in an environmental matter is to assume the due diligence provided by the other side was sufficient to catalog the universe of risk. It is essential that an attorney know what else to ask for and who else to talk to. Relying on the seller to provide everything you need to know is like looking to hit a fastball because the pitcher tells you one is coming.

In environmental law in particular, the risk of the unknown is great and comes from many sources: unidentified contamination, change in enforcement strategies because of a change in the administration, change in the cleanup standards, and arbitrary application of those standards. All of these place such emphasis on the adequacy of the due diligence. Once you identify the sources of uncertainty and potential liability, you can box the liability as above or, maybe better, transfer it away. Note that this works particularly well if you never operated the site. Once you no longer own it—and assuming you never operated it—you are out of the CERCLA liability chain described above.

The strategy of obtaining as much detailed information as possible applies to all my cases, regardless of who sits across the table. Indeed, the opposite party does not really affect the way I structure a typical environmental deal, unless that party is (1) a governmental entity or (2) a party with whom I have dealt before. With respect to the former, this owes to the restrictions placed on a government's ability to transfer contaminated properties (see the early transfer authority provisions of the CERCLA). With respect to the latter, you tend to already have the basics of an agreement in place. You know what definitions on which you can agree, which helps determine the scope of indemnity protection. The definition of environmental laws, hazardous materials, and, most importantly, cleanup standards to which the property must be remediated plays a strong role in structuring the deal.

David H. Quigley's practice covers an array of environmental matters, including transactional, enforcement litigation, regulatory compliance, lobbying, and legislative development. He has managed environmental due diligence in connection with acquisitions totaling more than $1 billion in assets. He drafts the environmental representations, warranties, and indemnities in complex mergers and acquisitions, and he has negotiated the scope of those provisions. He also assesses the scope of environmental liabilities faced by companies reorganizing under the U.S. Bankruptcy Code, and he drafts and evaluates environmental aspects of plans of reorganization. With respect to environmental litigation, he managed the discovery process in complex lawsuits filed under the Clean Air Act's new source review provisions and argued related motions in federal court. He developed fair notice and health effects defenses to the new source review suits, and he took and defended testimony related to these defenses both at deposition and at trial. He also has litigated a variety of environmental indemnity claims. Mr. Quigley's regulatory compliance *practice focuses on issues arising under the solid and hazardous waste regulations. He also advises clients on policy issues and represents clients regarding these issues before members of Congress, the Environmental Protection Agency, the Department of Energy, and the Department of Defense.*

Mr. Quigley received his B.S. with distinction in natural resources from Cornell University in 1995 and his J.D. in 1998 from Harvard Law School, where he served as a line editor of the Harvard Environmental Law Review. *He is a member of the District of Columbia, New York, and New Jersey Bars.*

Acknowledgment: *The author would like to thank Jasi Kamody for her assistance in completing this chapter.*

Creating a Win-Win Situation

Joseph D. Picciotti

Member and Leader, Environmental Practice Group

Harris Beach PLLC

The Importance of Early Involvement

My practice includes environmental litigation, as well as negotiating the sale and purchase of properties affected by environmental issues. For transactions that involve environmental issues, I add the most value when the client involves me in negotiations early on, so I have input on the basic structure of the purchase agreement. Thus, with early involvement, the transaction can be structured in a manner that best meets the client's needs by taking into account, among other factors, the client's appetite for risk, the time constraints for closing, and other critical factors. In fact, for this reason, some of the best transactions are those that don't close. If I am brought in early on—before the client becomes more financially and emotionally invested—I will be in a position to analyze available information and put the client in a position to allow him or her to walk away before additional time and money is invested in a deal that does not meet the client's needs.

Moreover, early involvement allows me to structure the agreement in a manner that allows the client to opt in or opt out of the transaction during the due diligence process based on test results or historic information that is developed. When appropriate, we structure the purchase agreement so that if during the due diligence period historic or analytical information (testing) identifies claims, potential claims, or other risks, the client can, at certain critical points, decide whether to continue toward closing, restructure the deal, or opt out of it. To adopt the appropriate structure for the purchase agreement, we first ascertain the client's appetite for risk, the availability of insurance that would provide coverage for investigating and/or remediating contamination, and the value of the property. Early involvement in the negotiating process allows the environmental lawyer to identify relevant information and analyze it so critical terms of the purchase agreement can be added (including indemnifications, representations and warranties, escrow provisions, and similar provisions) to ensure that the transaction is structured to meet the client's needs.

As a result, when representing a purchaser, the transaction should be structured so there is a series of decision points or milestones whereby the client can opt in or opt out of the transaction or seek to restructure it based on information developed through the due diligence process. In this regard, if during due diligence we identify a significant environmental issue that materially affects the value of the property or reveals contamination issues that must be addressed, we identify alternatives as to how to manage such risks. Thus, when significant environmental issues are identified there are any number of alternatives available to manage such risks, including testing to evaluate the nature and extent of the problem or entering into a government brownfield remediation program to obtain lucrative tax or other credits and to be eligible for applicable statutory defenses. In addition, there are other tools to manage risks associated with contamination, which range from escrow provisions whereby the purchaser or seller agrees to fund the investigation or cleanup or share the cost, to renegotiating the purchase price.

The principles articulated above concerning the strategy for a purchaser applies equally when representing a seller. For example, if through the due diligence process significant issues are identified from site testing that result in the purchaser seeking to restructure the transaction, or that might expose the seller post-closing to cleanup claims and the purchaser is unwilling to take on that responsibility, the seller must consider undertaking the cleanup prior to or following closing. When representing a seller, it should also be in a position to at critical milestones have the option of completing the transaction under the original terms, restructure it, or opt out, depending on the development of information during the due diligence period. Thus, from the seller's standpoint, if substantial environmental issues are discovered during the due diligence period that potentially have an impact on the value of the property and its sale price, the seller must also have the option to cancel the transaction or renegotiate it. As such, when it meets the client's needs we structure the purchase agreement so the seller also has the ability to opt out or continue based upon the seller's desire to perform the cleanup itself or pursue other alternatives to address issues identified during the due diligence process.

Thus, there are any number of tools available to address contamination concerns, including funding remediation and/or investigations through government programs identified during the due diligence process, including funding to address contamination identified during the due diligence process. In New York, the brownfield program can be quite lucrative for developers of contaminated sites, as upon completion of the remediation and development, lucrative tax credits are paid to the applicant based upon the cost of cleanup and development, as long as the cleanup is certified as meeting New York State Department of Environmental Conservation standards. New York Environmental Conservation Law §27–1419. A seller can use the credits that would be available under a government cleanup program to leverage its position when negotiating the purchase price for a property with environmental issues.

With the availability of such governmental cleanup programs, transactions dealing with these kinds of properties can be more attractive than some may realize. The tradeoff to entering your client into such programs is that it often takes significant time to complete the brownfield cleanup process, as not only must cleanup requirements be met and confirmed by follow-up testing, but also because there is usually a public process involved in selecting the remedy to investigate and remediate the property. Further, at least under New York's brownfield program, the person undertaking the cleanup does not receive any of the benefits (i.e., tax credits or limitations on liability) until the cleanup is completed and can be demonstrated to have met applicable standards. New York Environmental Conservation Law §27–1419.

Time is often a critical factor in any transaction, including those involving assets with environmental issues. If the environmental lawyer is brought in at the last minute simply to review due diligence information after the structure of the transaction has been finalized (i.e., representations and warranties have been negotiated, provisions for the shifting risk, including indemnification provisions, have been finalized), it may be too late to maximize the benefit of environmental counsel, and too late to get the best deal for the client. Thus, it is far more advantageous to the client to bring in the environmental lawyer early to allow him or her to quarterback the deal before the critical business terms of the purchase agreement are finalized. While environmental lawyers can always help identify issues and potential problems at any point in a transaction, bringing in environmental counsel at the eleventh hour to essentially bless or terminate a transaction based on previously developed due diligence information is not effective.

The Financial Value of an Environmental Lawyer

When considering the purchase of a property with environmental concerns, the biggest risk is that what appears to be an asset can at least potentially become a significant liability. The financial ramifications of environmental problems, including cleanup obligations and claims by off-site property owners, can be quite substantial if no provision is made to protect the client from such risks. As discussed previously, there are any number of tools that may be employed to address risks associated with information developed during the due diligence process.

For those transactions involving property that is even potentially affected by contamination, the purchaser must conduct due diligence so as to meet the federal "all appropriate inquiry" standard for the purchaser to be eligible for certain statutory defenses under federal law and (in many cases) for the purchaser to qualify for financing. This relatively new standard (previous iterations of this standard had been in effect over the last several years) is being adopted more by financial institutions as a condition precedent to financing transactions involving properties with environmental issues. Thus, the "all appropriate inquiry" standard identifies the criteria the purchaser must use to conduct due diligence on property, as such standard must be met for the purchaser to assert certain defenses under the Comprehensive Environmental Response, Compensation, and Liability Act of 1980 as amended. Title 42, Section 9601(35)(A)–(B). In essence, the new standard requires the prospective purchaser to seek specific information from the current owner and others regarding current and previous operations on the subject property and on adjacent properties. 40 Code of Federal Regulation §312 (ASTM E1527–05). Following the requirements of the standard allows the purchaser to assert certain defenses to cleanup obligations or off-site claims associated with previous contamination.

Nevertheless, complying with the requirements of the "all appropriate inquiry" standard will certainly not ultimately protect the client's interests and, at the very least, it could lose the purchase price, not to mention lost opportunity costs and the expenses and costs associated with having to assert the referenced defenses in any proceedings that may be initiated regarding the property. In fact, even an extended due diligence process that complies with the standard, including undertaking substantial testing, will not guarantee that the client will avoid risk associated with latent contamination.

Indeed, even for transactions in which substantial due diligence is undertaken, including completion of testing, sometimes there will not be a definitive answer as to the nature and extent of contamination. This is why it is important to identify for the client, even before the due diligence process is begun, options it may have to allocate risks of latent contamination, including establishing an escrow fund for addressing the contamination issues, requiring the seller to complete any remediation required prior to closing, or entering the property into a governmental cleanup program. Moreover, the structure of the entity taking title to such property must also be carefully considered to best protect the client's interests.

Thus, as indicated, simply walking away from a deal can sometimes be the best course of action, particularly where environmental concerns are identified during the due diligence process that significantly affect the value of the property or that would materially impact its intended use, and there are no appropriate alternatives available to address those concerns. This saves the client from larger costs down the road, particularly if the property would have required remediation by a regulator such as a state local or federal agency, or has the potential to become a subject of a claim by an off-site landowner. Clients who are in a position to enter into a state cleanup program and become eligible for credits will be able to at least potentially add value to a transaction with contamination issues, particularly one that involves significant development costs. In the event that a client does enter a cleanup program, it must be willing to invest the time necessary to progress the property through the often-extensive application process, and to complete the cleanup and other requirements before any credits are paid to the client.

Working Successfully with the Environmental Law Client

My background is rooted in environmental litigation, including defending clients in regulatory compliance prosecutions, and that background informs the strategy I employ in negotiating transactions involving environmental issues.

One of the biggest mistakes a property owner can make is to ignore potential environmental violations before they escalate. For example, a client owning an operation that is subject to environmental regulation where violations have been issued, but who has not addressed them, is risking the potential for a more significant fine or other punitive action by a regulator in the future. Ignoring such problems will eventually have ramifications in the form of fines, negative affects on financing or refinancing a property, as well as negatively affecting the sale price. If the client does not address the underlying practices that caused past violations, it is setting itself up from a fall later. When the client seeks to sell a property that has been the subject of such violations, the sale price can be substantially affected. An environmental lawyer should advise clients to look to address policies or procedures that spawned past violations and address the same to avoid future violations and the additional negative impacts associated with them.

At the outset of a transaction, it is essential for the circulation of a summary that identifies the material provisions of the purchase agreement to obtain consensus on those provisions on which the parties can agree so the transaction may move forward. On the other hand, the exchange of complete drafts of agreements before the parties agree on principal terms is a waste of time and resources. Thus, prior to the circulating of a draft of the entire agreement, we circulate a memorandum or at least an outline that identifies the principle areas of agreement and the contentions between the parties. From this memorandum, the parties of the transaction will be in a better position to draft a final agreement. While there will always be a period of revising and editing, the process outlined above at least avoids the parties expending the time and resources of exchanging draft agreements with diametrically opposed terms.

In any transactions, including those involving environmental issues, the ultimate arbiter of success is the client's level of satisfaction. There have been times when I have persuaded a client to cease pursuing a particular transaction that was not in its best interest, and while the client may not initially have been comfortable with his or her decision to walk away, in most cases they could at least appreciate my perspective. Sometimes my advice is followed, and sometimes it is not. Clients do not always understand what is best for them, but at the end of the day, it is the client's goals and objectives that must be met, and the ability to meet them ultimately determines whether you have undertaken a success transaction. If the lawyer does not understand those goals and structure advice accordingly, the client will not be well served.

To serve clients effectively, it is important for the environmental practitioner to not only meet professional requirements for obtaining sufficient continuing legal education credits, but also to periodically familiarize himself or herself with the latest precedents and rulings from courts and applicable regulators. This can be challenging, but it is a necessity for the environmental practitioner. Furthermore, it is beneficial for the environmental practitioner to get out into the community by participating in and conducting seminars on topical issues. These kinds of efforts help me stay focused on the relevant issues of the day and promote our practice.

Outlining Strategy

The client's risk tolerance is the most significant determinant of strategy in an environmental transaction. Also critical are the time constraints to finance and to close the deal. Additional factors that inform the strategy to employ when negotiating the agreement include the client's willingness to conduct environmental testing and due diligence and/or the client's willingness to manage ongoing environmental problems following closing (or, contrarily, the client's desire to put the transaction behind him or her and pay a premium to do so). There may be business pressures that prevent the client from completing a thorough due diligence process, including time constraints that prevent the undertaking of thorough testing of the subject property. Before addressing any of these issues, however, it is essential to understand the client's appetite for risk and the basic structure of the transaction with that risk tolerance in mind.

A client's risk tolerance will often depend on its assets, liquidity, and the potential availability of insurance that would cover contamination issues. As such, a well-heeled client with some experience in the environmental arena is less likely to be risk-averse. For example, a company that has acquired properties in the past that may have had environmental complications will have the benefit of experience, and knowing what to expect at each stage of the process. Contrarily, inexperienced clients for the most part are more likely to be risk-averse. However, a greater challenge is presented by those clients who are unfamiliar with environmental issues, and therefore do not appreciate the risks. Thus, inexperienced clients may be more willing to disregard such risks, but they do so because they do not have the background or experience to understand what those risks may entail. If I have not represented a client previously, in order to assess the client's appetite for risk, I ascertain what its past experience has been with environmental issues, if any, and its general business model. I attempt to educate the client on its potential risks by ascertaining its past environmental experience and its asset picture, insurances, etc., and in this way I can structure the transaction to meet the client's needs.

The Negotiation Process: The Importance of Applicable Law

Most transactions that are affected by environmental issues are principally governed by state law and applicable regulations. Federal law almost always applies to a certain degree, but applicable state law is the ultimate determining factor in the structure of a transaction in terms of the potential liabilities and responsibilities of the seller and buyer. When I look at a transaction involving New York law, I consider how New York law deals with disregarding corporate formalities and claims that arise out of environmental contamination. Furthermore, I must consider the potential for the client as the target of state or federal claims by not only the regulator, but also claims by private parties under applicable federal and/or state laws and statutes, if contamination is potentially emanating away from the property subject to purchase. From the purchaser's perspective, as indicated previously, the "all appropriate inquiry" standard forms the basic framework for due diligence required to be undertaken so that a perspective purchaser makes itself eligible for certain defenses, and in many cases, in order to meet conditions precedent to financing.

Needless to say, satisfying the all appropriate inquiry criteria without indemnifications and other risk shifting provisions will not protect the client's interests. Once I have a basic idea of how the transaction is impacted by particular state and federal laws, we look to other critical factors including the client's wherewithal and a client's leverage in the transaction (is the purchaser under a time constraint to purchase the property, or there are other potential buyers for the property, etc.) before negotiating critical terms of the purchase agreement. Additionally, the personalities behind the deal will have a significant impact on its shape and structure. The degree of openness, responsiveness, and flexibility of the parties will significantly affect how a transaction should proceed.

There are certain provisions for such agreements that tend to be less contentious to negotiate than others are. Purchasers and sellers tend to be fairly flexible in negotiating representations and warranties that may be conferred. Further most clients are flexible on the issue of establishing escrows, and other post closing arrangements where the parties recognize that cleanup will be required following the closing. On the other hand, the issue of financial guarantees, personal and otherwise, for indemnification and other funding obligations can be contentious. People tend to be very concerned with the nature of the guarantees, as well as the relationship between the seller and the guarantor. In today's business world, skepticism is on the rise, and negotiations are often more difficult and more contentious than they may have been twenty years ago.

During negotiations, if appropriate, I strive to handle as much of the deal as possible without directly involving the client. The atmosphere in which parties negotiate transactions is often different from that atmosphere which prevails when litigating a matter, where competition is often a factor. In a transaction setting, a lawyer will not be successful if he or she is principally concerned with prevailing over the other side as opposed to completing a transaction where common ground is achieved. I have been practicing since 1987, and my experience has taught me that the bottom line of a transaction is best handled through problem solving and cooperation. Being too contentious or competitive will only result in higher costs, a longer time frame, and at worst, a failed transaction.

The Client's Outlook

The attitude of the client can have a significant impact on strategy. Having experienced counsel on both sides of the transaction can remove some of the personal element that may be brought to a deal by clients. However, it is unavoidable that client personalities will affect negotiations. If the client is combative or confrontational, the negotiations will affected by such behavior. In those cases, where personalities may conflict, it is my job to prevent the client's negotiating style from hindering the deal. If I am working with a particularly difficult client, I will have to handle as much of the deal as possible without directly involving the client. Problems may arise when a client is overly concerned with its own level of involvement in negotiating the transaction.

In addition to the client's personality, its expectations have a significant effect on how the transaction is negotiated. Indeed, clients often have unrealistic expectations when it comes to completing a transaction involving contamination issues, including the amount of time it will take to complete due diligence (particularly if testing is required) and the time it will take to close such a transaction, particularly when financing is provided by a third party, which must satisfy its own due diligence standard. When a client approaches me with a goal of closing the transaction within an unrealistic time frame, it is my responsibility to explain the nature and extent of due diligence that should be undertaken in the time frame outlined. For each transaction, I outline a realistic time frame that balances the needs of the client with the realities of the due diligence process. In situations where the client is operating under significant time pressures, the client should be fully informed of the ramifications of the time frames at issue before the transaction proceeds, including the effect of a shortened time frame on completing due diligence.

My role on behalf of the client during the negotiations will also be determined by the client's goals for the transaction, the client's level of sophistication, and the amount of involvement the client wants to have in the negotiation. In addition, there are important ethical considerations by which we must abide concerning the negotiation process. If the opposing party in a transaction is represented, counsel may only communicate through opposing party's counsel, but this can be complicated by clients who like to be more involved in transactions, as such clients will sometimes attempt to speak directly opposing counsel without his or her own lawyer. For many reasons it is inadvisable for your client to speak with the other side's counsel and it places the lawyer so approached in a difficult position.

In addition, many clients involved in these kinds of transactions do not understand that property owners, consultants and others are required by certain state law, and in some cases federal law to disclose test results to a government agency. Too often clients are not aware of this obligation until after the tests are undertaken and unfavorable results are obtained that must be disclosed to a regulator. Thus, it is important for the client to understand the ramifications of testing and reporting obligations that may be triggered if substances above reporting levels are discovered in soils or groundwater.

Moreover, with the institution of the relatively new all appropriate inquiry standard, sellers must also understand that buyers (and financial institutions) are now required by federal law, 40 Code of Federal Regulation §312 (ASTM E1527-05), to make inquiries and attain information regarding among other issues, the past uses of the property and adjacent property. Again, it is important for counsel to inform a seller that it will be approached to respond to these kinds of inquiries. Prior to the transaction, environmental counsel should have a game plan for providing such information to buyers whether it is provided through counsel, including providing a written response to those issues that require a response to meet the all appropriate inquiry standard.

Advice for Other Environmental Lawyers

The most important factors when determining a strategy for a transaction are the client's goals and expectations based upon the client's appetite for risk and the time constraints associated with a particular transaction. Some clients may simply not be in a position to undertake a thorough due diligence process before closing a transaction. The client needs to understand the ramifications of failure to undertake a thorough due diligence and must appropriately structure the transaction to protect it as best as possible. For example, some clients simply want to put any contamination issues identified during the due diligence process behind them and close the transaction as quickly as possible and are willing to "pay a premium" to do so. The environmental lawyer should know the client's objectives and determine how to proceed with a transaction in the manner that meets those objectives.

Time pressures are the biggest cause of missteps for the environmental lawyer. Unfortunately, it is somewhat common for lawyers to misunderstand what a client is looking for in a transaction, particularly when the client is operating under time constraints. Lawyers may end up taking extreme positions in response to such time constraints, which only complicates the completing of the transaction. Furthermore, attorneys do not always pay enough attention to the information and documents that are identified during the due diligence process, particularly when time is an issue. Thus, if an important piece of information or a document is overlooked, or if counsel fails to provide such information to a qualified consultant for its analysis, it may come back to haunt the client. While time pressures must be taken into account, an attorney should never sacrifice his client's strategy or goals in order to meet unreasonable or unrealistic deadlines.

Furthermore, it can be quite a challenge to make a client appreciate the risks involved with a particular transaction. In reality, one can never be truly certain of all the risks inherent in a property with contamination issues, even if the proper due diligence and investigation is completed. You can comply with all of the regulations, laws, and guidelines, but the client may still be faced with a latent contamination issue long after the purchase of the property is closed. The threat of what is not known regarding a property and the potential for contamination that is not discoverable are factors that make practicing in this area so challenging.

The best piece of advice I can offer to another attorney in this area is to become involved in the negotiating process as early as possible, including in the drafting and structure of the purchase agreement. Purchasing or selling property with environmental issues carries tremendous potential risks, the biggest of which is turning an asset into a liability and exposing the client to potential claims. At the same time, there are opportunities for clients to enhance the value of property complicated by environmental concerns, including by taking advantage of lucrative tax credits under governmental cleanup programs. It is critical for the environmental lawyer to become involved early and fully understand the client's tolerance for risk and its goals for the transaction.

Joseph D. Picciotti is a partner of Harris Beach PLLC and leader of the firm's environmental practice group. He received his B.A. from the College of Wooster and his J.D. from the Albany Law School of Union University, and he was a note and comment editor for the Albany Law Review. *He is admitted to practice law in New York, Massachusetts, the U.S. District Court for the Western District of New York, and the U.S. Court of Appeals for the Third Circuit.*

Mr. Picciotti focuses his legal practice on environmental and commercial matters, including litigation. He has substantial experience representing companies and municipalities in hazardous waste site cleanup actions and prosecuting environmental claims on behalf of private parties and municipalities.

Mr. Picciotti's environmental practice includes counseling corporations on complying with federal and state requirements concerning storing, maintaining, and handling hazardous substances and hazardous wastes. He conducts environmental due diligence investigations pursuant to corporate transactions. He also assists companies in auditing their operations for such transactions, and in preparation for governmental audits and investigations. He also counsels clients concerning issues arising under the New York State Environmental Quality Review Act, including counseling clients on land use and zoning issues. He has had extensive experience in litigating such matters, as well as general trial and appellate work before state and federal courts. Mr. Picciotti has been a speaker at various seminars on a broad range of environmental issues.

Environmental Strategies in Deal-Making

Steven Humphreys
Special Counsel
Kelley Drye & Warren LLP

My practice falls into four main groups. The primary one is transactional. The others are litigation, compliance counseling, and legislative. The transactional work involves performing environmental due diligence for acquisitions, leases or financings and assisting with the negotiation of contractual provisions that allocate environmental risk among the parties to the transaction. Compliance counseling involves providing advice to companies on how to comply with the varied regulatory requirements that arise under federal, state, and local environmental laws. In the legislative area, I analyze statutory enactments, initiatives, and trends for clients to assist them in planning how their operations might be affected in the future.

Transactional Representation

In order to ensure that a proper contractual allocation of risks for environmental problems is achieved, parties to transactions involving known or potentially contaminated property will often look to specialized environmental counsel's expertise in assisting with the identification of environmental risk and the negotiation of contractual provisions that will meet the needs of the particular transaction. For example, in a real estate transaction, both the seller and purchaser will want to ensure that any indemnities and other contractual obligations pertaining to environmental concerns are drafted in accordance with the parties' expectations and to help them bridge the gap to reach an acceptable compromise where those expectations are at odds. The specific terms of any transaction will be influenced by the identifiable environmental risks associated with the property or business involved in the transaction, the objectives of the purchaser and seller in addressing those risks, the parties' relative bargaining leverage, and the relative skill and expertise of counsel.

I have represented the full gamut of parties in various kinds of business deals that involve environmental issues. Those may include, for example, a buyer or seller of real estate that potentially may be contaminated, or a company that is acquiring another company or business that may entail environmental impacts. In a loan transaction, I sometimes represent borrowers and other times lenders. All these clients have different goals and concerns in mind depending on their role in the transaction, but they all revolve around the same problem of how to assess the environmental risks that are associated with a particular transaction and how to manage and allocate those risks in the context of the contractual documents and other strategies to resolve environmental-related problems or concerns before the transaction is concluded. Sometimes, for example, though not often, it might be possible to take the environmental concerns out of the equation entirely by cleaning up the problem before the transaction closes. That is of course the optimal scenario, but that is usually not possible where the property being sold or used as collateral for a loan is extensively contaminated.

One question that sometimes arises during the course of a transactional representation is the degree of "lawyering" that takes place with regard to negotiating how environmental risks should be allocated in contract documents. Each lawyer has his or her own style, but as a rule it has been my experience that most attorneys who specialize in environmental law to be more in the mode of "problem solving" than "advantage seeking" when negotiating the environmental terms of an agreement. That is not to say, however, that there are no environmental attorneys whose style points more in the former direction. Whether to create pressure for a lower purchase price when representing a buyer or to gain an untoward advantage over an unsuspecting buyer, it is not unusual to encounter the occasional opposing environmental counsel who is bent on being obstreperous. Given the inherent scientific uncertainties associated with environmental contamination issues that typically arise during a transaction, there is quite often ample room for an attorney, or his or her client, to skew a particular environmental issue well beyond a realistic degree of relative risk. When dealing with a lawyer who is pursuing this approach, I have found that the best strategy is to keep the client well attuned to counsel's tactics, develop a reasonable, middle-of-the-road position, and then stick to it. That makes it difficult for an obstreperous opposing counsel to get much traction.

Another problem in dealing with opposing counsel arises where the attorney representing the other side has little or no training in environmental issues. While at first blush, it may seem that an environmental specialist will have an advantage over an opposing counsel with less experience or familiarity with environmental law, thereby allowing the parties to reach accommodation more readily, in practice it is usually more of a challenge. For example, the other counsel may not fully appreciate the need for careful study and understanding of environmental risk, or the various opportunities for the parties to work together to manage it on a collaborative basis. He or she may be more inclined in some circumstances to try to take more of a bullying or posturing approach, which can undermine efforts to cooperatively define the risk and manage it. In these situations, if opposing counsel is taking an unreasonable position or shooting from the hip, and they do not fully appreciate the complexity of the problem at hand, it is sometimes effective to turn the problem around by explaining why the problem presents a risk that the client is unwilling to absorb and ask counsel how they would propose that the client get comfortable with the risk. This approach sometimes forces them to go through the effort of analyzing the risk in order to present a defensible position, and sometimes leads them to suggest a compromise that will at least be a step in the right direction and which the parties can then work from to reach agreement. It also helps to have one or more "all hands" conference calls in which the clients, consultants, and attorneys participate in an effort to reach a broader conceptual agreement on how to allocate the risks. This approach tends to force all of the players to take more reasonable positions, for fear of appearing unreasonable or obstructionist.

More often than not, consistent with the client's desires, a collaborative and cooperative approach is the most fruitful from the perspective of all parties in terms of attorney time and simplicity. This approach entails everyone working together to identify the risk, assess its materiality, and how they are going to manage it between themselves. With all parties engaged in that process, and if the attorneys are truly acting in their clients' best interests, the endpoint is normally a win-win in which the business parties on both sides get something out of the deal, their interests are adequately protected, and both sides walk away feeling like they have accomplished their goals.

One very important component of resolving environmental issues in transactions involves taking what is learned about environmental risk through due diligence and incorporating it into an effective strategy for allocating the risk in the contractual documents. This is usually a very iterative process, since things change as the diligence process unfolds. As these developments occur, it is important to the collaborative process mentioned above that environmental counsel work cooperatively together so as to methodically and analytically understand and appreciate the risk and allocate it in accordance with the expectations of the business parties. At the end of the day, there is in every deal with environmental issues a set of problems that have to be resolved and there is a certain amount of work that must be accomplished to get to final agreement. If both sides are focused on getting through that process as efficiently as possible, it helps in the long run in order to get the deal done.

Most deals, of course, will fall somewhere between the two paradigms described above. Since every deal comes with its own mix of problems and personalities, each typically requires a different approach. Perhaps the most important variable involves the parties' relative bargaining power. It is invariably the case that one party has greater motivation than the other does to do the deal or has more resources to devote to the negotiation process than does the other. Depending on the degree to which this is the case, it should come as no surprise that an inequity in bargaining leverage can affect on how the parties and their counsel interact with regard to various deal issues. It can have an especially pronounced effect where the environmental issues of concern are particularly nettlesome. For example, if a buyer has relatively greater bargaining power, it may be able to obtain more significant contractual concessions from the purchaser that normally would be the case—even to the point of getting the seller to reduce the purchase price and/or exacting terms that could be considered draconian.

When confronted with such a situation, the counsel representing the party with the lesser bargaining power may need to employ other factors that are independent of the intrinsic deal issues to "keep" his or her adversary "honest." For example, counsel for a disadvantaged seller might be able to invoke the parties' long-standing business relationship (if that is the case) as a tool to remind his or her adversary that insisting on an unreasonable set of terms may do harm to the parties' relationship, which ultimately could have a negative effect on the clients' collective business interests. Conversely, counsel for a disadvantaged buyer might be able to invoke the need to satisfy requirements of a lender as an additional justification for including certain contractual protections, without which the deal might be economically infeasible.

In large measure, the success of a collaborative risk management strategy for resolving environmental issues is also dependent on the degree to which the business parties are able to build trust through a fruitful exchange of information and principled negotiations. In addition to the obvious importance of fair dealing and good-faith negotiating, the goal of building trust requires environmental counsel on both sides to establish a working relationship that is based on mutual respect and credibility. Credibility is enhanced where counsel representing the seller is conversant in the seller's business and its relevant environmental compliance obligations. By the same token, it is important for counsel representing buyers to fully understand, and appreciate the relative importance of, environmental problems identified through the due diligence process or otherwise.

In rare cases, counsel and their clients may become so uncooperative and untrustworthy that lack of trust becomes a business issue in and of itself. For example, a seller who stubbornly refuses to allow the purchaser to conduct adequate due diligence or who has deliberately withheld material information from the buyer about a potentially significant environmental concern may lose a deal if the purchaser becomes too wary of the seller's tactics.

The Due Diligence Process

Overall, the best advice to an attorney working on the environmental aspects of a business transaction is to study the risk, understand it, understand the client's business or the business/property the client is buying. An effective environmental attorney will understand these elements first, and then work rationally and logically with opposing counsel and their client to determine how the parties should allocate the risk.

The particular mix of environmental issues that will be relevant is, of course, transaction-specific. In real estate transactions, it is most important to focus primarily on the environmental condition of the property. If one is working on a deal that involves the purchase of a business or a stock deal or financing transaction, it is necessary to take the diligence a step further and look at regulatory compliance. Ask yourself whether the company is fully up to speed with all its environmental regulatory compliance obligations. Not every company is 100 percent on top of all of its environmental compliance obligations. In fact, it is probably fair to say that most companies are not in 100 percent compliance at any given time.

Many companies struggle to keep afloat with environmental compliance obligations because it is such a complicated area. A purchaser's counsel will have to know, for example, if the company has been operating without an air permit for several years. Otherwise, the client could find itself inheriting an environmental compliance problem and, henceforth, an enforcement problem, as well. You have to incorporate that additional dimension of compliance requirements when you are dealing with a stock deal or a purchase of a business or a financing transaction.

Under the ASTM E1527-05 standard for conducting a Phase I environmental site assessment, a typical investigation will include, among other things: (1) visually inspecting the property to identify any apparent indications of potential contamination (e.g., stained soils or concrete, stressed vegetation, evidence of underground storage tanks, vent or fill pipes, etc.); (2) reviewing documents maintained on-site in order to identify areas involving the use of hazardous substances, both present and past, and other potential environmental problems such as poor hazardous substances handling practices that may suggest the potential for on-site contamination; (3) interviewing employees of the company which owns the target property who are responsible for environmental matters; (4) reviewing relevant government documents and other publicly-available records (including information available through computer databases), which may reveal the presence of hazardous substance containment structures or spills at or near the property; (5) evaluating other historical documents concerning the site such as fire insurance maps, telephone directories and/or aerial photographs in order to identify prior uses of the property that potentially involved the use of hazardous substances; and (6) giving attention to potential environmental contamination at any surrounding properties that may affect the property.

Effective oversight of consultants assisting with the due diligence process is also important to a successful representation. If the consultant does not do the job he or she is tasked with doing, if they overlook a significant issue, and as a result the parties do not become aware of it until late in the transaction, it can require a significant renegotiation of the contracts or even put the transaction at risk. Allowing environmental counsel to select the consultant may serve to mitigate the risk of consultant error. Because of their frequent involvement in these matters, environmental counsel may be relied on to retain a consultant in a particular location or with a specific area of expertise related to the types of potential environmental concerns associated with a particular transaction. In addition, given their familiarity with particular consulting firms based on prior experience, environmental counsel can ensure that the consultant chosen will be fully qualified and capable for the task.

When representing a purchaser, the main investigation strategy that I use in any deal, as a rule, is to come to as thorough an understanding as quickly as possible of what the nature of the environmental risk is. This process may be influenced by a number of factors that vary significantly from one deal to the next.

The primary factor is the matter of what has happened at the property or group of properties historically. For example, was it historically pristine real estate, or was it an industrial operation going back thirty years or more, or at least back to a period of time in which they did not really have a very strong set of environmental regulations? If that is the case, then the task at hand is to characterize the degree of risk by having some type of invasive environmental investigation, such as soil borings or groundwater sampling.

The first step is to do a preliminary fact check. I will try to get the lay of the land by going onto a publicly available database, something like Environmental Data Resources. I will do some searches that focus on the property and some of the adjacent properties, and see if it has a regulatory profile with the environmental agencies. I will also try to understand the nature of the business, and the particular manufacturing process employed by the target involves the use of hazardous substances. If so, what kinds of hazardous substances are used? Does the company use a lot of solvents and degreasers—i.e., the "usual suspects" in very expensive cleanups?

Another particular risk factor is where the target is had fleet operations requiring vehicle maintenance areas, as well as large quantities of gasoline or diesel in underground storage tanks. If so, these can present a different set of problems as compared with solvents because petroleum constituents tend to behave differently in the environment. The types of substances involved also may dictate a different investigation approach.

Once I have that initial framework of the environmental risk under my belt, I will sit down with the client or talk to them on the phone, or maybe communicate with them by e-mail, to explain the risk. I will list what I see is the main potential problem areas and how they can be addressed most efficiently. Depending on the results of this discussion, we may elect do a Phase II investigation—i.e., actual sampling at the subject property. If that is the case, we will probably have to negotiate with the sellers as to the requirements they may have for allowing access to their property. For example, it may be necessary to provide the seller with certain contractual protections against risks associated with the investigation work.

Working with Clients

In eighteen years of practice, the instances in which I have seen clients get themselves into a pickle typically revolve around inattention to environmental considerations until late in the deal. Environmental risk in business transactions carries with it an element of uncertainty because of the very highly variable and uncertain nature of the science. Still, there is usually plenty of room for identifying the risk and negotiating an effective approach to resolve most environmental problems that arise, provided that the process is started as early as possible. If the call to get environmental counsel involved comes a couple of weeks or a month before the closing, then the client is going to be at a disadvantage right out of the box, whether they be the seller or buyer. They will not have adequate time to study the problem, identify the issues, formulate a strategy, and then implement it. With a truncated time frame, all of these tasks will have to be compressed, and there is a clear trade-off between the amount of time to work through the tasks and the quality of information obtained with which to inform the process for problem solving negotiating risk allocation issues.

From time to time, clients may want to change their strategy for allocating risk mid-deal. For example, a client who is purchasing property or a business might say, "Well, I know I insisted on an indemnification, but I think now I need to change that position because of certain business considerations." Such a fundamental alteration in the terms of the deal will in turn put greater pressure on the diligence process, to ensure that the client is not incurring a "bet-the-store" level of risk. It may also be necessary to consider other potential solutions, such as purchasing environmental insurance to absorb the excess risk.

Some clients are very "hands-on" and like to get very involved in the due diligence process and contract negotiations. Others fall on the opposite end of the spectrum, and it may even be difficult in some cases to get their attention when it's necessary to focus attention on a problem. Most clients, of course, fall somewhere between those two parameters. In the general, the more involved that a client is, the better. For those clients who are too preoccupied with other matters to be very involved, it's best to keep them fully updated on developments by summarizing them in a quick e-mail. This will help to ensure that the client is aware of what's happening on an ongoing basis, and understand the potential ramifications of the various environmental issues. Otherwise, at the end of the process, all they will see is a black box and will not understand or appreciate how they got to where they are or fully understand what their post-closing obligations are. Of course, one should always provide additional guidance post-closing, but it is always better if the client is at least minimally engaged in the deal negotiation process.

Contractual Risk Allocation

Once the risk has been relatively well characterized, the next task is to incorporate the risk into a set of contractual provisions that allocate how the risk is going to be managed over time. Typically, an environmental problem has to be managed over time. If it is a significant problem, it can often take a matter of years to resolve. This usually means that the parties in the deal are going to have an ongoing contractual relationship to manage the remedial project over time. The one significant exception to this is where the purchaser sells the property under an "as-is, where-is" arrangement, under which the buyer normally gets an offsetting advantage in return, such as a significant reduction in purchase price. In such a case, the purchaser might even go so far as to take back either a release of liability or an indemnification from the buyer so they can walk away. Such a risk transfer arrangement happens rarely, but it might happen where the property is being sold has been well investigated so that the risk is well characterized and there is a significant market upside for the purchaser to offset the environmental risk.

If the deal is something short of a risk transfer in the "as-is, where-is" model, then in the normal course the seller is going to retain some responsibility, and will quite often want to retain the control over the management or remediation of the condition after closing. If the seller does retain control, then it will be in the best position to minimize the cost associated with the remedy, and thereby the amount of its indemnification obligation. Remedies for environmental contamination can get very expensive very quickly and there are typically a range of different possible technical approaches to employ, some of which are more expensive than others. If the deal is set up so the purchaser gets, in effect, a "blank check" from the seller to pay for the cost of the purchaser's remediation, that is obviously not a good situation for a seller, since the purchaser then has every incentive to employ a "gold-plated" remedy at the site. More typically then, the seller will have an ongoing remedial obligation after the closing and will retain some degree of control over the ultimate remedy.

It is a rare case where the deal could not get done because of the complexity or size of the environmental problems, as it is normally just a question of manpower and time to get them resolved. Instead, the most challenging problems in completing a deal arise where there time frame for completing the due diligence process has been compressed. This goes back to the earlier point that if the deal must close by a date certain and the due diligence process is started only a month or two months out from that date, it can present a significant challenge to complete the necessary work within the given time frame. It is not just a matter of getting more attorneys or environmental consultants involved; timing constraints often make it difficult to line up schedules of contractors and their sub-contractors, who will have competing demands on their time, as well as get sampling data turned around from the laboratory.

The jurisdiction in which the subject property is located is an important element that can greatly influence strategy and how the deal is structured. States have developed a very disparate approach to dealing with environmental contamination issues. There are many similarities, but there are also many differences that affect how the parties negotiate and resolve their risk allocation decisions. To give an example of this, New Jersey has a statute that is somewhat unusual, known as the Industrial Site Recovery Act, which requires that any time an industrial establishment, as defined in the statute, is sold or transferred, the transferor must undergo a regulatory process requiring them to investigate and possibly remediate contamination on that property. (Connecticut has a similar statute.) Consequently, this results in a situation where a regulatory process is superimposed over the transactional process, and the parties can take advantage of that to some extent.

There are also regional differences and local differences in how environmental statutes are enforced. If you are dealing with a property out west, for example, it may have a lot of contamination from mining wastes on it and the parties tend to approach it differently than they might a contaminated property in the east. Some states are also less aggressive than others are, so that parties in those states may not give as much attention to environmental risk as they do in others.

Negotiations

Most parties to transactions start from the operating premise that what they are buying is not a set of environmental problems, but a property—or property associated with a business that is being purchased—that is fully functional on which they can operate a business. In the normal case, purchasers do not expect getting stuck with environmental liabilities that are associated with the seller's operations, and sellers generally recognized that fact. Consequently, allocating environmental risk to a seller for conditions that it caused is usually an area where the parties can come to agreement without much difficulty.

By contrast, sellers and purchasers more frequently find themselves at odds where the contamination was caused by someone other than the seller, such as a prior owner or operator of the property, or the owner or operating of a neighboring property from which contamination has migrated onto the subject property. It is not uncommon for the buyer and seller to address this issue by reaching a compromise of some sort, under which both parties share in the associated costs and/or liability risks. In that case, they may wish to develop a balanced set of environmental provisions in the purchase contract that will govern the parties' interactions post-closing in a way that protects both their interests and requires them to cooperate with each other. If the parties are still at loggerheads, it also may also be possible to help bridge the gap with the use of a third-party liability transfer like an environmental insurance policy, which serves to allocate certain risks to the carrier or other third party in exchange for a premium.

Until recently, obtaining environmental insurance to cover environmental liability risks associated with properties involved in transactions was a largely futile effort. In most cases, the few policies available for such risks were prohibitively expensive and riddled with exclusions rendering them of little use in providing adequate protection. More recently, however, with the advent of state and federal programs aimed at promoting the redevelopment of brownfields and a general maturing of the science of environmental site assessment, a number of leading major carriers have started offering less expensive insurance products intended to tap into this growing market.

In general, there are two types of insurance policies that may be used to offset a purchaser's environmental risk in a brownfields transaction: Pollution Legal Liability (PLL) policies and Cost Cap or Remediation Stop-Loss policies. PLL policies are designed to protect the insured from the risk of incurring environment-related liability for property that may be contaminated from prior uses of the property, but for which there is generally no currently identified contamination requiring active remediation. Cost Cap policies, on the other hand, provide coverage to ensure that the cost of specific environmental remediation activities at sites with known contamination will not exceed a certain amount.

Conclusion

During each phase of a transaction involving the transfer of contaminated or potentially contaminated property, the transaction team for the purchaser or seller will benefit greatly from a working familiarity with the practical issues and concerns that typically arise in the course of such transactions. In addition, armed with an in-depth understanding of the pertinent regulatory and liability regimes at the federal, state and local levels and any particular property transfer laws that may apply to the deal, as well as case law trends and policy developments that may impinge on the specific liability risks posed by the transaction, parties to these transactions will be in a position to craft an effective strategy for dealing with environmental problems as they arise during the course of the transaction and after closing. These parties, therefore, should work closely with environmental counsel who can provide practical advice on how these various laws will affect their respective rights and obligations and on their implications for any specific transaction. In this way, purchasers and sellers can best ensure that the impacts of contamination in such transactions will be properly identified and incorporated into the framework of a workable agreement that properly protects their interests.

Steven Humphreys serves as special counsel with the law firm of Kelley Drye & Warren LLP, where he specializes in environmental law. He counsels corporate and institutional clients in all aspects of environmental law, including emerging regulatory initiatives and business challenges associated with climate change. A primary focus of his practice has involved advising clients with respect to the purchase and sale of environmentally contaminated real estate, conducting associated environmental due diligence investigations of target properties, and negotiating third-party risk transfer agreements and contractual provisions relating to the allocation of environmental risk. He also counsels clients with respect to compliance obligations arising under such federal statutes as the Comprehensive Environmental Response and Liability Act, the Resource Conservation and Recovery Act, the Clean Air Act, the Clean Water Act, as well as various state and local environmental laws.

Mr. Humphreys received a J.D., cum laude, from the American University Washington College of Law and a B.S. from the University of Maryland, and is a member of the New Jersey, District of Columbia, and Maryland bars, as well as the American Bar Association's section on natural resources, energy, and environmental law. He has also served for eight years as the chairman of the environmental law committee of the Federal Bar Association's section on environment, energy, and natural resources.

Transactional Environmental Law Strategies: Getting the Deal Done

Lewis T. Putman

Partner

Milbank, Tweed, Hadley & McCloy LLP

The Role of an Environmental Transactional Lawyer

As an environmental transactional attorney, I consider myself both a corporate lawyer and an environmental lawyer because the practice of environmental transactional law sits at the intersection of traditional environmental and corporate law practices. Attorneys like myself who practice environmental transactional law provide legal advice and counseling to clients (including venture capitalists, private equity and hedge funds, and lending institutions) on environmental risks in corporate and financing transactions and bankruptcy and workout proceedings. In this role, I represent clients on environmental matters in transactions and proceedings that involve global industries in sectors such as oil and gas exploration, development and refining, heavy manufacturing, mining, power generation and transmission, transportation and renewable energy. Specifically, my role as an environmental transactional lawyer is to identify the environmental risks of the business at question through due diligence review and to craft and implement strategies to manage those risks through contract drafting and negotiation and the use of insurance and other risk management tools.

Creating Client Value

Environmental attorneys working in the context of corporate and other transactions create value for clients in several important ways. In the broad sense, I add client value by understanding client goals and crafting a transactional strategy to reach those goals. To do this, I must remain focused on the "big picture" and what the particular client hopes to achieve from the transaction. For example, in an acquisition or investment by a private equity fund, I structure due diligence and focus on environmental risk issues that are relevant in light of the anticipated investment horizon and ultimate exit strategy.

Equally important are strong skills as a counselor—the ability to help clients understand the complexities of environmental law and the portfolio of options to manage risks in a corporate or financing transaction. Understanding environmental risks in the transactional context is essential to the overall strategy for negotiating a transaction and anticipating and managing environmental risks in the future. To effectively manage environmental risk in the transactional context you must understand not only the magnitude but also the timing and type of obligations associated with environmental liabilities. Timing of obligations is relevant because some liabilities are more near term, and thus more amenable to a contractual indemnity or escrow, whereas others are more long-term, and may be more amenable to a purchase price reduction. The nature of liabilities is important, for example, because only certain unknown and known risks are insurable under policies of environmental insurance. Offering high-level strategic legal advice on the portfolio of options for managing different types of environmental risks provides great assistance and value to my corporate clients.

The Nature of Environmental Transaction Support

As an environmental transaction attorney, I provide the following main areas of support during corporate and financing transactions:

1. I define the nature, scope, and magnitude of environmental risks in a transaction.
2. I craft contractual mechanisms for managing and allocating environmental risk.
3. I develop strategies for presenting and packaging environmental risks for divestitures.
4. I identify non-contractual mechanisms for managing environmental risk, such as environmental insurance and other risk transfer mechanisms.
5. I counsel clients on environmental compliance and permitting.

Sources of Environmental Risk

The focus of client representation in the transaction context is identifying and quantifying environmental risk. Environmental risk arises from the following sources:

1. Liability relating to known and unknown contamination and other environmental conditions (e.g., wetlands, endangered species, and sensitive ecological or cultural issues) at real properties.

2. Liability relating to non-compliance with environmental laws and environmental permits, including possible fines and penalties and capital expenditures for corrective action.

3. Environmental litigation risk, including the risk of personal injury or property damage claims from the release of hazardous substances (commonly known as "toxic tort" actions), the manufacture, use, or distribution of products containing asbestos, asbestos-containing materials in facilities, and liability for the off-site arrangement for disposal or release of hazardous substances (e.g., "Superfund" liability in the United States.).

4. Permitting and change of law risks arising from more stringent environmental laws and permit requirements or changes in operational limitations during future permit renewals or approvals.

5. Environmental "legacy" liabilities arising from former, closed or divested real properties, and past corporate divestitures and acquisitions.

Evaluation of Environmental Risk for Clients

To evaluate the scope and magnitude of these environmental risks in the transactional context, I provide the following advice, counsel, and support for clients during acquisitions:

1. **Contamination Risk**: I retain, on behalf of clients, environmental consultants to conduct a technical assessment of these potential environmental risks (commonly known as a "Phase I Environmental Assessment") and supervise environmental review of the target real properties to identify and, if possible, quantify environmental liability associated with known and unknown on-site contamination and other environmental conditions.

2. **Non-Compliance Risk**: I retain, on behalf of clients, environmental consultants to assist me with a review of the environmental compliance of target operations to identify current non-compliance issues and the scope and possible costs of corrective action necessary to reach or maintain compliance with environmental laws.

3. **Environmental Litigation Risk**: I review and analyze existing and threatened environmental claims and litigation through docket and public record searches and discussions with target in-house and outside counsel. I also use the results of the consultant's environmental review to develop an environmental risk profile for the target's facilities and operations (e.g., Are there off-site releases of hazardous substances, or if asbestos exists in buildings, is it damaged and posing an exposure risk to occupants?).

4. **Permitting and Change of Law Risk**: I review and analyze, from a legal standpoint, all current permits held by the operations for (i) status and timing of renewal, (ii) potentially onerous limitations and (ii) current policies and laws that could result in significantly changed conditions upon permit renewal.

5. **Environmental "Legacy" Liability Risk**: I research the corporate history of target companies, including all past acquisitions and divestures, looking for retained or assumed liabilities in purchase and sale agreements and liabilities the target could have by operation of law. I also coordinate searches of publicly available environmental records for information on environmental problems with closed and/or divested facilities.

Financial Implications of Environmental Liability

Each category of liability listed above—(i) on-site conditions, (ii) compliance, (iii) litigation, (iv) permitting, and (v) legacy liabilities—can give rise to significant liabilities to a purchaser of operating companies and real property. These same liabilities can hinder or prevent the financing or sale of a business or real property. I add value to clients by helping executives and investors understand the implications of environmental risk in financial terms. Understanding the financial implications of environmental liabilities requires that I understand how the timing and nature of cash flows from environmental liabilities are relevant to the investment or financing decision. For example, although liabilities from costs to investigate and remediate on-site or off-site contamination can be high (e.g., many millions of dollars), the cash flows associated with contamination liabilities are usually spread out over a long period of time, typically ten to thirty years.

On the other hand, liabilities arising from current non-compliance or from future anticipated legal changes that could increase the cost of compliance or give rise to significant capital expenditures are more near term, typically one to five years. Further, from an accounting, tax, and valuation standpoint, liabilities that consist of recurring annual expenses are treated differently than capital investments. This difference in the timing and nature of cash flows associated with environmental liabilities is particularly relevant to private equity investors that may only have a three to eight year ownership horizon in a particular business or to lenders that may only loan to a business for a short period of time.

How I Address Issues Often Overlooked By Clients

One area of environmental risk often overlooked by clients in the transaction context arises after a transaction closes and involves a lack of follow through on issues identified in the transaction. An example is when a purchaser acquires a real property or operation with environmental compliance or contamination issues but does not follow through and correct the issues after acquiring the business or operation. Over time, the issues persist, and when the purchaser tries to sell the property or operation, it then is faced with having to deal with these same issues in the sale context. This may mean a reduced sale price to account for the environmental issues or having to provide an indemnity for the environmental liabilities to the subsequent purchaser. The same issue can also arise during financing transactions, where the lenders will need to be comfortable with environmental risks. In this context, the failure of a purchaser to proactively correct known environmental issues can be viewed negatively by future lenders and their counsel. This mistake can be particularly acute in the private equity context, where the fund acquiring a business or property is typically involved over a short investment horizon before it sells or refinances the property or operation.

Another area often overlooked by clients is realizing the value of contractual indemnities after a transaction closes. It is common for large companies to acquire numerous businesses over the years—each with environmental issues and each with some form of contractual indemnity from the sellers in those acquisitions. Many of these companies do not realize the full potential of environmental indemnities because they do not follow through with claims against the indemnitors. This issue arises for a variety of reasons, including limited knowledge about contractual protection, corporate culture or a relationship with the indemnitor that inhibits aggressive prosecution of indemnity claims or a lack of a third party claim, enforcement action or other external motivation for pursuing recovery. The downside is that indemnities for environmental matters often have finite survival periods, so failure to act to preserve rights can result in loss of valuable contractual rights to protection.

There are several steps that I take in my practice to address these commonly overlooked issues. One step is to draft a summary of the key contractual terms for the client's legal staff. Legal staff can use the summary as a starting point to become informed on the scope and limitations of contractual indemnities for environmental matters. On the compliance front, I sometimes draft a confidential post-closing memorandum created under the attorney-client privilege and directed to an environmental compliance officer, alerting the officer to action items identified during the due diligence review. To the extent applicable, such a memorandum often includes advice on self-reporting and other penalty mitigation policies available from governmental environmental authorities.

Personal Strategies for Success

One effective strategy for success is to get an understanding of the environmental issues and the overall environmental risk profile of a business quickly and flagging potentially material issues from the outset. This provides several benefits. First, it allows due diligence to be structured to focus on the issues of potentially material concern. Second, it provides an early indication of the structure of environmental risk allocation for the deal agreements, which often are drafted and exchanged early in the transaction process. Ultimately, this proactive approach reduces the risk for surprises later in the transaction.

The ability to be a counselor to clients by providing clear and sound advice on environmental matters is one primary element that dictates success in environmental transactional law. A client needs to understand in clear, business-friendly terms the bottom line risks involved in a transaction and the portfolio of options based on a professional's experience as to how to address those risks. Being a counselor means not being shy about conveying a confident appraisal of the risks and speaking from the position of experience as to how environmental issues are typically dealt with in similar transactions.

Staying Current

The field of environmental law has changed dramatically over the years and will continue to constantly evolve in ways that tend to become more complex and challenging for legal practitioners and corporate managers. In order to stay apprised of new developments in the industry, I keep in touch with a network of environmental attorneys throughout the world as to developments and trends in environmental policy and issues relevant to the practice of environmental law. I also closely monitor major state and federal regulatory, legislative and policy developments and decisions by the courts interpreting existing statutes, regulations, and contracts that allocate environmental risk.

These tactics have helped me greatly throughout my career. An example of where current knowledge is essential is in the area of global climate change. The topic of greenhouse gases, or global warming as it is commonly known, is not only an issue of truly global dimension, but it is also the hot environmental issue *de jour* and the focus of many articles in magazines and the popular press. Accordingly, misconceptions and inaccuracies tend to circulate about the legal initiatives in the area of global warming—particularly in the United States. For example, I have been involved in discussions with foreign investors in power projects located in the United States who expect that the United States, having long been at the forefront of global environmental policy and regulation, has some form of federal or comprehensive state greenhouse gas legislation. That is not yet the case. My research and study in the area of global warming allows me to educate these investors on the current climate change polices in the United States and the prospect for comprehensive federal and state regulation of greenhouse gases in the future.

Determining Strategy

The first step I take in any transaction is to become very familiar with the business (whether it is a business targeted for acquisition or a business that is being sold or financed) and the structure of the anticipated transaction (e.g., stock or asset acquisition or merger; long or short-term financing). Knowledge of the business at issue and how the transaction will be structured is of primary importance because this understanding governs all other aspects of the transactional process—from the structure and scope of the due diligence review to the drafting and negotiation of transaction documents. Becoming familiar with the business and its potential environmental risks requires answering the following questions, among others: How old is the business? What is the corporate history of the business? Was it part of a major conglomerate that was broken up? Has it bought and sold other businesses? How many facilities does it have? How old are those facilities, and where are those facilities located? What is the nature of operations at those facilities? Are the facilities owned or leased? Does it have former or non-operational facilities? Does it have any material known environmental problems? How is environmental management structured? Early knowledge of the business and its facilities allows an attorney to flag leading deal issues, such as the relevance of transaction-triggered environmental laws in New Jersey (the Industrial Site Recovery Act) and Connecticut (the Connecticut Transfer Act).

The structure of the transaction determines whether the liabilities will flow with the business (e.g., in the case of stock acquisitions and mergers) or whether the liabilities can be excluded from the transaction (e.g., asset acquisitions). Because of the risk to an asset buyer for successor liability, the mere fact that a transaction is structured as an asset sale does not eliminate the need for due diligence on the part of a buyer.

The sophistication of the opposing party on environmental matters is the basic factor in overall deal strategy. If I am dealing with a counsel who is seasoned in environmental transactional law, I am typically able to cut through most of the problem areas fairly easily. However, if the person on the other side is a corporate or real estate attorney with little environmental background, then the negotiation of the deal and resolution of issues are often more difficult and time-consuming.

The basic way to neutralize a hostile opposing party is to realize what they want out of the deal and then offer a solution that gives them what they want in a way that is also favorable to my client. An example is a buyer that is demanding full environmental indemnification from a seller. When representing the seller in this instance, I may suggest environmental insurance as a substitute for an indemnity from the seller as a way to get the buyer comfortable on the terms of a deal without saddling the seller with a long-term indemnity obligation.

The ultimate sign of success in my practice is getting the deal done. If the deal gets done and all of the environmental hurdles and roadblocks are cleared away, I rest assured that the parties accomplished what they desired.

United States Environmental Law

Historically, the United States' environmental law at the heart of environmental due diligence and risk in the transactional context has been the Comprehensive Environmental Response Compensation and Liability Act of 1981 (CERCLA) (42 U.S.C. § 9601 *et seq.*), also commonly known as the "Superfund" law. CERCLA and many similar state counterparts impose retroactive liability without regard to fault (so called "strict" liability) on the present owners and operators (e.g., lessees) of contaminated real property. Because of CERCLA, purchasers of real properties and operations in the United States are at risk for the costs to clean up contamination that may be unknown at the time of purchase and caused by unrelated prior owners and operators.

I say this with the following caveat regarding my use of "historically" in the statement above. In many ways, the field of environmental transaction law has grown and become more complicated and sophisticated as the environmental laws have grown in scope and complexity. CERCLA was the stringboard for the field of environmental transaction law. Today, site contamination is one of many environmental risks and concerns that include permitting risks and risks from constantly changing and increasingly stringent environmental laws, particularly in the areas of air permitting, emissions credits and trading, global climate change, greenhouse gas regulation, and environmental justice concerns. CERCLA has also changed, and now provides certain safe harbors for the liability of lenders, and defenses to liability for purchasers who conduct "all appropriate inquiry" into the environmental condition of acquired real properties. The practice of transactional environmental law today has CERCLA at its core, but also requires an in-depth knowledge and understanding of a wide range of regulatory programs covering pollution and the protection of health, safety, air, water, natural resources, wildlife, and cultural resources.

State-by-State Practice

I practice in Washington, DC, so my main focus is on federal environmental laws and policies. This, I believe, is ideal because the federal environmental regulatory system is the template upon which many state and local environmental laws have developed and matured. This is particularly true in the area of air emission regulation. Under the federal Clean Air Act, the states are directed to implement the federal Clean Air Act programs through what are known as State Implementation Plans or "SIPs." SIPs can be no less stringent than the federal legislation. However, the states are free to enact environmental legislation or regulations that are more stringent than those of the federal government. This is particularly true in the area of regulation of mercury emissions from coal-fired power plants. Many states have enacted more stringent and ambitious (as far as timing) standards for mercury from coal-fired power facilities due to local health, public policy, or political concerns.

Understanding state and local laws and international laws and treaties are a common part of my practice. What I find most fascinating and intellectually challenging is understanding the patchwork of laws and programs across all 50 states in areas that have traditionally been the domain of state and local regulation, such as underground storage tank programs, site remediation programs, site use, and zoning.

Structuring a Deal

The single biggest factor in how to structure a deal from the environmental standpoint is whether the target business has the potential for significant legacy liabilities; that is, liabilities associated with a long history of operations and many former facilities and operations that may have known or unknown contamination. An asset deal allows the buyer to exclude liabilities associated with such historical baggage and assume only those liabilities relating to the acquired sites, for which, under CERCLA, an asset buyer would have liability anyway. A caveat to this is the common law theory of successor liability, which holds even an asset buyer responsible for the liabilities of the seller if the transaction if is deemed a *"de facto merger"* or if the buyer is deemed a "continuing enterprise" of the seller. Under these theories, successor liability risk arises when (i) a plaintiff has a claim against the seller, and (ii) the seller is judgment proof or simply no longer exists. In this case, the plaintiff many look to the purchaser of assets for possible recovery under a successor liability theory. Although successor liability is dependent on the law of a particular state, in essence to find successor liability based on a theory of *de facto* merger or continuing enterprise, a plaintiff must show that there are significant communalities between the defunct seller and the buyer (e.g., same name, same management, same facilities, same products and product names, and in some cases, same or similar ownership) or that the buyer holds themselves out as a mere continuation of the seller (e.g., a buyer using the name and goodwill associated with a company that had a 100 year history of operations—"quality since 1888").

The risk of successor liability aside, an asset deal does provide a mechanism for a buyer to cut off "liability tails" associated with historical company operations, which, in many cases are difficult to due diligence and have nothing to do with the present-day operations of the business. On the other hand, a stock acquisition of a company with a long history of operations and potentially significant legacy liabilities would theoretically have the buyer acquiring those liabilities (unless a specific indemnity in the nature of a "retained liability" for such risks is provided by the selling shareholders). These liabilities are often difficult to assess because former properties are not accessible for review, the corporate history may be unclear, and the risks acquired and retained in past transactions may not be well understood. Ultimately, the final decision on structure comes down to whether the magnitude of potential environmental risk outweighs the increased transaction costs and administrative difficulties (e.g., having to transfer environmental permits). This evaluation should also consider any tax or other structure considerations and transaction costs raised by structuring the transaction as an asset acquisition verses a stock acquisition.

Factors Influencing Deal Strategy

There are several important factors that influence strategy. First, the nature of the client. Is the client a financial (e.g., private equity) or a strategic (e.g., corporate) acquirer or seller? Financial buyers and sellers and strategic buyers and sellers often approach transactions from different viewpoints. For instance, a financial buyer rarely sells a business as a going concern in an asset sale, whereas strategic sellers often sell assets of divisions in divestiture transactions.

Second, what is your client's understanding of and tolerance for environmental risk? Does the client buy and sell businesses with environmental problems, or is it new to the environmental risk arena? Understanding a client's tolerance for and knowledge of environmental risk governs the desired approach for due diligence review and how to best describe the environmental risks to the client, structure the transaction, and allocate environmental risk.

Third, how big is the transaction? The answer to this question provides an essential understanding as to what is considered a "material" or significant environmental risk from the standpoint of the parties. An environmental risk that is material to a $20 million transaction may not even bear scrutiny in a $2 billion transaction. Proper calibration of the environmental materiality threshold avoids missed client expectations and stress in the transaction context from overreaching in the due diligence process.

Fourth, are third parties, such as co-investors or lenders, involved in the transaction? This is essential to structuring and documenting the due diligence process. If other parties need to become comfortable with environmental risk then it is important in most cases to have third party environmental assessments (e.g., Phase I Environmental Assessments) and more detailed presentations of the environmental risks.

The Negotiations

The most important environmental issue negotiated in any transaction is the allocation of environmental risk. The various sources of environmental risk (known and unknown on-site contamination, compliance and permitting flaws and issues, off-site waste disposal liability, toxic tort suits and other environmental litigation, and former facilities and operations and other legacy liabilities) need to be allocated between the buyer and the seller. This requires an answer to the sometimes difficult question: which party is going to assume, retain, and/or indemnify for environmental risk? This is typically decided as a big picture business matter by the parties on each side. It is up to the transactional environmental lawyers to draft and negotiate the mechanisms for achieving the overall risk allocation (e.g., representation-based vs. straight indemnities, purchase price reductions, escrows or holdbacks) and the fundamental terms for the allocation (e.g., survival of indemnity and/or escrow provisions). Appendix K provides an example of environmental provisions that are typical of those used in corporate transaction documents by buyers to allocate environmental risks.

In my experience, it has been rare for open hostility to erupt between parties to a transaction over environmental issues. However, environmental matters can arouse the passions of the parties and result in heated discussions. One way contention commonly arises is from a misunderstanding between the business principals on the terms of the environmental risk allocation "deal." For instance, when one party agrees to keep risks for "contamination" did they mean on-site and off-site contamination, known and unknown contamination, or some subset of these categories? The misunderstanding first comes to light when the transactional environmental attorneys sit down to draft and negotiate the deal. This misunderstanding and the subsequent discussions, often at a high level, that take place to sort out the business understandings of the parties on the nuances of environmental risk allocation can be the most contentious part of negotiations.

The second common area of disagreement, and the most hotly and heavily negotiated environmental concept, relates to special procedures that apply to indemnification claims for contamination at owned or leased real properties. This arises when a buyer receives an indemnity from the seller for known and/or unknown contamination at an acquired faculty or site. Often the seller will want full control of the cleanup after closing given that the seller's money is being spent. Conversely, the buyer typically wants full control of cleanup because it now owns the property subject to the transaction. Further, when the seller is on the hook for unknown, undiscovered environmental problems, often the seller will want to restrict the buyer's ability to look for problems (using so called "no-dig" provisions), the nuances of which often give rise to the most discussed and negotiated provisions in a contract. Appendix L provides an overview of the typical competing positions of buyers and sellers on special environmental procedures. Appendix M provides example special environmental procedural provisions that reflect a commonly negotiated middle-ground between a buyer and seller on these often contentious procedural rights.

Maximizing Deal Success

The key to deal success is being candid with the client with respect to the environmental risks and options for dealing with these risks. This requires the superb counseling skills that I spoke of earlier. The clients need to appreciate the magnitude and timing of costs associated with environmental risk and the uncertainties (e.g., from changing regularity schemes or limited due diligence information) arising from those risks.

I gauge from my client how aggressive to be in a transaction. If an issue is important for the client, I take an aggressive position. If an issue is less important, I tend to take a more conciliatory position. The ultimate goal is to get the deal done, and getting the deal done requires listening to the positions of opposing counsel and clearly articulating to the client the opposing party's position and options for a response. For instance, one of the big mistakes an environmental transaction attorney can make is to overplay or puff up an insignificant issue in a negotiation without a strategic purpose. My view is that the force of negotiations should be brought to bear on the most important, non-trivial aspects of the deal agreements.

I learned early on in my career that you need to be thoroughly prepared before entering a negotiation. Being prepared means knowing the business deal of the parties to a transaction, what issues the opposing party has raised, and my client's response is to those issues. Early in a transaction, my approach is to take the position that everything that I propose in the transaction documents is structured to meet the understanding of both parties to an agreement. This does several things. First, it provides a position of strength from which to negotiate (How can the opposing party disagree if the language merely accomplishes the intent of the parties?). Second, it flags areas where the opposing party may have a difference of understanding as to the fundamental business deal.

Later in the transaction, when a few points remain for resolution, I tend to rely on more common negotiating tactics, such as making a non-important point seem significant so I can trade it for agreement on another point, which may be actually more significant to the client, and starting negotiations with areas of agreement before raising areas of disagreement.

As an attorney, first and foremost I owe an obligation to zealously represent the client's interests. What this means in practice is that any point or position the client wants to take, I take and fight hard to prevail. As I noted earlier, some clients are more risk averse than others when it comes to environmental matters. Understanding the client's sensitivity and risk aversion is the key to understanding on how to approach a negotiation. You can't know when to hold or fold unless you know the wishes of the client and its relative bargaining position. One principle that I follow is to realize that it is my duty as a counselor to educate, inform, and advise the client on environmental matters, not to substitute my judgment for that of the client's.

Negotiation Challenges

The negative attributes of my negotiating style are usually driven by over-reaching prompted by the desires of a client. For instance, a client may want to win on every point no matter how significant. Pushing full bore on all points in a "take it or leave it" approach can cause you to lose credibility with the opposing party to the negotiation and can create an acrimonious environment that may disrupt, delay and complicate a transaction. In these cases, it is important for the environmental transactional attorney to step up as a counselor and guide the client to focus on the issues of material concern.

Protecting the Client as Purchaser

When representing a purchaser, the two fundamental sources of protection are (i) due diligence and (ii) contractual protection (e.g., indemnity). The amount of focus allocated to due diligence verses contractual protection sits as a single point on a spectrum with 100% due diligence-0% contractual protection on one end (e.g., an "as is" deal) and 100% contractual protection-0% due diligence on the other. Most transactions end up somewhere in the middle of this spectrum. Where there is little information provided or little opportunity to conduct due diligence, you generally want more in the way of contractual protection to cover for this uncertainty.

Walking Away

Walking away can be a useful negotiating tool in a transactional context, but only where the party who walks away has a superior bargaining position. If a seller is desperate to sell and the buyer knows this, the buyer should not be under pressure to compromise on important points. Walking away in this context as a means of getting the seller back to the table on terms favorable to the buyer may then be an effective way to proceed. The risk (and reality) is that it is often hard to gauge the relative bargaining strength of the opposing party. This is complicated by bidding wars for companies, which is a fairly common practice used by sellers to create a real (or artificial) superior bargaining position.

Minimizing Deal-Related Risks

The main deal-related risks and pitfalls are: (i) not doing enough due diligence to please lenders, co-investors, and other relevant third parties; (ii) not fully understanding the goals and the business deal of the parties to a transaction; (iii) placing too much emphasis on trivial issues; and (iv) not structuring due diligence review in relation to the risks. Gaps or a lack of thoroughness in due diligence can often present the greatest challenges and risks. Often the client and its counsel are only afforded an opportunity to conduct a high-level, "kick the tires" type of review given a short time period for the transaction and/or information asymmetry, flow, and disclosure issues. Having an experienced environmental transaction counsel who knows the risks inherent in certain types of businesses and can quickly get to the heart of environmental risks in a transaction is often helpful to overcome these risks.

Mid-Deal Changes

In my view, the client is always free to change the environmental deal and any other terms of a transaction up until the closing. The downside is that last minute changes, particularly those not triggered by newly revealed or discovered information (such as a new item appearing on a disclosure schedule) can throw a deal into disarray and give rise to allegations of "retrading" of key business points already decided. Sometimes buyers will use a change in deal terms as a way to reopen discussions on the purchase price based on changes in economic conditions since the start of the transaction.

In some cases, the parties can even reach agreement on amendments to environmental provisions after closing, although this is much harder to accomplish and tends to require some ongoing business relationship or common interconnection between the parties. For example, it is not unheard of for parties to "cash out" of a contractual indemnity obligation years after a deal closes. This typically arises when the seller is paying for environmental work on behalf of the buyer and tensions arise as to the goals and performance of the work. Often the buyer may decide it is best to liquidate the seller's obligations (using information typically gained after closing) and take on the work and obligations itself.

Strategic Challenges

The challenges of strategy come down to the client and available information. If the client is not engaged in the process and/or not committed to a certain approach to environmental matters, it can lead to the deal drifting along without progress. Another issue is no or limited information with which to evaluate environmental risk. If the company is closely held and little public information is available, or the company is being sold in a bid contest where the flow of information is tightly controlled, then it can be hard to get anything accomplished. These situations place a greater emphasis on creativity in client management and due diligence. On the client management side, I have learned to keep clients engaged in the process through regular e-mails updating the client on the status of the environmental aspects of the transaction and significant issues. Such messages need to be brief and narrowly focused to grab a busy client's attention. The message should also specifically ask for direction or response from the client—such as identifying an issue and specifically asking the client how the client would like risks to be allocated for that issue. On the issue of limited information for conducting due diligence, a number of publicly-available database resources exist and environmental database vendors are available to search records of contamination and compliance on companies in the United States. While database searches are not a full-proof method of for conducting due diligence alone, such searches can provide a nice starting point for orienting and structuring a due diligence review.

Major Strategy Mistakes

The biggest single strategy mistake I have seen other attorneys make is failure to "see the forest thought the trees" by focusing on minor or trivial matters to the exclusion of the real and significant issues. I believe this mistake arises from a lack of communication between the environmental transaction attorney and the client as to the materiality threshold and environmental concerns for the transaction. Such a mistake results in additional cost and expense, inefficiencies in the deal process, and possible delay in getting the deal done.

Special Deal Considerations Raised by Environmental Law

There are two aspects of environmental law that lead to special and unique considerations in transactions: (i) strict liability under CERCLA and (ii) the fact that the events and conditions that cause environmental liability are often separated in time from when the liability arises. The first point requires that environmental provisions not be couched only in terms of whether or not the target company complied, but also whether or not there are facts, events, or conditions that could give rise to liability. The second point requires finesse in drafting environmental provisions in a way that allocates risk based on when the facts or events that underlie environmental liability exist or occur rather than on when the actual liability arises. Both points shape the conduct of environmental due diligence because historical and unknown, undiscovered conditions and occurrences are relevant to the overall environmental risk profile of a business. (*See* Appendix K).

Advice for Attorneys

Trust, but verify. Trust what you are told regarding environmental risk, but verify through independent sources, such as database searches or independent consultant review. Most information received in a transaction is reliable, but there still is a fair amount of gamesmanship on the part of sellers with the disclosure of environmental information. This gets to the heart of one of the biggest challenges in any transaction: information asymmetry between the seller, who has all the information, and the buyer, who has little. Often sellers will prepare seller-friendly environmental assessment reports and ask that buyers rely on these reports in lieu of doing their own due diligence review. I always counsel against wholesale reliance on environmental reports prepared by a consultant retained by the seller that may have been massaged by the seller or its counsel. These reports tend to present issues in a way that belie the true nature of the problems. Overcoming this information asymmetry when representing the buyer is challenging, particularly in a bid contest where access to and the flow of information is tightly controlled by the investment bankers in order to give all bidders an even playing field.

It is most important for attorneys to understand the client, the deal, and the desired outcome. This basic knowledge is essential to success in environmental transaction law, because if an attorney does not understand these basic factors and goals, the attorney's work may unknowingly be at cross purposes from the interests of the transactional client.

Lewis T. Putman is a partner in the global corporate group of the international law firm of Milbank, Tweed, Hadley & McCloy LLP. He is resident in Milbank's Washington, D.C., office, where he is the head of Milbank's global environmental and natural resource practices. His practice focuses on international environmental transactional law and environmental risk management. Since 1994, he has advised corporations, private equity firms, and lenders on complex environmental liability, compliance, and permitting issues during mergers, acquisitions, divestitures, public and private financing transactions, bankruptcies, restructurings, and workouts. His commercial and environmental law practice focuses on identifying and quantifying environmental risks through legal due diligence on corporate history, structure, operations and management and the accounting treatment of environmental liabilities; coordinating technical due diligence on environmental risks; communicating environmental liability and compliance risks to clients; and drafting and negotiating contract language for environmental risk allocation.

Dedication: *To my wife, Megan, who I cherish above all others, and Audrey, Hannah, Jessica, Kelly, and Jack, my lovely children who make everyday an adventure.*

From Fear to Greed: The Business of Environmental Law

Andrew N. Davis, Ph.D.

Partner

Dewey & LeBoeuf LLP

Introduction

This essay is offered in the context of hopefully providing thought-provoking guidance in the area of environmental business counseling and transactional matters. My environmental law practice, and the skill sets I bring to the table on behalf of clients, have their origins in almost 30 years of training and experience as both a scientist and environmental lawyer. As a non-contentious environmental lawyer (i.e., non-litigator), my practice focuses on identifying, quantifying and developing strategies to manage environmental risks—what is known as the "business of environmental law." This generally falls into two areas of environmental legal practice: (1) domestic and cross-border corporate, real estate and energy transactions; and (2) compliance/business counseling. While these non-litigation aspects of environmental law are by no means new, the demands presented by the business world are dynamically imposing a new construct on, and portend a new paradigm for, environmental lawyers. Environmental issues are increasingly being seen as business issues, and C-level executives and their in-house counsel demand that their environmental lawyers add value, in a measurable way, beyond traditional approaches.

A brief aside about the somewhat provocative title is warranted. There is increasing recognition that the role and function of the environmental lawyer is evolving. While the field of environmental law is relatively new in context of the overall legal profession, the focus of environmental law has changed over the past 30-plus years. For perspective, 1970 is viewed as the birth of the field of modern environmental law with the creation of the U.S. Environmental Protection Agency (EPA) through an executive reorganization plan. The 1970s also saw the enactment of major new federal environmental laws and important amendments to older laws that greatly expanded EPA's responsibilities, and it was not until 1980 that this country saw a comprehensive federal environmental cleanup statute.

In the past, many environmental lawyers were viewed as using "fear" as a basis for client advice—focusing on what costs/liabilities would be associated with cleanup obligations at a Superfund/CERCLA site; or what penalties could be incurred for violations of "end-of-the-pipe" environmental laws, such as the Clean Water and Clean Air Acts. In fact, it may be safe to say (and some business lawyers may still think this way) that environmental lawyers were often only called on—somewhat reluctantly I might add—at the proverbial "eleventh hour" of a deal as a necessary evil, in order to quickly review the environmental aspects of the transaction, identify any major environmental issues, and offer ways to minimize the potential for subtraction from the bottom line—but never, ever, to add to the bottom line. This construct was self-fulfilling; the environmental lawyer had little time and room to maneuver to truly add value—and in the post-game locker room evaluation of the deal, that would be what was remembered. Further, the desire by clients and their business counsel to "get the deal done" and view environmental issues as merely impediments to the transaction could lead to the potential for missing (or mismanaging) critical environmental risks that could be material or, in the worst-case, turn a transaction upside down.

On the other hand, business/corporate lawyers have always focused on the "bottom line"—the value added/financial aspects of a business transaction. The corporate lawyer did, and continues to, look for ways to maximize shareholder value and return on investment; in other words, using "greed" (in the non-judgmental sense) as the basis for client advice.

While there are still (and will continue to be) opportunities for traditional environmental law practice, we are increasingly seeing changes to traditional media-based (air, water, soil) "command and control" environmental laws, where the government determines that a particular substance is hazardous to human health or the environment, and sets standards for the maximum amount that can be discharged into the environment, what are known as "end-of-the-pipe" controls. In fact, while further engineering controls demanded by traditional environmental law constructs are technically feasible, the environmental benefits of such controls are shrinking in relation to the greater dollars needed to achieve the desired pollution reductions. Thus, future national and international laws need to embrace "before-the-pipe" concepts and will undoubtedly focus on pollution prevention, conservation, recycling and renewable energy issues. Importantly, future developments in environmental law must also address the world's real problem: too many people consuming limited resources— the "tragedy of the commons."

Critically, we are seeing the investing world—both institutional investors and individual shareholders alike—driving the evolution of the role of the environmental lawyer and the development and application of new environmental laws (e.g., the Carbon Disclosure Project—*see* www.cdproject.net). Because of this, in part, corporate attitudes toward the environment have changed. Companies now recognize the importance of sustainable development in the context of their manufacturing/energy supply activities; thus, compliance with environmental laws, and the utilization of best management practices, is becoming *de rigueur*. (Not to mention that all of the major U.S. environmental laws today contain provisions that can impose criminal sanctions—jail time and fines—on C-level executives for noncompliance with environmental laws, including seemingly benign activities such as recordkeeping and reporting.) The circle is complete—shareholder demands are driving corporations to be better environmental citizens, and environmental lawyers are being asked to assist in this process and identify ways to increase shareholder value (i.e., play to the "greed" factor).

Today, pervasive environmental problems top political, social, and legal agendas globally, and environmental lawyers are being asked to add value in non-traditional environmental areas, such as: establishing corporate policies/governance structures and advising on the regulatory compliance issues under the Kyoto Protocol (in force globally but not yet in the United States), and state/regional initiatives such as the California Global Warming Solutions Act and the east coast's Regional Greenhouse Gas Initiative (RGGI), disclosure obligations, and other risks presented by climate change; advising on other climate change agenda items, such as investment strategies, emissions trading and "carbon footprint" reduction projects, development and permitting of alternative energy sources such as wind farms and carbon capture and storage projects; advising property owners, tenants and developers, building contractors, and architects on voluntary or mandatory green building issues associated with carbon reduction and other environmental agendas; developing risk/liability transfer or "exit" strategies for boxing-in remediation obligations and associated potential environmental liabilities; advising on tax benefits/credits, public-private partnerships, and other financial/economic programs and incentives to facilitate cleanup efforts to redevelop historically contaminated sites (e.g., "brownfields"); assisting clients with satisfying natural resource damage assessment (NRDA) and restoration obligations under federal and state laws; helping clients identify environmental and natural resource aspects of their businesses/properties that can be viewed and valued as assets (such as carbon credits, wetland banking credits, and natural resource damage offsets); advising on EHS issues associated with nanotechnology R&D and manufacturing; advising corporations on environmental aspects of corporate, social responsibility and concepts of sustainability; and advising clients on the implications of and steps needed to ensure compliance with a range of emerging EU legislation such as directives concerning Waste Electrical and Electronic Equipment (WEEE), restrictions of the use of certain hazardous substances (RoHS) and the chemicals reforms under the Registration, Evaluation and Authorization of Chemicals (REACH) regulation, which requires industry to register all existing and future new substances with a new European chemicals agency.

These types of issues are very different from the assignments most environmental lawyers are familiar with; suffice it to say that the environmental lawyer who does not "evolve" to handle these new opportunities will find him/herself out of the mainstream and going the way of the dodo bird and dinosaurs.

The Role of the Non-Contentious Environmental Lawyer: Transactional Law

Virtually all transactions, whether for assets or stock, have liability components associated with past and future environmental, health, and safety (EHS) activities and conditions associated with currently or formerly owned and operated properties and/or assets. As a transactional lawyer, my role is to assist the multidisciplinary corporate deal team that handles complex country-specific and cross-border mergers, acquisitions, and divestitures with environmental risk identification, allocation, and avoidance strategies to minimize the potential for EHS issues to be "deal killers." This "front-end" work is also important in that it can help identify issues early on that need to be resolved in order to avoid the potential for litigation down the road.

In the environmental due diligence context, my practice encompasses all transaction phases. In addition to traditional due diligence activities, this can also generally entail assisting with project development and land use/siting issues; the application and structuring of environmental insurance; and advising on a "target's" compliance with federal, state and local EHS regulatory and permitting requirements. We are typically brought in at an early stage to assist in formulating a strategy that minimizes potential liabilities, such as to: design the appropriate nature, scope, and timing of the environmental due diligence effort; advise on the use of environmental consultants/engineering firms or others with special expertise to interface with the deal parties, lenders/investors, and possibly environmental regulators; and negotiate the risk allocation and management strategies appropriate to meet the client's business objectives.

The Role of the Non-Contentious Environmental Lawyer: Environmental Business/Compliance Counseling

The second prong of my practice encompasses business counseling, which includes: (1) regulatory compliance counseling, permitting, and assisting with the identification and reporting of environmental risks and satisfying applicable disclosure obligations; and (2) assisting clients (such as marine insurers/insureds and manufacturers) with oil and chemical spill response/casualty events; and the assessment and restoration of natural resource damages (NRD).

Environmental compliance/permitting counseling encompasses the mandates of key federal EHS laws (and their implementing regulations) in the United States, including the Clean Air Act (CAA); Clean Water Act (CWA); Resource Conservation and Recovery Act (RCRA); Toxic Substances Control Act (TSCA); Comprehensive Environmental Response, Compensation and Liability Act (CERCLA or Superfund); the Oil Pollution Act of 1990 (OPA); the Occupational Safety and Health Act (OSHA); state law counterparts; and unique state property transfer laws such as the Connecticut Transfer Act and the New Jersey Industrial Site Recovery Act (ISRA). In addition, clients frequently seek advice with respect to financial disclosure and reporting obligations associated with environmental issues, which have become closely scrutinized in the United States following the passage of the Sarbanes-Oxley Act of 2002 and the development/clarification of various accounting standards (such as FAS 143 and FIN 47) that have environmental implications. As a business lawyer, clients frequently seek counsel on developing and implementing proactive, preventive business strategies that meet the environmental requirements of the above-referenced laws and regulations, and minimize potential exposure to costly criminal, administrative, and civil governmental compliance actions—all without unduly restricting business objectives.

In the area of NRD, legislation such as CERCLA, OPA and the EU Environmental Liability Directive (ELD) make responsible parties liable for not only the costs incurred to clean up a contaminated site or waters affected by hazardous substances or an oil spill, but also for the NRD (or biodiversity damage) suffered by the environment as a result of that pollution incident. While the statutory authority to pursue NRD claims has existed for some time in the United States, under OPA, significant marine casualties (collisions, explosions, oil spills, and groundings) routinely involve NRD claims, and, under CERCLA and state analogs, aggressive Attorneys General in several jurisdictions are increasingly pursuing NRD claims, even at sites that had been remediated many years ago.

Across the pond in Europe, the EU's ELD is just now imposing similar obligations across the EU's member states (from 30 April 2007) on those that cause pollution leading to biodiversity damage. For example, the key Annex II to the ELD (which provides a framework for selection of suitable primary, complementary, and compensatory remedial measures) is heavily based on the U.S. OPA regulations for carrying out NRDAs.

Success in managing multifaceted defense strategies in NRD cases, whether under OPA or CERCLA, has led to assignments to defend some of the most significant marine pollution incidents that have occurred recently in the United States. For example, over the course of the cases we have handled, we have constructed a scientifically-based claims avoidance/mitigation strategy employed during the all-important NRDA phase which has won praise from our clients and respect from government regulators (known as "trustees" in the NRDA context). Examples of our work in this emerging area include advising a leading marine insurer and its insureds on the OPA (and state law) spill response and NRDA process for marine oil spills and casualty events in locations throughout the United States, including: Buzzards Bay, Massachusetts; Point Judith, Rhode Island; Puget Sound, Washington; Mississippi River, New Orleans, Louisiana; Gulf of Mexico, Texas and Louisiana; Portland, Maine; and Staten Island, New York.

Environmental Law Deal Strategies

In the deal context, it is important to stress a few basics about my philosophy and approach to environmental issues in transactions and the concept of risk. Environmental due diligence in a corporate or real estate transaction necessarily focuses on the identification of environmental risks, and the facilitation of the disclosure of the nature and scope of those risks. However, just because something is identified as an environmental issue or risk does not mean it is necessarily a deal killer or significant problem in a particular situation. Rather it becomes a problem for the client, whose risk tolerance (see below) you must understand, when it presents risks that are unacceptable (from a financial, human health, or public relations perspective) or cannot otherwise be managed. Environmental issues should never be "overwhelming" to a client, and as their trusted environmental advisor, you should not let them become such. If environmental issues were major issues in every transaction, few deals would close. Fortunately, that is not the case, nor should it be. Every deal that has real property or other assets may have environmental risks. Although they need to be taken seriously, most can be managed and need not kill a deal. While occasionally a deal may fall apart due to an environmental problem, in most situations environmental issues need not be "deal stoppers."

Given this background, below are offered some of the lessons learned from experience with environmental transactional/due diligence matters. These transactional considerations are vital to environmental law deal strategies—and importantly, but disconcertedly, none of these are taught in law school.

There is risk, and there is risk that matters. Virtually every choice in life presents risks and benefits. The key is being able to distinguish minor risks from major ones—and in the end, the only critical risks are the unacceptable ones. As your client's trusted environmental counsel, your role is to identify all of the risks, separate out the "significant" ones, and present options to creatively manage them. For example, in the real estate arena, the key is to develop innovative solutions to environmental issues, which often pose significant obstacles to real estate conveyance, development, and construction. While risk allocation can be accomplished by using traditional contractual negotiations, environmental laws also present opportunities for utilization of environmental insurance to "shift" risk (see below), entering into creative public/private partnerships with environmental agencies for voluntary cleanups based on site-specific risk assessments, and taking advantage of brownfield funding mechanisms. To do this, you need to have an understanding of all potential risk identification and management tools in the tool box, from traditional pre-contract environmental due diligence structuring (which can vary significantly, depending on the client's role in the transaction—whether buyer, seller, lender/investor—and can involve traditional environmental due diligence (EDD) techniques such as transaction screens, Phase I (or greater) environmental site assessments, or the emerging environmental disclosure due diligence (EDDD) approach that has come to life in this post-Sarbanes Oxley world of environmental disclosure); to contractual strategies (such as environmental representations and warranties, covenants, indemnities, environmental escrows, and post-closing access/remediation side agreements); to more creative tools such as environmental insurance (cost-cap/stop loss or pollution legal liability policies), risk/liability transfer strategies (such as guaranteed fixed-price remediation contracts, with or without the backing of environmental insurance) and corporate structuring strategies. The bottom line is simple: environmental issues can be managed in many different ways and need not—in fact should not—become the tail that wags the proverbial dog in a transaction.

Begin with the end in mind. Not every environmental issue is a risk in every transaction. Knowing the future use of the site can be critical in this context. For example, if the future use of the site will be industrial/commercial, the evaluation of the environmental risks and cleanup strategy will be very different than if the future use will be residential. If there is a type of contamination in the soil and/or groundwater that poses no risks to human health, given the absence of human receptors or a pathway to sensitive environmental resources (e.g., it is of a type that is not volatile and thus poses no indoor air risks through today's buzz word of vapor intrusion, or the groundwater is not used for consumptive purposes), then leaving residual contamination in place, that is still protective of human health and the environment, may be appropriate and acceptable to the environmental regulatory agency with jurisdiction and the parties to the transaction. Further, there can be tremendous synergies in cost and time savings in, for example, a brownfield redevelopment context, by combining and/or coordinating many of the remediation tasks with redevelopment/construction plans (particularly with respect to soil moving/removing activities as well as utilizing construction elements, such as parking lots, as "caps" for soil with residual contamination to minimize off-site transportation and disposal costs).

Environmental counsel should be consulted early in the process. While the tendency is to be cost-conscious in the early stages of the transaction (such as during the negotiations of the fundamental business terms or a letter of intent) and not involve environmental counsel at that time, early involvement can be essential, as the key strategic framework is often set at this time, and it becomes more difficult (if not impossible) for the environmental lawyer to be creative (i.e., add "real" value) later on if the business framework is set in stone. At that point, the assistance environmental counsel can add will be limited to being reactive to decisions that have already been made, and solutions will be focused on risk minimization/damage control rather than having the opportunity to creatively shape the environmental aspects of the deal and offer creative risk management options that can box in the environmental risks/costs (see discussion about environmental insurance and risk/liability transfer options below). Environmental issues need to be integrated into all of the deal documents, such as: the letter of intent; the purchase agreement; any scope of work or remediation agreement; environmental insurance policy; post-closing access/remediation/environmental escrow agreement; and voluntary cleanup order with an environmental regulatory agency. Given the breadth of this undertaking, consultation with environmental counsel should be like voting—early and often—so that environmental issues do not become a "drag" on the transaction.

Pick experienced environmental consultants/experts. Consultants who have generic science backgrounds and little business savvy will be less successful in interacting with the legal and non-legal business team members than those who are well-credentialed, experienced in the transactional setting, and who possess the specialized expertise for the issues at hand. In my experience, environmental consultants have a significant role and are made a valued part of the deal team, including being apprised of the key transactional documents and client's business drivers. This team effort is critical in that clients today demand that the environmental lawyer be conversant with environmental consultant "speak," and be able to assist in translating the technical issues into creative business solutions for the matter at hand.

Define the risk, know the hot-bed jurisdictional issues, and understand the remediation options. In the old days, soil remediation was traditionally done by the "dig and haul" method, affectionately known as "remediation by Bubba"—where Bubba drove the backhoe and removed all "dirty" dirt (i.e., contaminated soil) to background levels. Today, in many jurisdictions, it is "remediation by RBCA" (phonetically Rebecca). That term does not refer to a matter of the advancement of women's rights; rather, many jurisdictions have cleanup programs that permit the use of risk-based cleanup approaches (hence the RBCA) that allow cleanups to satisfy less onerous, risk-based standards, utilizing monitored natural attenuation, engineering controls (e.g., vapor barriers), and institutional controls (e.g., site-wide or localized activity or use limitations that are memorialized in deed restrictions placed on the land records) in lieu of the application of more rigorous cleanup standards that would require more extensive and expensive active remediation.

Environmental issues need not be deal killers. In many deals, environmental, lawyers are often seen, sometimes appropriately, as impediments to the deal progressing. Further, many environmental lawyers who I have sat across the table from treat a transaction as a litigation matter, and feel they must "fight to the death" over environmental issues and risk allocation. In my experience, this is unnecessary and unwarranted. These are transactions, not litigation—the role of the environmental lawyer is to turn the rocks over, identify the risks that may lurk there under, advise their clients of those risks, and offer creative risk allocation and management strategies, with the goal of closing the deal. In the end, which environmental risks are acceptable and how they are allocated are business decisions made ultimately by clients, not environmental lawyers. Good environmental lawyers recognize this, and work across the table from each other, representing their clients well, but negotiating in good faith within the deal constraints to further the overriding goal of creating a "win-win" scenario to allow the transaction to proceed.

Understand your client's business. While this seems obvious, it is critical to understand your client's business, whether: for real estate market clients, its sector or role as a developer, landlord or lender/investor; or, for manufacturing clients, its industry sector, the raw materials it uses, products it manufactures, the wastes it generates and where they go, the overall corporate management structure, and its environmental management philosophy and system (if any).

Understand the full deal context and the client's level of risk tolerance. Many times I have been asked to assist in a transaction and "just review the environmental provisions" of the deal document(s). In fact, the environmental sections are the last provisions I review (and I train my associates to do so as well). It is critical to review the entire deal document (or documents, as the case may be, including any letters of intent or related financing agreements) to understand: the type of transaction (e.g., asset vs. stock vs. debt or equity financing vs. securitization deal); dollar value of the deal and the overall deal structure (i.e., an arms-length one-off deal or a bid situation); who the various parties are (and importantly, where our client fits in and what entity(ies) will survive post-closing); whether a due diligence data room (real or virtual) has been set up, or how environmental issues are otherwise being disclosed; how other (non-environmental) risks are being handled/allocated; the length and scope of any allowable environmental due diligence opportunity; how long the representations, warranties, and covenants survive; whether there are any indemnification obligations, and the details of same; how the various defined terms are used in the non-environmental provisions as well as in the environmental provisions; whether there is an "off-ramp" or other mechanism (e.g., price adjustment, environmental escrow) that can be triggered in case material issues (whether environmental or otherwise) are identified; whether a materiality threshold has been agreed to; etc.

Similarly, it is critical to understand the client's risk tolerance generally, and in the context of the specifics of the transaction. While this is typically a dollar or materiality threshold for environmental risks (e.g., a $25,000 leaking underground storage tank issue may be acceptable in a $50 million deal), increasingly clients (particularly publicly-traded companies) are also concerned about reputational issues in the context of corporate social responsibility and disclosure obligations. Without an understanding of the client's risk tolerance, the environmental lawyer is operating in a vacuum and cannot provide tailored business guidance and advice that is useful for the business lawyers (internal and external) and, importantly, the non-legal members of the client's team.

Tell the client what they need to hear, not what they want to hear. This cannot be overemphasized. I have too often seen, and heard, environmental lawyers "soft-selling" the environmental risks of a deal. That is not in our job description—we are the messenger, and the goal is to be thorough and rational, not to ensure that your client likes you because of the message you are delivering. While it is great when it works out that what you tell the client is what they want to hear, it is critical to be honest and direct with clients in discussing the potential environmental risks and liabilities of their deal. Equally as important, the good environmental deal lawyer will have in his/her arsenal risk elimination and/or mitigation strategies that can be employed to "box-in" the potential risks, understand where and how risks can become liabilities, and look down the road to devise an acceptable path forward to allow the deal to close.

Environmental insurance can be a useful tool to help manage risks and bridge the gap in risk allocation. The development and creative use of innovative environmental insurance products can be valuable in managing environmental risks and liabilities. While these risks and liabilities can be daunting, they are almost always manageable when approached creatively. Environmental insurance can be employed with great success to address environmental risks in a variety of business contexts, including: real estate transactions/brownfield redevelopment; corporate mergers and acquisitions/divestitures; balance sheet management; corporate insurance restructuring (i.e., coverage disputes); and resolution of responsible parties' liabilities at hazardous waste sites.

While environmental insurance is not necessary or even available (nor cost-effective) for every situation (such as when the expected cleanup cost is small and/or well-defined, or the cost of the premium for the environmental insurance policy is disproportionate to the value of the deal), the key is to identify environmental risks at the earliest stage possible, and then to craft solutions tailored specifically to the client's business priorities. The goal is to maximize the use of the array of environmental insurance products available for the benefit of clients, using manuscripted policy forms. This is an area where many practitioners fall short; an environmental insurance policy (with its attendant endorsements), in its essence, is a contract, and needs to be negotiated and tailored to the specifics of the transaction and the underlying cleanup or other environmental risks, just like any other deal document. Off-the-shelf, template or specimen policies are not acceptable in this context, and should be avoided. The relevant types of policies include manuscripted pollution legal liability (PLL); cleanup cost cap/stop loss; and secured creditor (or any combination thereof) policies. Environmental insurance policies, if properly structured, can be written to cover a broad spectrum of potential exposures, including property damage and bodily injury ("toxic tort" coverages); cleanup obligations and cost overruns; natural resource damages; liability associated with transportation and disposal of hazardous wastes/substances; project delays and business interruption; loss of collateral value; contract liability; and legal defense costs. Environmental insurance can be used to cap remediation costs and provide long-term (10 or more years) third-party liability protection at a single site or for a portfolio of impacted properties across one or many states in favor of a single entity, lenders/investors, all parties to a transaction, or a group of potentially responsible parties (PRPs).

Evaluate the use of risk/liability transfer options where technically feasible and cost-effective. A risk/liability transfer is a risk-allocation strategy that allows for the complete *contractual* resolution of environmental liabilities that may be associated with the conditions of a property, or a portfolio of properties. Applied properly, a risk/liability transfer can function to "take environmental issues off the table." As the name suggests, a risk/liability transfer involves the contractual transfer of all liabilities associated with pre-existing environmental conditions (e.g., third-party, toxic tort liabilities, cleanup obligations) at a site or a portfolio of sites to a third-party contractor/insurer team. Such transfer is typically pre-funded and supported with a guaranteed-fixed price remediation contract/scope of work backed by a parent-level indemnity from the environmental contractor, as well as a long-term (e.g., 10 or more years) comprehensive environmental insurance policy (often combining both cost-cap/stop loss and PLL coverages) from a financially secure insurer. In some instances, the environmental contractor will enter into a cleanup consent order or voluntary cleanup program with the environmental regulatory agency with jurisdiction. It is important to recognize that each risk/liability transfer is negotiated extensively to meet a client's goals for the specific risks associated with the specific sites involved in the deal.

Andrew N. Davis, Ph.D. is a partner in the environmental/health and safety practice group of the international law firm of Dewey & LeBoeuf LLP. He counsels clients in transactional, permitting, compliance, and enforcement matters under federal and state health and safety, hazardous waste, air and water pollution, site development, and property transfer laws. He provides due diligence support in domestic and cross-border energy, corporate, and real estate transactions, and assists clients with the development and performance of environmental insurance policies, site assessments, and engineering contracts related to the investigation and remediation of brownfield properties. He assists clients with environmental auditing, reporting, recordkeeping, and other compliance obligations under programs governing asbestos, lead, mold, and other indoor air issues. He also assists marine insurers, their members, and others with oil and chemical spill response, casualty events, and the assessment and restoration of natural resource damages in locations throughout the United States and in foreign waters.

Dr. Davis serves on the board of directors of the Ocean Technology Foundation, the executive committee of the University of Connecticut Real Estate Center Council, the steering committee of the Great Lakes Natural Resource Damage Assessment Advisory Group, and is a member of several national and international environmental organizations, is a frequent speaker on a variety of topics, and has been recently recognized as one of the leading environmental lawyers by Chambers & Partners' Guide to America's Leading Business Lawyers—Environment *(2007–2008). He is the author of two books and numerous articles and chapters on his areas of expertise. He is an adjunct professor of environmental studies/law and policy at Connecticut College. He holds a B.S. in biology from Trinity College, an M.S. and Ph.D. in botany/marine ecology from the University of Massachusetts at Amherst, and a J.D. from George Washington University. He is admitted to practice in Connecticut and Massachusetts. He can be contacted at adavis@dl.com or 860/293-3514.*

Successfully Minimizing Risk

Eric B. Rothenberg

Partner

O'Melveny & Meyers LLP

When first meeting with a new client, I look for an opportunity to speak with the target's environmental management team to understand the current and past structure of the organization, audit programs, the location of key environmental assessments, permits, and compliance files. I prefer this method to an electronic question-and-answer process, which other firms use. This initial discussion is usually done as a call or meeting in conjunction with other initial meetings with management.

Laws of Note

More than most areas of practice, each deal brings a unique matrix of potentially applicable international, federal, state, and local law (including common law) concerns.

For most current transactions, we will be looking to evaluate remedial and compliance risk in conjunction with the law that applies in jurisdictions where the facilities are located. Absent meaningful local law, we will look to the law of the United States, European Union, and certain of its member states (notably Dutch cleanup standards) to benchmark. Some examples of recent developments that broadly affect transactions in the industrial sector would include global and U.S. regulatory requirements for greenhouse gas controls, the EU REACH chemical registration law that requires first filings in June of 2008, and newly emerging European contaminated land cleanup regimes.

State Level

In the U.S., certain states impose unique requirements on transactions. These include "transfer laws" requiring pre-deal approval by the environmental regulatory authority (notably New Jersey and Connecticut), cessation of business laws where a shut down is contemplated (e.g., in Ohio), and laws which provide for a greater measure of protection as to pre-existing conditions depending on the nature of diligence conducted (e.g., in Michigan).

Where the parties to a deal understand that a cleanup is in prospect, we will also look at the degree to which state law provides for expedited remediation through voluntary remediation and brownfield development programs. Brownfield programs are largely based on a USEPA program first created in 1995 with the objective of redeveloping an estimated 450,000 abandoned or underutilized contaminated properties to active use through facilitated remediation. As of the end of 2006, EPA announced that it had completed 1,000 brownfield projects, creating 80,000 jobs and $2.7 billion of annual income. Site number 1000 is a 450-acre former defense department facility in Charleston that was cleaned up at an estimated cost of $9.5 million and is slated for a $6 billion multi-use redevelopment. The success of EPA and its government and business partners has been the product of several statutory, policy and economic initiatives, the most significant of which are summarized in this handbook: (1) creation of a "bona fide purchaser" (BFP) liability exemption for post January 11, 2002, asset purchasers; (2) issuance of a form EPA agreement and covenant not to sue for BFP's willing to perform remedial work; (3) enactment of a Superfund amendment which, *inter alia*, provides protection to secured creditors that provide financing for development of contaminated sites, (4) creation of a liability exemption and USEPA enforcement policy not to prosecute owners of land whose groundwater is contaminate from off-site sources, (5) issuance of USEPA policies for use of "ready for reuse" or RFR certification and no further action or comfort letters in circumstances where a liability exemption is not available, (6) taxpayer relief legislation making environmental remediation expense deductible in the year incurred, (7) guidance and legislation on federal certification and funding of state brownfield programs, (8) pilot grant funding more than 300 regional projects at up to $200,000 each to date (and expanded through 2007 for up to $350,000) and $1 million per site for site assessment and remediation, respectively; (9) elimination of inactive sites from USEPA's contaminated properties database, the Comprehensive Environmental Response Compensation and Liability Information System (CERCLIS), (10) establishment of exemptions for small business and non-profit organizations responsible for only *de minimis* waste contributions, (11) issuance of a policies allowing for "brownfield" remediation of Superfund sites currently treated under the Resource Conservation and Recovery Act (RCRA) or under the joint jurisdiction of other agencies.

Diligence

The scope of extent of diligence is influenced first by the nature of the client's own resources to evaluate environmental, safety, and health concerns—many corporate clients will have already conducted very sophisticated diligence. Database and public information searches are done on virtually every deal. The decision to perform Phase I (site visits without invasive sampling) reviews at all sites and Phase II (invasive sampling) at certain sites will be driven by the potential materiality of on-site remediation/compliance concerns relative to deal value, needs of lenders and, sometimes, by a desire to have diligence qualify under the 2002 Bone Fide Purchaser defense available under the US Superfund program described above. Generally, we seek to accomplish certain minimum levels of diligence on all deals, including public database and document reviews and representative site visits. If there is one thing I would tell a new attorney, it would be dig into the detail. There is no substitute for reviewing the remediation documents, the permit conditions, the terms of the consent decrees/order and the applicable laws, rules and regulations.

Negotiation Strategies

We prefer to negotiate issues before looking at contract language. This is often accomplished by creating an issues chart that includes statements of respective party positions. Negotiated contract provisions include:

1. Statement of excluded liabilities (including former sites, pre-existing conditions at current sites, toxic tort and products liability claims),
2. Environmental Safety and Health Representations (Reps) and related Reps on litigation, real estate, permits, historic insurance and material contracts (including environmental indemnity obligations and rights),
3. Covenants related to pre-closing environmental diligence and "chemical cleanup" obligations,
4. Indemnity for pre-closing contamination and non-compliance, including baskets and caps and conduct which is permissible for trigger of indemnities and
5. Right to assign indemnities.

Negotiation of duration of reps, baskets (deductibles), and caps (maximum indemnity amount) is often part of the larger deal terms negotiation.

Typically, the more sophisticated the opposing party, the faster we can get through the required diligence and effect viable deal documentation.

Structuring the Deal

Structure is almost always driven by corporate and tax concerns. In circumstances where significant legacy liabilities are apparent from historic operations at former sites, our preference is to structure as an asset deal. (acquisition of stated parcels and improvements rather than stock of an operating entity). Stock transactions will generally require the acquirer to assume responsibility for legacy liabilities, including former and off-site contaminated properties.

Generally, there are opportunities to test the initial representations of target's environmental management against public files and the diligence materials provided. As discrepancies arise, there is further opportunity to reflect on the nature of qualifications that are permissible in connection with environmental reps.

Risk

All clients have different levels of "risk tolerance" and differing affinities for ways to deal with risk. We have clients that are inclined to acquire cost cap and/or pollution legal liability insurance as a way to quantify and transfer risk. A public company will need to consider how liabilities of the acquired concern will be reflected in public disclosures.

Risks generally fall into several categories:

1. Costs of current and foreseeable environmental compliance (including climate change regulation, process safety management, EU REACH, waste recycling and electronic component obligations, site security, and other newly emerging regulation)
2. Current and foreseeable costs of remediation on site, at former sites and at off-site locations to which hazardous materials may have been sent for treatment, storage, disposal or handling
3. Toxic tort and product liability risk

4. Pending or threatened litigation including civil/criminal enforcement

5. Accounting issues including obligations of public companies to make disclosure as to environmental expense, including in connection with asset retirement obligations

6. Consideration of indemnity and/or insurance applicable to disclosed risks

Challenges

Adequate quantification (often with present value adjustment) is often the greatest challenge. The buyer will typically want dollar estimates for the potential remediation and compliance matters uncovered through diligence, and model the same over a stated investment or ownership period (i.e., one to five years, twenty years in five-year increments). This exercise may also be necessary to assist in the development of reserves for public reporting companies, fixing the value of environmental escrow accounts and placing "risk transfer" insurance policies, i.e., insurance which will either place a cap on remediation costs and/or provide coverage for future governmental and third-party claims.

Conclusion

More than most areas of legal practice, environmental transactional practice requires a large measure of resilience: resilience to adapt to a rapidly changing regulatory/enforcement landscape and corresponding adoptions in deal documentation.

Eric B. Rothenberg is a partner in O'Melveny & Myers LLP's New York office and directs the firm's environmental practice. He represents business and financial institutions in a broad range of adversarial environmental matters, including Superfund proceedings, related toxic tort claims, and private cost recovery actions.

Drawing upon prior experience as a graduate-degree environmental engineer, Mr. Rothenberg directs diligence and documentation of transactions and financings involving industrial allocation counsel at national priorities list Superfund sites, and defense counsel in toxic tort proceedings. He is a frequent speaker and author of numerous publications including current U.S. and international environmental law summaries for the PLI Corporate Legal Counsel series. He is recognized in the current International Who's Who as one of the leading U.S. environmental lawyers. He earned his A.B. and M.S. degrees from Harvard University and his J.D. from Northeastern University.

Appendices

APPENDIX A

EXCERPTS FROM PROPERTY SALE REQUIRING BUYER TO REMEDIATE PROPERTY PRIOR TO ITS REDEVELOPMENT

Sale and Purchase of Property Agreement

THIS SALE AND PURCHASE OF PROPERTY AGREEMENT, made and entered into this ___ day of _____, 2000, between Seller and Buyer.

RECITALS

Buyer desires to purchase and accept from Seller, and Seller desires to sell and convey to Buyer, approximately ___ acres of that certain real property described on Exhibit A.

THEREFORE, in consideration of the terms, covenants, warranties and conditions hereinafter set forth, the parties, intending to be legally bound, mutually agree as follows.

ARTICLE I
SALE AND PURCHASE OF PROPERTY

Subject to the terms of this Agreement, Seller shall sell, transfer, assign, and deliver to Buyer on the Closing Date (as defined in Section 12.01), and Buyer agrees to purchase and accept from Seller on the Closing Date, certain real property and all rights, interests and appurtenances therein or thereto pertaining, which real property is further described on Exhibit A attached hereto (collectively, the "Real Property"). Additionally, Seller agrees to convey to Buyer the right to make ___ divisions to the Real Property under Section 108 of the Land Division Act, Act No. 288 of Public Acts of 1967, as amended.

ARTICLE II
PURCHASE PRICE OF THE PROPERTY

*   *   *

SECTION 2.04. Agreement Regarding Remediating Landfill. As a further condition to the sale of the Real Property, on the Closing Date, Buyer and Seller shall enter into an agreement substantially in the form attached as Exhibit C (the "Restrictions Agreement") imposing restrictions on the use and sale of the Landfill (as defined in Section 9.02) and setting forth Buyer's obligations regarding the Landfill. The Restrictions Agreement shall be placed in escrow with Seller's counsel. In the event that Buyer does not submit to and obtain the approval by the Michigan Department of Environmental Quality within eighteen (18) months following the date of Closing of a remedial action plan with respect to the Landfill, Seller's counsel shall record the Restrictions Agreement.

*   *   *

ARTICLE IX
DISCLAIMER OF WARRANTIES

SECTION 9.01. Disclaimer. Except as otherwise expressly and explicitly provided herein, Buyer agrees to accept the Real Property on an "AS IS, WHERE IS" basis. Except as otherwise expressly and explicitly provided herein, with respect to the Real Property, SELLER DISCLAIMS ANY AND ALL WARRANTIES, EXPRESS OR IMPLIED, REGARDING THE REAL PROPERTY, INCLUDING, BUT NOT LIMITED TO, ITS PHYSICAL OR ENVIRONMENTAL CONDITION, AND MAKES NO WARRANTY OF MERCHANTABILITY OR FITNESS OF THE REAL PROPERTY FOR ANY PARTICULAR PURPOSE, EXPRESS OR IMPLIED. BUYER RELEASES SELLER FROM ANY AND ALL CLAIMS AT LAW OR EQUITY REGARDING THE REAL PROPERTY AND ITS PHYSICAL OR ENVIRONMENTAL CONDITION, MERCHANTABILITY, OR FITNESS FOR ANY PARTICULAR PURPOSE.

SECTION 9.02. Landfill. Seller discloses and Buyer accepts the condition of the Real Property as disclosed in the Summary Report regarding the Real Property conducted by _____ (the "Environmental Report") prepared with Buyer's knowledge. Buyer affirms that it understands the condition of the Real Property and more particularly the presence of the Landfill on a portion thereof, and understands that Seller disclaims any and all warranties, express or implied, regarding the Real Property, the location of the Landfill, and the physical or environmental condition of the Real Property. Buyer releases and shall indemnify, defend and hold harmless Seller from any and all claims at law or in equity regarding the Landfill, its location, physical or environmental condition, merchantability, or fitness for any particular purpose.

ARTICLE X
BUYER'S PRIVILEGES PENDING CLOSING;
OPPORTUNITY TO TERMINATE

SECTION 10.01. Access to Real Property. Buyer has previously inspected the Real Property and been provided with the results of the Environmental Report. Buyer has found the Real Property to be acceptable to Buyer, subject to Section 10.02 below. From and after the execution date of this Agreement until the Closing Date, Seller shall permit Buyer's representatives to have access to the Real Property at all reasonable times and upon reasonable notice as mutually agreeable to the parties, for the purposes of inspecting (including obtaining soil and groundwater samples) and monitoring the Real Property. Buyer agrees to indemnify and hold harmless Seller for any losses, claims, damages, liabilities, fines, penalties, costs, or expenses (including attorneys' fees or expenses) arising out of or relating to Buyer's access to the Real Property, whether occurring prior to or after the date of this Agreement.

SECTION 10.02. Termination Events. Notwithstanding any other term of this Agreement, (a) Buyer shall have no right to terminate this Agreement due to any physical or environmental condition of the Real Property known to Buyer at the execution date of this Agreement or otherwise disclosed in the Environmental Report and (b) either Buyer or Seller may terminate this Agreement (by written notice to the other within thirty (30) days following the date of this Agreement and without further liability to the other) due to any physical or environmental condition of the Real Property discovered after this Agreement has been executed and not disclosed in the Environmental Report which causes or may cause the physical or environmental condition of the Real Property to be materially worse than that disclosed in the Environmental Report.

ARTICLE XII
CLOSING

*　　　*　　　*

SECTION 12.03. Buyer's Obligation to Seller at Closing. On the Closing Date, Buyer shall deliver to Seller the following:

*　　　*　　　*

(c)　　The Restrictions Agreement required pursuant to Section 2.04, signed and dated by both parties.

*　　　*　　　*

ARTICLE XIII
INDEMNIFICATION

SECTION 13.01. Indemnity. Buyer shall defend, exonerate, indemnify, and hold harmless Seller and its directors, officers, employees, agents, and representatives from and against all causes of action, debts, losses, claims, damages, demands, liabilities, injuries, fines, penalties, costs, or expenses (including attorneys' fees or consultants' fees and remedial, removal, or other response costs and costs of defense), suits or obligations of any and every nature whatsoever arising out of or in any manner connected with the operation or ownership of the Real Property and the conduct of business therein, thereabout, thereon, or with regard thereto, at all times after the Closing Date, including, without limiting the generality of the foregoing, remedial, personal injury, and property damage claims (including stigma damage claims), suits, cases, or charges, including those arising from or related to the Landfill that arise from damages first incurred after the

Closing Date. Nothing herein shall obligated Buyer to indemnify or otherwise protect Seller with respect to any obligation not required by law.

SECTION 13.02. Notice. Seller agrees to promptly give Buyer notice of any claim of indemnification arising under this Article.

SECTION 13.03. Survival. The obligations of Buyer under the foregoing indemnification provision shall survive the Closing Date.

Courtesy of Sharon R. Newlon, Dickinson Wright PLLC

APPENDIX B

AGREEMENT REGARDING RESTRICTIONS ON TRANSFER AND USE OF REAL PROPERTY

This Agreement is entered into this __ day of _____, 2000, between Seller and Buyer.

On _____ 2000, Seller sold and Buyer purchased real property described in Exhibit A pursuant to a Sale and Purchase of Property Agreement dated _____, 2000 (the "Purchase Agreement"), between Buyer and Seller. As more fully set out in the Purchase Agreement, Buyer is aware of the presence of a landfill on a portion of the real property which is the subject of the Purchase Agreement and is more particularly described in Exhibit B (the "Landfill Area"), as described in the Summary Report prepared by _____(the "Environmental Report"). As a condition to the purchase, Buyer is to enter into and undertake to perform its obligations under this Agreement.

Buyer agrees to pursue environmental closure of the Landfill Area, pursuant to Part 201 of the Natural Resources and Environmental Protection Act ("Part 201"), by submitting to the Michigan Department of Environmental Quality ("MDEQ") a remedial action plan ("RAP") for the remediation of the Landfill to levels acceptable to MDEQ for a limited or unlimited residential cleanup under Part 201 The RAP shall include all requirements of Part 201, which may include a land use restriction which runs with the land, in a form acceptable to MDEQ. Buyer shall execute and record any such land use restriction with the Register of Deeds in the timeframe specified in the RAP. Buyer shall submit the RAP to MDEQ for approval within 12 months after the Closing Date. Buyer shall diligently take all steps reasonably necessary to obtain MDEQ approval of the RAP and shall implement the RAP in accordance with the schedule contained in the approved RAP.

Restriction on Transfer of Property. Buyer agrees that it shall not sell, lease, or transfer any interest in the Landfill Area, nor shall Buyer build upon or otherwise develop the Landfill Area, for any use inconsistent with the approved RAP. Moreover Buyer agrees that it shall not sell, lease, or transfer any interest in the Landfill Area, nor shall Buyer build upon or otherwise develop the Landfill Area until Buyer has: (1) received MDEQ approval of the RAP (as to the Landfill Area), (2) completed all response activity required under the approved RAP as to the Landfill Area, (3) executed and recorded any land use restriction required by the RAP as to the Landfill Area, and (4) requested and received a document from MDEQ, pursuant to Section 20114(5) of Part 201, stating that all response activities required in the approved RAP as to the Landfill Area have been completed. When Buyer receives MDEQ's acknowledgment that all response activities required in the approved RAP as to the Landfill Area have been completed, Buyer shall record certification of that fact with the Register of Deeds, in a manner similar to that described in Section 20116(2) of Part 201. Buyer agrees to execute and record notice of this restriction at Closing through the Memorandum Of Agreement Regarding Restrictions On Transfer And Use Of Property of even date herewith. Seller and Buyer also agree to execute and place into escrow the Release of Restrictions on Transfer of Property. Seller and Buyer agree that this Release is to be held by the Escrow Agent and provided to Buyer upon presentation to the Escrow Agent of a certification of MDEQ's acknowledgment that all response activities required in the approved RAP as to the Landfill Area have been completed. Buyer agrees that it shall record this Release upon receipt of the Release from the Escrow Agent.

Restriction on Use of Property. Buyer further agrees that it shall not use, build upon or otherwise develop the Landfill Area for any use within the "Residential" Land Use Category or the "Commercial" Land Use Category, Subcategory I, set forth in Section 20120a(1) of Part 201 of NREPA, as amended in June 1995, and the Operational Memoranda issued thereunder, using the definitions of those terms in effect as of the date this Agreement is first recorded unless the Landfill Area is remediated to levels at or below the applicable generic residential cleanup criteria under Part 201 ("unlimited residential cleanup"), or unless the only limitation on the residential cleanup is a deed restriction prohibiting the use of the groundwater in the Landfill Area for the purposes of drinking water or irrigation. This restriction shall not prohibit the use of or construction upon the Landfill Area of any use under the "Recreational" Land Use Category. However, any such recreational use shall still be subject to the restrictions set forth in the previous paragraph of this Agreement. This restriction against Residential and Commercial I uses of the Landfill Area shall be binding upon Buyer and its successors in interest and shall run with the land. Buyer agrees to execute and record notice of this restriction at Closing through the Memorandum Of Agreement Regarding Restrictions On Transfer And Use Of Property of even date herewith. Seller and Buyer also agree to execute and place into escrow the Release of Restrictions on Transfer and Use of Property. Seller and Buyer agree that this Release is to be held by the Escrow Agent and provided to Buyer upon presentation to the Escrow Agent of: (1) a certification of MDEQ's acknowledgment that all response activities required in the approved RAP as to the Landfill Area have been completed, and (2) a certification by Buyer or its designate that the Landfill Area has been remediated to levels at or below the applicable generic residential cleanup criteria under Part 201 or that the only limitation on the residential cleanup is a deed restriction prohibiting the use of the groundwater in the Landfill Area for the purposes of drinking water or irrigation. Buyer agrees that it shall record this Release upon receipt of the Release from the Escrow Agent.

If Buyer defaults in performing its obligations hereunder, Seller may resort to any remedy available to Seller at law, in equity or by statute, including but not limited to, specific performance of a residential cleanup approved by MDEQ and monetary damages.

This Agreement shall run with the land, and be binding on all successors and assigns of Buyer. The Parties shall execute and record with the Register of Deeds either this Agreement or a memorandum evidencing the restrictions contained in this Agreement.

IN WITNESS WHEREOF, the parties hereto have caused this Agreement to be executed on the day and year first above written.

WITNESSES:

BUYER.

_____

By: _____

Print Name: _____

Print Name: _____

Its: _____

WITNESSES:

SELLER

_____

By: _____

Print Name: _____

Print Name: _____

Its: _____

Courtesy of Sharon R. Newlon, Dickinson Wright PLLC

APPENDIX C

MEMORANDUM OF AGREEMENT REGARDING RESTRICTIONS ON TRANSFER AND USE OF PROPERTY

NOTICE is given of an Agreement Regarding Restrictions on Transfer and Use of Property, dated _____, 2000 (the "Agreement"), between Seller and Buyer regarding certain property described in Exhibit A hereto (the "Property").

Under the terms of the Agreement, Buyer agrees not to sell, lease or transfer any interest in the Property or build upon or otherwise develop the Property unless and until Buyer has completed certain response activities as set forth in the Agreement (the "Restrictions on Transfer of Property"). Buyer also agrees that it shall not use the Property for certain uses set forth in the Agreement unless and until Buyer has completed certain response activities as set forth in the Agreement (the "Restrictions on Use of Property"). As set forth in the Agreement, these restrictions shall be binding on successors and shall run with the land unless and until Seller and Buyer execute a release or releases of the Restrictions on Transfer of Property and the Restrictions on Use of Property.

Dated this ___day of _____, 2000.

WITNESSES:

_____

Print Name: _____

BUYER.

By: _____

Print Name: _____

Its: _____

WITNESSES:

_____

Print Name: _____

SELLER

By: _____

Print Name: _____

Its: _____

Courtesy of Sharon R. Newlon, Dickinson Wright PLLC

APPENDIX D

RELEASE OF RESTRICTIONS ON TRANSFER AND USE OF PROPERTY

THIS RELEASE is executed as of this __ day of _____, 2000, but made as of _____, 20__, by and between Seller and Buyer.

RECITALS

A.   Seller and Buyer entered into a certain Agreement Regarding Restrictions on Transfer and Use of Property (the "Agreement") dated _____, 2000, which was referenced in a Memorandum of Agreement between the parties recorded _____, 2000, in Liber ___, Page ___, pertaining to property described in Exhibit A attached hereto and made a part hereof (the "Property").

B.   The Agreement prohibits Buyer from selling or transferring any interest in the Property prior to the satisfaction of certain conditions as more fully set forth therein (the "Restrictions on Transfer of Property").

C.   The Agreement also prohibits Buyer from using the Property for certain restricted uses set forth in the Agreement prior to the satisfaction of certain conditions as more fully set forth therein (the "Restrictions on Use of Property").

D.   The conditions relating to the Restrictions on Transfer of Property and the Restrictions on Use of Property have now been satisfied.

NOW, THEREFORE, Seller and Buyer release the Restrictions on Transfer of Property and the Restrictions on Use of Property, and Seller agrees and acknowledges that Buyer may freely sell, transfer, and use the Property.

Executed this __ day of _____, 2000.

WITNESSES:

_____

Print Name: _____

BUYER.

By: _____

Print Name: _____

Its: _____

WITNESSES:

_____

Print Name: _____

SELLER

By: _____

Print Name: _____

Its: _____

Courtesy of Sharon R. Newlon, Dickinson Wright PLLC

APPENDIX E

EXCERPTS FROM PURCHASE AGREEMENT REQUIRING BUYER TO QUALIFY FOR ENVIRONMENTAL LIABILITY EXEMPTION BY SUBMITTING DUE DILIGENCE REPORT TO STATE

Purchase and Sale Agreement

THIS AGREEMENT, made and entered into this _____ day of _____, 2006, by and between Purchaser and Seller.

W I T N E S S E T H:

WHEREAS, Seller is the owner of premises situated in the City of Francoise, legally described in Exhibit A; and

WHEREAS, Seller desires to sell and Purchaser desires to purchase all of Seller's rights in such premises, on an AS IS, WHERE IS basis, including (i) all of Seller's rights in the land described in Exhibit A (the "Land"), (ii) all of Seller's rights in the buildings and all other improvements thereon (the "Improvements"), (iii) all of Seller's rights in easements, rights-of-way, tenements, hereditaments, appurtenances, licenses and privileges belonging or in any way appertaining to the Land (the "Easements and Ownership Rights"), (iv) all air, subsurface and mineral rights of Seller relating to the Land except as the same may have been transferred of record prior to the date of this agreement (the "Air and Subsurface Rights"), (v) and all fixtures owned by Seller and on the date of closing of the purchase located in and affixed to the Land or the Improvements, or any part thereof, if any, including without limitation any heating, lighting, incinerating, refrigerating, ventilating, air conditioning, air cooling, plumbing, gas, water and electrical equipment, elevators and escalators (the "Personal Property"), all of the foregoing land and premises rights described in this paragraph, consisting collectively of the Land, Improvements, Easements and Ownership Rights, Air and Subsurface Rights, and Personal Property, being referred to as the "Property";

NOW, THEREFORE, in consideration of the mutual covenants and agreements contained in this Agreement and of the benefits to be derived herefrom, receipt of which is severally acknowledged, Seller and Purchaser hereby agree as follows:

* * *

6. **Inspection and Investigation by Purchaser.** Purchaser and its agents shall have until 12:00 noon, E.S.T. on _____, 2006 to inspect and investigate or cause to be inspected or investigated all aspects and conditions of the Property, to enter the Property and make such soil borings, environmental assessments and other tests as Purchaser may deem necessary or desirable, and otherwise to determine the suitability of the Property for use by Purchaser, in Purchaser's sole discretion, including, without limitation, verification of environmental and building condition, taxes, availability of utilities, business and use permits and zoning classification. All testing, inspections and investigations shall be conducted at Purchaser's sole cost and expense. Purchaser, at its sole cost and expense, shall restore and pay Seller for any and all damage whatsoever caused by such tests, inspection, investigation, entry or access to the Property, including only by way of example and not of limitation, any damage caused by cutting or drilling, or otherwise sampling, testing, investigating, inspecting, disrupting or disassembling any ventilation system, ceiling, wall, building system, door, lock, floor, dry well, support structure, ground, equipment or any other portion of the Property whatsoever. Purchaser's consultant shall carry a minimum of $2,000,000 in professional liability insurance and shall name Purchaser and Seller as additional insureds with respect to any work performed at the Property. Purchaser shall deliver to Seller copies of all reports, studies and tests regarding the Property which it possesses or obtains, and shall provide for Seller's ability to rely on any such reports. Purchaser hereby indemnifies Seller, its agents, brokers, or representatives (representatives and agents include without limitation all company directors, officers, employees, shareholders, members, attorneys, consultants and other representatives and agents), and holds Seller, its agents, brokers or representatives harmless against any loss or damage arising out of such testing, inspections and investigation and any claim related to the reports, studies or tests delivered by Seller, its agents, brokers or representatives or the accuracy of the information contained therein.

If Purchaser is not satisfied, in Purchaser's sole discretion, with the results of the inspections and tests or with the suitability of the Property for Purchaser's use, Purchaser may rescind this transaction by mailing, faxing or hand delivering written notice to Seller at its address set forth above to be received by Seller on or before 12:00 noon E.S.T. on _____, 2006, in which case this Agreement shall be terminated and Purchaser shall be entitled to a refund of the Deposit. If this Agreement is terminated pursuant to the provisions of this paragraph, Purchaser shall return to Seller all surveys and other information previously delivered to Purchaser by Seller. In the event that Purchaser fails to deliver written notice to Seller rescinding this transaction within the time period stated above, the parties shall proceed to Closing and disposition of the Deposit shall be governed by paragraph 11 or 12, as applicable. Both parties understand and agree that the Deposit becomes non-refundable on and after _____, 2006.

*   *   *

7.   Conditions Precedent to Purchaser's Obligations. The obligation of Purchaser to proceed to consummate this transaction shall be conditioned upon each of the following conditions precedent:

*   *   *

C.   Purchaser shall be satisfied with Purchaser's due diligence investigation of the Property as described in paragraph 6 of this Agreement. Notwithstanding the foregoing, this condition shall expire, be fully and effectively waived by Purchaser, and be of no further effect if Purchaser does not deliver, mail or fax to Seller written notice of termination on or before 12:00 noon E.S.T. on _____, 2006.

8.   Documents to be Furnished by Seller/Purchaser on Closing Date. On the Closing date, Seller/Purchaser (as indicated) shall deliver to Purchaser the following documents, each of which shall be in a form reasonably satisfac¬tory to counsel for Seller and Purchaser:

*   *   *

E. (Purchaser) A Baseline Environmental Assessment as to the Property in form acceptable to Seller and its counsel, and evidence of submission of the same to the State of Michigan Department of Environmental Quality.

*   *   *

9.   Environmental Assessments/Conditions Precedent to Seller's Obligations. Purchaser acknowledges receipt of the environmental reports listed in Exhibit B of this Agreement. Seller has provided these reports for Purchaser's information only, and to satisfy any obligations it may have under MCL 324.20116, and Seller does not warrant the information contained therein. Purchaser agrees that it will conduct its own due diligence with respect to the environmental conditions at the Property, in accordance with paragraph 6. Purchaser agrees that if it determines, based on that due diligence, that the property is a "facility" as that term is defined in MCL 324.20101, Purchaser will prepare a Baseline Environmental Assessment report and cause it to be filed with the Michigan Department of Environmental Quality pursuant to the timeframe set forth in paragraph 8. Purchaser also agrees that it will prepare a due care plan for the Property, in accordance with the requirements of MCL 324.20107a.

If Purchaser closes on the purchase of the Property, (a) Purchaser releases Seller, its agents, brokers, or representatives (representatives and agents include without limitation all company directors, officers, employees, shareholders, members, attorneys, consultants and other representatives and agents), from any liability then existing or arising thereafter related to the environmental condition of the Property; and (b) Purchaser does and shall indemnify and hold Seller, its agents, brokers, or representatives (representatives and agents include without limitation all company directors, officers, employees, shareholders, members, attorneys, consultants and other representatives and agents), harmless against any loss or damage arising out of the environmental condition of the property at the time of the Closing and thereafter. The foregoing provisions shall survive closing and shall be included in a written affirmation of indemnities and releases signed by Purchaser at Closing.

*   *   *

17.   Condition of Property. Notwithstanding anything herein to the contrary contained, Purchaser acknowledges and agrees that Seller has been, is and remains unwilling to make any projection, warranty or representation whatsoever with respect to the nature, type, extent, condition, size, use, fitness for a particular purpose, merchantability, zoning, permitting or any other aspect of the Property other than as may be expressly set forth in the numbered paragraphs of this Agreement. Furthermore, Purchaser has had the right to inspect the Property and shall continue to have the right to inspect the Property in accordance with the provisions of this Agreement. Purchaser acknowledges and represents that it has not relied upon any written or verbal representations made by the Seller or its agents, brokers, or representatives (representatives and agents include without limitation all company directors, officers, employees, shareholders, members, attorneys, consultants and other representatives and agents), but has independently investigated and verified each and every fact it deems relevant related to the Property. Accordingly, Purchaser acknowledges that if it waives its right to terminate its purchase of the Property pursuant to the provisions of paragraph 6, Purchaser shall acquire the Property "as is, where is, with all faults and defects, latent or patent, known or unknown" confirming thereby that it is fully familiar with the condition of the Property, structurally, legally, environmentally and economically, the Purchaser having satisfied itself concerning all aspects of the Property by investigating the same, and will not rely upon facts, information, statements or other communications supplied or furnished by Seller, its agents, brokers or representatives except for any warranties or representations expressly set forth in writing in this Agreement.

Courtesy of Sharon R. Newlon, Dickinson Wright PLLC

APPENDIX F

ASSET PURCHASE AGREEMENT
(BUYER-FAVORABLE, NO REAL ESTATE SOLD)

AGREEMENT made as of this _____ day of _____, 20_____, (the "Agreement") and effective as of 12:01 a.m. on _____ ___, 20___ (the "Effective Date") by and between [_____], a corporation organized and existing under the laws of [_____] ("Buyer"), [_____], a corporation organized and existing under the laws of [_____] ("Seller"), and [_____], an individual, and the [_____] (the [_____] hereafter collectively the "Stockholders").

RECITALS:

Seller is engaged in the business of manufacturing [_____] (the "Business"). Seller desires to sell, and Buyer desires to acquire, the assets comprising the Business, upon the terms and conditions set forth herein.

IN CONSIDERATION of the mutual covenants, agreements, representations and warranties set forth herein, and in reliance thereon, the parties agree as follows:

SECTION 1. DEFINITIONS

The capitalized and certain other terms used herein shall have the meanings ascribed to them in Schedule 1 to this Agreement.

SECTION 2. THE PROPOSED TRANSACTION

2.1 Assets To Be Acquired. Subject to the terms and conditions of this Agreement, and in reliance on the representations, warranties and covenants contained herein, on and as of the Closing Date, Seller will sell, convey, assign, transfer and deliver to Buyer, and Buyer will purchase and acquire, the Business as a going concern and all of Seller's right, title and interest in and to the Purchased Assets, as the same shall exist as of the

Closing Date (excluding the Excluded Assets listed in Section 2.02), including without limitation:

(a)   cash and cash equivalents on hand or in depository or other accounts which relate to the Business;

(b)   all Accounts Receivable;

(c)   all Inventory;

(d)   all Equipment, a list of which is set forth in Schedule 2.01(d);

(e)   all Intellectual Property, a list of which is set forth in Schedule 2.01(e), together with the goodwill associated therewith and symbolized thereby; and any licenses relating to the Intellectual Property used in or useful to the Business, whether to or from Seller and all income, royalties, damages and payments due or payable with respect to any time on or after the Closing Date, including, without limitation, damages and payments for infringements or misappropriations of any thereof throughout the world after the Closing Date; and all rights of Seller in and to, including rights to enforce the terms of, confidentiality agreements and noncompetition agreements of, and any agreements relating to the assignment of Intellectual Property made by, prior and present employees of Seller and any such agreements with any other Person with respect to the Intellectual Property;

(f)   all Technical Information;

(g)   all Computer Software Assets, a list of which is set forth in Schedule 2.01(g);

(h)   all Prepaid Expenses;

(i)   [reserved]

(j)   all Contracts and Leases;

(k)   all Open Orders;

(l)   all Permits, a list of which is set forth in Schedule 2.01(l) except to the extent any such permits are not assignable as marked on Schedule 2.1(l);

(m)   all Books and Records; all property, records and copies of personnel records of employees who become Hired Employees after the Closing Date, and all office supplies and the right to receive and retain mail and other communications relating to the Business;

(n)   all certifications, ratings, listings and similar benefits from any product or quality control certification organization and all systems and manuals related thereto;

(o)   all memberships of Seller relating to the Business in, and all rights as a member of, the industry, trade, civic, social and other associations, organizations and clubs listed in Schedule 2.01(o); and

(p)   all other assets (including causes of action, rights of action, contract rights and warranty and product liability claims against third parties) relating to the Purchased Assets or the Business.

2.2   Excluded Assets. Notwithstanding Section 2.01, the following assets shall be excluded from this Agreement and shall not be sold, conveyed, assigned, transferred or delivered to Buyer pursuant hereto:

(a)   Seller's Real Property;

(b)   Any insurance policies maintained by Seller with respect to the Business and any prepaid insurance expenses;

(c)   Seller's franchise to be a corporation, its certificates of incorporation, bylaws, minutes books and other records having to do with the organization and capitalization of Seller;

(d)   Any claims and rights against third parties (including, without limitation, insurance carriers), to the extent they relate to liabilities or obligations that are not assumed by Buyer (except to the extent Buyer shall have incurred costs and expenses with respect to such claims and rights);

(e)   All payments made by Seller which constitute prepaid Taxes of the Business and all claims for refunds of Taxes and other governmental charges to the extent such refunds relate to periods ending on or prior to the Closing Date;

(f)   Any pension, health or welfare plans, any post retirement benefits for any employees of Seller who do not become Hired Employees and all payments made by Seller which constitute prepaid expenses of the Business relating to such excluded employee benefits;

(g)   Seller's depository and other accounts (but not including the cash to be transferred to Buyer as contemplated by Section 2.01(a));

(h)   All assets listed in Schedule 2.02(h); and

2.3   Consideration for the Purchased Assets. Subject to the terms and conditions of this Agreement, and in reliance on the representations, warranties and covenants contained herein, in consideration of the sale, conveyance, assignment, transfer and delivery of the Purchased Assets, Buyer agrees (a) subject to adjustment pursuant to Section 2.05, to pay and deliver to Seller on the Closing Date the Purchase Price, as set forth in Section 2.04, and (b) to assume as of the Closing Date the Assumed Liabilities, as set forth in Section 2.06.

2.4   Purchase Price. The Purchase Price shall consist of the payment by Buyer of $[_____] by wire transfer of immediately available funds to Seller's bank account (or bank accounts of creditors of Seller, other third parties, for the benefit of Seller) as designated by notice to the Buyer at least three (3) days before the Closing Date.

2.5   Adjustments to the Purchase Price to Reflect Closing Net Book Value.

* * *

2.6   Assumed Liabilities. On and subject to the terms and conditions set forth in this Agreement, as additional consideration for the Purchased Assets, on the Closing Date Buyer shall undertake, assume, perform and otherwise pay, satisfy and discharge, and hold the Seller harmless from the following liabilities and obligations of Seller relating to the Business:

(a)   the liabilities and obligations relating to the Business to the extent incurred in the ordinary course of business and reflected on the liability side of the Final Closing Balance Sheet, including, to the extent of the warranty reserve set forth in the Final Closing Balance Sheet, any Warranty Claims but excluding any debt payable to First Union as set forth in Section 2.7(n); and

(b)   the liabilities and obligations arising pursuant to Open Orders, Contracts, Leases and Permits, but not including any liability or obligation arising out of or in connection with any breach thereof occurring prior to the Closing Date.

2.7   Excluded Liabilities. Notwithstanding anything to the contrary contained in this Agreement, Buyer will not assume or in any way become liable for, and Seller shall retain, all of Seller's and its Affiliates' debts, liabilities and obligations of any nature whatsoever (other than the Assumed Liabilities), whether accrued, absolute or contingent, whether known or unknown, whether due or to become due, including, without limitation, the following:

(a)   the liabilities or obligations of Seller to its stockholders respecting dividends, distributions to its stockholders in liquidation, redemptions of stock or otherwise;

(b)   liabilities or obligations of Seller arising out of any transactions occurring, or liabilities or obligations incurred, after the Closing Date, other than relating to Buyer's use or operation of the Purchased Assets or the Assumed Liabilities after the Closing Date;

(c)   any liabilities or obligations of Seller for expenses, Taxes or fees incident to or arising out of the negotiation, preparation, approval or authorization of this Agreement or the consummation of the transactions contemplated hereby, including, without limitation, all of its attorneys, and accountants, fees and all brokers, or finders, fees or commissions payable by Seller;

(d)   any liabilities or obligations of Seller under or arising out of this Agreement;

(e)   liabilities or obligations against which Seller is insured or otherwise indemnified or which would have been covered by insurance (or indemnification) but for a claim by the insurer (or the indemnitor) that the insured (or the indemnitee) had breached its obligations under the policy of insurance (or the contract of indemnity) or had committed fraud in the insurance application or in entering unto the indemnity agreement;

(f)   any liabilities or obligations of the Business to Seller or any Affiliates of Seller, except payables for products sold or shipped to the Business by Seller or an Affiliate of Seller after the Closing Date;

(g)   any liabilities and obligations of Seller to indemnify its officers, directors, employees or agents;

(h)   all Taxes imposed on Seller (including any Taxes of any other corporation) and any Taxes assessed against Seller by virtue of its status as a member of any consolidated group of which such other corporation was also a member;

(i)   all liabilities and obligations of the Business for Warranty Claims with respect to products manufactured, repaired, sold or delivered by Seller prior to the Closing Date to the extent they in the aggregate exceed the warranty reserve set forth in the Final Closing Balance Sheet; and

(j)   all liabilities and obligations of Seller relating to any collective bargaining agreement by and between Seller and any certified collective bargaining unit;

(k)   all liabilities and obligations arising under or imposed pursuant to Environmental Laws, whether or not attributable to actions or failures to act by Seller, with respect to the ownership of, operation of, or properties utilized in connection with, the Business at any time prior to the Closing Date, or to any property being transferred or leased to Buyer pursuant to this Agreement;

(l)   all liabilities and obligations for employee benefits of the Business incurred prior to the Closing Date;

(m)   all other liabilities or obligations of Seller arising out of its conduct of the Business prior to the Closing Date, including without limitation, Product Liabilities; liabilities or obligations related to the infringement by Seller of any intellectual property of another Person; liabilities or obligations of Seller relating to any Environmental Laws including but limited to liabilities or obligations for remediation of contamination identified in the reports listed in Schedule 4.27(c); and any liabilities or obligations related to any lawsuit, cause of action, litigation or legal proceeding with respect to any losses, occurrences or events occurring prior to the Closing Date, whether commenced prior to or after the Closing Date, except for those liabilities or obligations constituting a part of the Assumed Liabilities.

2.8   Allocation of Consideration. Seller and Buyer agree that the Purchase Price and the amount of the Assumed Liabilities shall be allocated to the various assets comprising the Purchased Assets for all purposes (including tax and financial accounting purposes) in a manner to be determined in writing by Buyer and Seller as soon as practicable following the final determination of Final Closing Net Book Value. Seller and Buyer acknowledge that such allocation is intended to comply with the requirements of Section 1060 of the Code and shall be binding upon the parties for all applicable federal, state, local and foreign tax purposes. Seller and Buyer covenant and agree to report gain or loss or cost basis, as the case may be, in a manner consistent with such allocation on all tax returns filed by either of them subsequent to the Closing Date and not to take voluntarily any inconsistent position therewith in any administrative or judicial proceeding relating to such returns, except if, in the opinion of counsel reasonably acceptable to the other party, there has been a change in applicable law since the Closing Date. Seller and Buyer shall exchange mutually acceptable completed IRS Forms 8594 (including any Supplemental IRS Forms 8594 that they mutually deem necessary to reflect adjustments to the Purchase Price and to the amount of Assumed Liabilities), which they shall use to report the transaction contemplated hereunder to the Internal Revenue Service in accordance with such allocation.

SECTION 3. CLOSING

The Closing of the transactions contemplated by this Agreement shall take place at [_____] in [_____], [_____] at the offices of [_____] on the later of (a) _____ ___, 20___ and (b) the fifth business day following the date when all of the conditions to the Closing specified in Sections 8 and 9 have been satisfied or waived, or such other date as the parties may mutually agree to in writing, but in no event later than _____ ___, 20___.

SECTION 4. REPRESENTATIONS AND WARRANTIES OF SELLER AND STOCKHOLDERS

Seller and Stockholders, jointly and severally, hereby represent and warrant, to Buyer that:

4.1   Organization and Good Standing. Seller is a corporation duly organized, validly existing and in good standing under the laws of the State of [_____], with full corporate power and authority to carry on the Business as presently conducted by it, and Seller is qualified to do business in the states listed in Schedule 4.01, which constitute all of the states where the failure to be so qualified would adversely affect the condition (financial or otherwise), prospects, properties, assets or operations of the Business. Seller has delivered to Buyer copies, true and correct as of the date hereof, of its Certificate of Incorporation, duly certified by the Secretary of the State of [_____], its state of incorporation, and of its By-laws, duly certified by its Secretary, and certificates or other evidence of good standing in each state listed in Schedule 4.01.

4.2   Subsidiaries. The Seller has no subsidiaries.

4.3   Names. Seller has not conducted the Business under any name other than [_____].

4.4   Certain Business Relationships. Except as noted in Schedule 4.04, none of the Stockholders or any Affiliate of Seller has been involved in any business arrangement, contract or relationship with Seller or the Business (other than as a stockholder, director, officer or employee), and none of the Stockholders or any Affiliate of Seller owns any asset, tangible or intangible, which is used in the Business.

4.5   Corporate Authority. Seller has full corporate power and authority to execute and deliver this Agreement and the instruments of transfer and other documents delivered or to be delivered pursuant hereto, to perform all the terms and conditions hereof and thereof to be performed by it, and to consummate the transactions contemplated hereby and thereby. This Agreement and all instruments of transfer and other documents delivered or to be delivered by Seller in connection with this Agreement have been duly authorized and approved by all necessary and proper corporate action of Seller (including all necessary shareholder action) and constitute, and will constitute, the valid and binding obligations of Seller enforceable against Seller in accordance with their respective terms.

4.6   No Violation. Except as noted in Schedule 4.06, neither the execution and delivery by Seller of this Agreement or the instruments of transfer and other documents delivered or to be delivered pursuant hereto by Seller and the performance by Seller hereunder or thereunder, nor the consummation of the transactions contemplated hereby or thereby, will violate, conflict with, result in the breach of, or accelerate the performance required by any of the terms, conditions or provisions of the Certificate of

Incorporation or Bylaws of Seller or any covenant, agreement or understanding to which Seller is a party or any order, ruling, decree, judgment, arbitration award or stipulation to which Seller is subject, or constitute a default thereunder or result in the creation or imposition of any Lien upon any of the Purchased Assets, or allow any Person to accelerate any debt owed by Seller or secured by any Purchased Asset, or allow any Person to interfere with Buyer's full use and enjoyment of any of the Purchased Assets and operation of the Business.

4.7   Consents and Approvals of Governmental Authorities and Others. Except as noted in Schedule 4.07, no approval or authorization of, filing or registration with, or notification to, any Governmental Authority is required in connection with the execution and delivery of this Agreement by Seller or the performance of its obligations hereunder or the consummation of the transactions contemplated hereby. Except as noted in Schedule 4.07, no consent, approval or authorization of any Person is required in connection with the execution or delivery of this Agreement by Seller, the transfer to Buyer of the Purchased Assets, or the performance by Seller of any other obligation under this Agreement, except where the failure to obtain such consent or approval would not have a material adverse effect on the Business or the Purchased Assets.

4.8   Financial Statements; Books and Records.

(a)   Seller has delivered to Buyer balance sheets of the Business as of December 31, _____ and December 31, _____ and statements of income, changes in stockholders' equity and cash flow for the years then ended, together with the report of [_____] with respect thereto. The Financial Statements have been prepared in accordance with GAAP consistently applied throughout the periods involved, are true and correct in all respects and present fairly Seller's financial condition as of the dates thereof and results of its operations for such periods.

(b)   Seller has no liabilities or obligations relating to the Business, except:

(i)   those liabilities and obligations set forth on the Financial Statements and not heretofore paid or discharged;

(ii)   those liabilities and obligations arising in the ordinary course of business consistent with past practice under any Contract, Lease, Open Order or other commitment specifically disclosed in the Schedules hereto; and

(iii)   those liabilities and obligations incurred in the ordinary course of business consistent with past practice since the Bid Balance Sheet Date.

(c)   All Books and Records are complete and correct with respect to all information and time periods covered thereby. All of the Books and Records have been prepared and maintained, where applicable, in conformity with GAAP and in compliance with applicable laws, regulations and other requirements.

4.9   **Events Subsequent to Bid Balance Sheet Date.** Except as set forth in the Financial Statements or as noted in Schedule 4.09, there has not been since the Bid Balance Sheet Date any material adverse change in the condition (financial or other), properties, assets, liabilities or prospects of Seller or the Business. Without limiting the generality of the foregoing, since that date:

* * *

4.10   **Accounts Receivable.** All of the Accounts Receivable arose in bona fide transactions and are good and collectible in full at the recorded amounts thereof in the Books and Records in the ordinary course of business without resort to legal proceedings, net of an aggregate amount equal to reserves for doubtful accounts and bill back items, as reflected in the Financial Statements.

4.11   **Inventory.** The Inventory consists of items which are merchantable and fit for the purposes intended and the quantity thereof is at levels appropriate and adequate for Buyer to conduct the Business following the Closing Date. The Inventory is carried in the Books and Records at an amount that is not in excess of the lower of its cost or its current fair market value and is saleable at prices at least equal to the value thereof in the Books and Records.

4.12 Tangible Purchased Assets.

(a)   Schedules 2.01(d) and 2.01(e) set forth a list of all Equipment and Real Property, respectively, owned by Seller and included in the Purchased Assets. Except as noted in Schedule 4.12(a), on the Closing Date, Seller shall have good and marketable title to, and all right, title and interest in, all Equipment, Real Property and other Tangible Purchased Assets, real and personal, owned by it, and will transfer and convey such properties and assets to the Buyer, free and clear of all Liens (other than those relating to Assumed Liabilities). None of the Tangible Purchased Assets owned by Seller was purchased by the Seller in a bulk sale.

(b)   Schedule 4.12(b) sets forth a list of all Leased Real Property, Equipment and other Tangible Purchased Assets leased by Seller and the Leases pursuant to which such Tangible Purchased Assets are leased. Except as noted in Schedule 4.12(b), all Leases relating to Leased Real Property, Equipment or other Tangible Purchased Assets, real or personal, leased by Seller are valid and enforceable by Seller in accordance with their respective terms. There is not, under any Lease relating to Leased Real Property, Equipment or other Tangible Purchased Asset, any existing default by Seller or any existing default by any other party thereto, or any circumstance known to Seller that could give rise to a default by the Seller or any other party to such Lease. All commissions payable by Seller under or with respect to any such Leases have been paid.

(c)   Except as noted in Schedule 4.12(c), the uses to which the Tangible Purchased Assets are put are not subject to any restriction or condition and conform in all respects to zoning, subdivision and/or planning regulations, fire and safety regulations, and all other regulations or requirements of the relevant federal, state or local authorities and to all statutes or laws governing such assets or the use thereof and are not temporary uses. All of the Tangible Purchased Assets may be used for the purposes of the Business. All certificates of occupancy and necessary consents of Governmental Authorities or other Persons to such existing uses have been obtained. Seller has not received notice of violation of any such regulation, ordinance or other law, order or requirement from any court or Governmental Authority or of taking by eminent domain or condemnation proceeding.

(d)   All the Tangible Purchased Assets of the Seller are in good operating order and condition and are suitable for their intended uses.

(e)   The Tangible Purchased Assets include all tangible personal property necessary to permit Buyer to carry on the Business following the Closing Date in substantially the same manner as the Business is currently conducted by Seller.

4.13   Intellectual Property. * * *

4.14   Solvency. * * *

4.15   No Prior Sale or Licensing of Purchased Assets. * * *

4.16   Tax Matters. * * *

4.17   Contracts. * * *

4.18   Open Orders. * * *

4.19   Permits. Schedule 4.19 sets forth a list of all Permits (other than Environmental Permits) required or useful in the conduct of the Business. All Permits are in full force and effect and no suspension or cancellation of any have been threatened. No Permits or parts thereof are subject to loss by reason of dormancy or non use. No claims have been made by any Governmental Authority or any Person relating to the Permits and no such claim is contemplated by any Governmental Authority or other Person, nor does any basis therefor exist. Except as noted in Schedule 4.19, no Permit will be terminated or require the consent of the issuer to continue in effect as a result of the execution of this Agreement or the consummation of the transactions contemplated herein.

4.20   Technical Information. * * *

4.21   Computer Hardware and Software; Embedded Controls. * * *

4.22   Depositary Accounts, Etc. * * *

4.23   Insurance. * * *

4.24   Compliance with Laws; Litigation. Seller has been, and is, operating the Business in compliance with the requirements of all federal, state and local laws, regulations, judgments, injunctions, decrees, court orders and administrative orders regarding such operations. Except as noted in Schedule 4.24, Seller is not engaged in, or a party to, or threatened with, any legal action, suit, investigation or other proceeding by or before any court, arbitrator or administrative agency, and after due inquiry, Seller does not know of any basis for any such action, investigation or proceeding. There are no outstanding orders, rulings, decrees, judgments, stipulations or proceedings to which Seller is a party or by which Seller is bound, by or with any court, arbitrator or administrative agency.

4.25   Warranties; Product Liability. * * *

4.26   Absence of Sensitive Payments. * * *

4.27   Environmental Matters.

(a)   Except as noted in Schedule 4.27(a), Seller has conducted all activities of the Business in compliance with, and all properties owned, leased or operated by Seller in connection with the Business comply with, all Environmental Laws. Except as noted in Schedule 4.27(a), no facts, events or conditions relating to the facilities, properties or operations of the Business will prevent,

199

hinder or limit continued compliance with any Environmental Laws.

(b)   Schedule 4.27(b) sets forth a true and complete list of the Environmental Permits which have been obtained by Seller. Except as noted in Schedule 4.27(b), all Environmental Permits are in full force and effect and are not subject to any appeals or further proceedings or to any unsatisfied conditions. No modification, suspension, rescission, relocation or cancellation of any Environmental Permit is pending or threatened, and no Environmental Permit will be cancelled or withdrawn, or otherwise adversely affected by the execution of this Agreement or the consummation of the transactions contemplated hereby. Except as noted in Schedule 4.27(b), Seller has made or caused to have been made all notifications and done all other things necessary to ensure that, following the consummation of the transactions contemplated by this Agreement, all previously issued Environmental Permits shall remain in full force and effect or shall be reissued or amended to permit Buyer to operate the Business as operated by Seller.

(c)   Except as noted in Schedule 4.27(c), no Contamination is present or has emanated from or at any property now or previously owned, leased or operated by Seller in connection with the Business. Except as noted in Schedule 4.27(c), no property now owned, leased or operated by Seller in connection with the Business is subject to an environmental Lien. Except as identified in Schedule 4.27(c), Seller has not incurred costs or liabilities, and has not been ordered to investigate, remediate or otherwise respond to a potential environmental threat of Contamination in connection with the Business.

(d)   Schedule 4.27(d) sets forth a true and correct list of all sites at or to which any waste generated by or on behalf of Seller, or otherwise, in connection with any of its operations has been transported, stored, treated or disposed and all arrangements for such disposal. Except as noted in Schedule 4.27(d):

(i)   To the knowledge of Seller and Stockholders, none of the sites identified in Schedule 4.27(d) is or may become the subject of a response action under CERCLA or any similar federal, state or local law imposing liability for remediation;

(ii)   Seller has not, in connection with the Business, received (A) a request for information from any Governmental Authority with respect to any discharge or removal of any Hazardous Substance, or (B) other notice that it has been identified in any litigation, administrative proceeding or investigation as a responsible party or a potentially responsible party for any liability under any Environmental Law or in connection with any Hazardous Substance.

(iii)   Seller has not filed any notice under any federal, state or local law, regulation or order reporting a release of Hazardous Substances in connection with the Business or any property owned, leased or operated by the Business except for the filing required by the Act as contemplated by Section 6.6; and

(iv)   (i)   Seller has not entered into any negotiations or agreements with any Person relating to any response action or other cleanup or remediation of any Hazardous Substance.

(e)   Except as noted in Schedule 4.27(e), no portion of any property owned, leased or operated by Seller contains any of the following:

(i)   polychlorinated biphenyls or substances containing polychlorinated biphenyls;

(ii)   asbestos or materials containing asbestos;

(iii)   urea formaldehyde foam insulation;

(iv)   radon gas or the presence of the radioactive decay products of radon in excess of an air concentration of four picocuries/liter; or

(v)   tanks presently or formerly used for the storage of any Hazardous Substance or any other liquid or gas above or below ground.

(f)   Except as noted in Schedule 4.27(f), no portion of any property owned, leased or operated by Seller constitutes any of the following:

(i)   a wetland or other "water of the United States" for purposes of Section 404 of the Federal Clean Water Act, or any similar area regulated under any applicable state or local law or regulation;

(ii)   a floodplain or other flood hazard area;

(iii)   a portion of the coastal zone for purposes of the Federal Coastal Zone Management Act or similar state law; or

(iv)   any other area development of which is specifically restricted under applicable law by reason of its physical characteristics or prior use.

(g)   Except as noted in Schedule 4.27(g), Seller has not, in connection with the Business, either expressly or by operation or law, assumed or undertaken any liability or corrective or response action obligation of any other Person relating to Environmental Laws.

(h)   Except as noted in Schedule 4.27(h), Seller is not aware of any costs that Seller expects the Business will be likely to incur to achieve or maintain compliance with Environmental Laws or to respond to Contamination.

4.28   Benefit Plans and Employment Arrangements. * * *

4.29   Obligations to Pay Fees. * * *

4.30   Completeness of Disclosure. The representations and warranties contained in this Section 4 and in the Schedules delivered pursuant hereto do not contain any untrue statement of a material fact or omit to state any material fact necessary in order to make the statements and information contained in this Section 4 and such Schedules not misleading.

SECTION 5. REPRESENTATIONS AND WARRANTIES OF BUYER

Buyer represents and warrants to Seller as follows:

5.1   Organization, Good Standing, and Corporate Authority. Buyer is a corporation duly incorporated, validly existing and in good standing under the laws of the State of [_____], and has full corporate power and authority to execute this Agreement and the other documents delivered or to be delivered pursuant hereto, to perform all the terms and conditions hereof and thereof to be performed by it, and to consummate the transactions contemplated hereby and thereby. This Agreement and the other documents delivered or to be delivered by Buyer in connection with this Agreement have been duly authorized and approved by all necessary and proper corporate action and constitute, and will constitute the valid and binding obligations of Buyer, enforceable against Buyer in accordance with their respective terms.

5.2   No Violation. Neither the execution and delivery by Buyer of this Agreement or the other documents delivered or to be delivered pursuant hereto by Buyer and the performance by Buyer hereunder or thereunder, nor the consummation of the transactions contemplated hereby or thereby, will violate, conflict with, result in the breach of, or accelerate the performance required by any of the terms, conditions or provisions of the Certificate of Incorporation or Bylaws of Buyer or any covenant, agreement or understanding to which Buyer is a party or any order, ruling, decree, judgment, arbitration award or stipulation to which Buyer is subject, or constitute a default thereunder.

5.3   Consents and Approvals of Governmental Authorities and Others. Except as noted in Schedule 5.03, no approval or authorization of, filing or registration with, or notification to, any Governmental Authority is required in connection with the execution and delivery of this Agreement by Buyer or the performance of its obligations hereunder or the consummation of the transactions contemplated hereby. Except as noted in Schedule 5.03, no consent, approval or authorization of any Person is required in connection with the execution or delivery of this Agreement by Buyer, the purchase by Buyer of the Business and the Purchased Assets, or the performance by Buyer of any other obligation under this Agreement.

5.4   Obligation to Pay Certain Fees. Neither Buyer nor any of its officers, directors, employees or Affiliates has agreed to pay any fees or commissions to fees or commissions to any investment banker, broker, finder or agent with respect to the transactions contemplated by this Agreement for which Seller could become liable or obligated.

5.5   Litigation. There are no actions, suits or proceedings pending, or, threatened, by any Person or Governmental Authority challenging the legality, validity or propriety of the transactions contemplated by this Agreement.

5.6   Completeness of Disclosure. The representations and warranties contained in this Section 5 and in the Schedules delivered pursuant hereto do not contain any untrue statement of a material fact or omit to state any material fact necessary in order to make the statements and information contained in this Section 5 and such Schedules not misleading.

SECTION 6. COVENANTS OF SELLER

6.1   Employees. Seller shall permit Buyer to discuss the possibility of employment with current employees of the Business, and shall not interfere with or impede the Buyer's right to do so, either directly or indirectly.

6.2   Taxes. Seller or Stockholders shall pay all Taxes arising from the sale of the Purchased Assets pursuant hereto.

6.3   Access to Offices, Officers, Accountants, Etc. Seller will afford to, and will cause its Affiliates to afford to, the officers and authorized representatives of Buyer (including without limitation, attorneys, accountants, surveyors, building inspectors, engineers, environmental consultants, insurance brokers, financial advisors and bankers) access to the offices, officers, properties, Books and Records of Seller and the Business, and to the attorneys, accountants and other representatives of Seller and its Affiliates and with any and all Persons Buyer deems appropriate in order to enable it to consummate the transactions contemplated hereby, and will furnish Buyer with such additional financial and operating data and other information as to the Business and Purchased Assets as Buyer may from time to time reasonably request. Seller will cooperate with Buyer to facilitate Buyer's contacting vendors, dealers, customers and such other Persons as Buyer and its representatives may desire to contact in connection with Buyer's investigation of the Business at such time and in such manner as shall be reasonably acceptable to Buyer and Seller

6.4   Cooperation in Buyer's Environmental Investigation. In connection with Buyer's Environmental Investigation Seller will:

(a)   comply fully and completely with any request for information made by Buyer or its agents in connection with any such investigation;

(b)   assist Buyer or its agents to obtain any records pertaining to Seller or to properties owned, leased or operated by Seller in connection with such an investigation; and

(c)   accord Buyer and its agents access to all areas of the properties owned or operated by Seller in connection with any such investigation.

6.5   Approvals; Consents. Seller will use its best efforts to obtain the consents of all other parties to all Contracts, Open Orders, Permits, Environmental Permits and other rights of Seller, which require the consent of such parties for the consummation of the transactions contemplated hereby.

6.6 Seller's Environmental Obligations.

(a)   Seller will take in a timely manner any and all corrective, response or other actions necessary or appropriate to correct any violations of the Environmental Laws relating to the Business, or to address any Contamination present at or emanating from any Real Property, Leased Real Property or other real property operated by Seller in connection with the Business, and attributable to any actions taken by Seller or conditions occurring on or prior to the Closing Date (whether or not disclosed by Buyer's Environmental Investigation), so as to conform to any applicable requirements or guidelines (including but not limited to procedures, schedules and cleanup levels) for such corrective or response actions. Without limiting the generality of the foregoing, Seller shall assume all liabilities, duties and responsibilities imposed by or arising from the Connecticut Transfer Act, Conn. Gen. Stat. Section 22a-134 et seq., as amended (the "Act"). Such compliance shall include, but not be limited to, signing and delivering to Buyer a Form I or Form II, as those terms are defined in the Act; and, if Seller is unable to delivery to Buyer a Form I or Form II, preparing and signing the Form III or Form IV, whichever is applicable, as the "certifying party," as that term is defined in the Act, and filing such Form III or Form IV with the commissioner of environmental protection, along with the environmental condition assessment form, as required by the Act, and paying all required fees. Seller shall indemnify and hold Buyer harmless for any claims, losses, damages, liabilities, costs and other expenses related to non-compliance with the Act. If Seller does not make a filing pursuant to the Act, Seller shall provide at closing an opinion of environmental counsel that the Act does not apply to this transaction.

(b)   Seller will provide Buyer with reasonable advance notice of any activities Seller proposes to take in compliance with subsection (a) above on or affecting any Real Property, Leased Real Property or other properly operated by Seller in connection with the Business. Seller shall undertake these activities in a manner which minimizes any interference with the Buyer's use or enjoyment of or operations on the property following the Closing Date.

(c)   Seller will keep Buyer reasonably informed of the initiation, progress and completion of any corrective or response action Seller undertakes in compliance with subsection (a) above. Seller will provide to Buyer copies of all documents and correspondence submitted to and received from third parties, including Governmental Authorities, in connection therewith.

6.7   Preservation of Business Organization. * * *

6.8   Change of the Seller's Name. * * *

6.9   Approval of Certain Transactions. * * *

6.10   Exclusive Dealing. * * *

6.11   Seller's Insurance. * * *

6.12   Update Schedules. Prior to the Closing Date, Seller shall disclose to Buyer any information contained in the representations and warranties of Seller contained in Section 4 or in the Schedules delivered pursuant thereto which is no longer true or complete. Any such disclosure shall not be deemed to modify, amend or supplement the Seller's representations and warranties unless otherwise agreed in writing by Buyer.

6.13   Employees; WARN. * * *

6.14   Further Assurances. From time to time after the Closing, at Buyer's request and without further consideration, Seller will execute and deliver such other and further instruments of conveyance, assignment and transfer, and take such other action as Buyer may reasonably request for the more effective conveyance, transfer and enjoyment of the Purchased Assets to Buyer. To the extent that the assignment of confidentiality and noncompetition agreements to Buyer is not enforceable against the other parties to such agreements, Seller will use its best efforts to enforce such agreements with respect to the Business for Buyer's benefit. Seller will cooperate with Buyer in obtaining execution of any documents by current or prior employees of Seller with respect to inventions, invention disclosures and patent applications for goods or processes invented prior to the Closing Date.

SECTION 7. COVENANTS OF BUYER

7.1   Confidentiality. If the transactions provided for herein are not consummated, unless otherwise required by law, Buyer and its officers, agents and representatives will hold in strict confidence all information obtained from Seller and its officers, agents or representatives and will promptly return to Seller, all documents obtained from Seller and its officers, agents or representatives and all copies of such documents made by Buyer and its officers, agents and representatives, or, alternatively, if requested by Seller, will destroy all such documents and copies, as well as all analysis, compilations, summaries, studies or other documents prepared by Buyer or its officers, agents and representatives which contain information obtained from Seller or its officers, agents or representatives; provided, Buyer may retain any documents obtained from Seller or prepared by Buyer if Buyer reasonably determines that litigation may result from the failure to consummate the transactions and such documents may be relevant in such litigation.

7.2   Access to Offices, Officers, Accountants, Etc. Buyer will afford to and will cause its Affiliates to afford to, the officers and authorized representatives of Seller (including without limitation, attorneys and accountants) access to the offices, officers, properties, Books and Records of Buyer and the Business, and to the attorneys, accountants and other representatives of Buyer and its Affiliates and with any and all Persons Seller deems appropriate in order to enable it to adequately review the Final Closing Balance Sheet and Buyer's Calculation of the Final Closing Net Book Value for the purpose of determining the adjustment to Purchase Price as set forth in Section 2.5, such access to be at such time and in such manner as shall be reasonably acceptable to Buyer.

7.3   Hired Employees. Except as noted in Schedule 7.3, the Buyer will offer employment to all of Seller's employees, on terms and conditions determined by Buyer, except that such terms shall include provision for vacation and holiday time at least comparable to any accrued but unused vacation and holiday time to which any Hired Employee is entitled from Seller as of the Closing Date.

SECTION 8. NON-COMPETITION

* * *

SECTION 9. CONDITIONS PRECEDENT TO
THE OBLIGATIONS OF BUYER

The obligation of Buyer to acquire the Purchased Assets, pay the Purchase Price and assume the Assumed Liabilities is subject to the satisfaction or waiver in writing by the Buyer, on or prior to the Closing Date, of each of the following express conditions precedent:

9.1   Corporate Action. All corporate and other actions necessary to authorize and effectuate the consummation of the transactions contemplated hereby by Seller shall have been duly taken prior to the Closing, and Seller shall have delivered to Buyer a certificate of a duly authorized officer of Seller to that effect with respect to Seller.

9.2   Representations and Warranties. The representations and warranties of Seller made in or pursuant to this Agreement (without giving any effect to the modifications to the Schedules contemplated in Section 6.12) shall be true and correct on and as of the Closing Date with the same effect as though all such representations and warranties had been made on and as of such date (except for representations and warranties that expressly relate to a specified date, which need be true and correct only as of the specified date), and there shall have been delivered to Buyer a certificate to that effect, dated the Closing Date, signed by a duly authorized officer of Seller.

9.3   Performance of Obligations. Each and all of the covenants and agreements of Seller to be performed or complied with pursuant to this Agreement on or prior to the Closing Date shall have been duly performed and complied with or duly waived and there shall have been delivered to

Buyer a certificate to that effect, dated the Closing Date, signed by a duly authorized officer of Seller.

9.4   Due Diligence Investigation. The results of Buyer's due diligence investigation, including, but not limited to, the Environmental Investigation, shall have been satisfactory to Buyer.

9.5   Instruments of Conveyance, Etc. Seller shall have executed and delivered such bills of sale, assignments and other instruments of transfer and conveyance, certificates of title and other documents, as shall be reasonably required by Buyer for the transfer to the Buyer of all of Seller's right, title, and interest to and in the Purchased Assets, free and clear of any Liens (other than those relating to the Assumed Liabilities) or shall have delivered, with such instruments and documents, financing statement releases or termination statements with respect to any security interests constituting Liens on the Purchased Assets.

9.6   Lease for Real Property. Seller shall have signed and delivered to Buyer a lease for the Real Property in the form of Exhibit A, attached hereto.

9.7   Delivery of Physical Possession. Seller shall have delivered physical possession of all Equipment, Inventory, Technical Information and Tangible Purchased Assets and any tangible evidence of all Intellectual Property, Open Orders and Accounts Receivable to Buyer.

9.8   Opinion of Counsel. Buyer shall have been provided with an opinion of Seller's counsel substantially in the form of Exhibit B, attached hereto.

9.9   Required Consents. Seller shall have obtained all consents and approvals of all Persons and all Governmental Authorities required for the transactions contemplated hereby, and all waiting periods specified by law (including any extensions thereof) the expiration of which is necessary for the consummation of such transactions shall have expired or been otherwise terminated, including but not limited to the consent of [_____] to the assignment by Seller to Buyer of all Open Orders issued by [_____] to Seller, and any long term agreements between [_____] and Seller in effect as of the Closing Date.

9.10   Litigation. No order of any court or administrative agency shall be in effect which restrains or prohibits the transactions contemplated hereby and there shall not have been threatened, nor shall there be pending, any action or proceeding by or before any court or governmental agency or other regulatory or administrative agency or commission (a) challenging any of the transactions contemplated by this Agreement; (b) seeking monetary relief by reason of the consummation of such transactions; or (c) which would adversely affect the Purchased Assets or the Business following the Closing Date.

9.11   UCC-3 Lien Release. The pay-off statements and UCC-3 termination statements and/or mortgage satisfaction pieces releasing and terminating any liens and security interests on the Assets identified on Schedule 9.11 attached hereto.

9.12   Governmental Action; Damage to Property. There shall not have occurred any (a) seizure by any Governmental Authority of all or a portion of the Purchased Assets, or (b) damage, destruction or other impairment of or to all or a portion of the Purchased Assets including, without limitation, damage, destruction or other impairment caused by theft, fire, any casualty or the negligence of any Person, including Seller.

9.13   No Adverse Change. There have been no material adverse changes to the financial condition of Seller or the Business.

SECTION 10. CONDITIONS PRECEDENT TO THE OBLIGATIONS OF SELLER

The obligation of Seller to sell or otherwise transfer the Purchased Assets hereunder is subject to the satisfaction, or waiver in writing by Seller, on or prior to the Closing Date, of each of the following express conditions precedent:

10.1   Corporate Action. All corporate and other actions necessary to authorize and effectuate the consummation of the transactions contemplated hereby by Buyer shall have been duly taken prior to the Closing, and Buyer shall have delivered to Seller a certificate of a duly authorized officer of Buyer to that effect.

10.2   Representations and Warranties. The representations and warranties of Buyer made in or pursuant to this Agreement shall be true and correct on and as of the Closing Date with the same effect as though all such representations and warranties had been made on and as of such date and there shall have been delivered to Seller a certificate to that effect, dated the Closing Date, signed by a duly authorized officer of Buyer.

10.3   Performance of Obligations. Each and all of the covenants and agreements of Buyer to be performed or complied with pursuant to this Agreement on or prior to the Closing Date shall have been duly performed or complied with or duly waived and there shall have delivered to Seller a certificate to such effect, dated the Closing Date, signed by a duly authorized officer of Buyer.

10.4   Payment. Buyer shall have paid the Purchase Price to Seller in accordance with Section 2.04 of this Agreement.

10.5   Documents. Buyer shall have executed and delivered such agreements and undertakings confirming Buyer's assumption of the Assumed Liabilities as Seller shall reasonably request.

10.6   Litigation. No order of any court or administrative agency shall be in effect which restrains or prohibits the transactions contemplated hereby, and there shall not have been threatened, nor shall there be pending, any action or proceeding by or before any court or governmental agency or other regulatory or administrative agency or commission: (a) challenging any of the transactions contemplated by this Agreement or (b) seeking monetary relief by reason of the consummation of such transactions.

SECTION 11. SURVIVAL OF REPRESENTATIONS, WARRANTIES, AND COVENANTS

All representations and warranties made by Seller, Stockholders or Buyer as to any fact or condition existing on or before the Closing Date in this

Agreement, in any exhibit, schedule or in any certificate delivered pursuant hereto shall survive the Closing for a period of two years, except the representations and warranties in Section 4.16, which shall survive for the applicable limitations period, and in Section 4.27, which shall survive without time limit; provided, that there shall be no termination of any such representation or warranty as to which a claim has been asserted in writing prior to the termination of any such survival period. All such representations and warranties shall be unaffected by any investigation made by or on behalf of Buyer or Seller or by any knowledge obtained as a result thereof or otherwise. Except as otherwise expressly provided in this Agreement, all covenants, agreements, undertakings and indemnities set forth in this Agreement shall survive indefinitely.

SECTION 12. INDEMNIFICATION

12.1   Indemnity by Seller and Stockholders. Seller and Stockholders, jointly and severally, shall defend, indemnify and hold Buyer, its officers, directors, employees, subsidiaries and Affiliates harmless from and against all Losses arising out of or resulting from:

(a)   any breach of the representations and warranties made by Seller in or pursuant to this Agreement or the failure of such representations and warranties to be true and correct;

(b)   any failure by Seller to carry out, perform, satisfy and discharge any of its covenants, agreements, undertakings, liabilities or obligations under this Agreement or under any of the documents delivered by Seller pursuant to this Agreement;

(c)   any infringement of any patent, trademark, copyright and/or unfair competition rights arising out of Seller or its Affiliates' or customers' use of any Intellectual Property, Technical Information or Computer Software Assets, or the manufacture, use, or sale by Seller or its Affiliates or customers of any products or services incorporating or reflecting any Intellectual Property or Technical Information;

(d)   any failure by Seller to comply with or have complied with any Environmental Laws, or from any Contamination resulting from Seller's operation of the Business or present at, threatening or emanating from any property which the Business has owned, leased or operated and attributable in any way to actions occurring or conditions existing prior to the Closing Date, including, but not limited to Contamination described in Schedule 4.27(c).

(e)   any failure of Seller to pay and discharge any Excluded Liabilities;

(f)   any Product Liabilities;

(g)   any claims asserted by third parties against Buyer relating to the ownership, occupation and/or operation of the Business, the Purchased Assets or any other property occupied by Seller in connection with the Business prior to the Closing Date;

(h)   any suit, action or other proceeding brought by any Person or Governmental Authority asserting any of the matters referred to in this Section 11.01.

12.2   Indemnity by Buyer. Buyer will indemnify and hold Seller harmless from and against all Losses arising out of or resulting from:

(a)   any breach of any representations and warranties made by the Buyer in or pursuant to this Agreement or the failure of such representations and warranties to be true and correct;

(b)   any failure by Buyer to carry out, perform, satisfy and discharge any of its respective covenants, agreements, undertakings, liabilities or obligations under this Agreement or any of the documents and materials delivered by Buyer pursuant to this Agreement;

(c)   the failure by Buyer to pay, discharge or perform any Assumed Liabilities;

(d)   any claims asserted by third parties against Seller relating to the ownership, occupation or operation of the Business or the Purchased Assets by Buyer after the Closing Date; and

(e)   any suit, action, or other proceeding brought by any Person or Governmental Authority asserting any of the matters referred to in this Section 11.02.

12.3   Notice of Claim. The indemnified party shall promptly notify the indemnifying party in writing in reasonable detail of any claim, demand, action or proceeding for which indemnification will be sought under this Section 11. If such claim, demand, action or proceeding is a third party claim, demand, action or proceeding (a "Third Party Claim"), the indemnifying party will have the right at its expense to assume the defense thereof using counsel reasonably acceptable to the indemnified party. The indemnified party shall have the right to participate, at its own expense, with respect to any such Third Party Claim. In connection with any such Third Party Claim, the parties shall cooperate with each other and provide each other with access to relevant books and records in their possession. No such Third Party Claim shall be settled without the prior written consent of the indemnified party. If a firm written agreement is made by, or with the approval of the indemnifying party to settle any such Third Party Claim and the indemnified party unreasonably refuses to consent to such settlement, then: (a) the indemnifying party shall be excused from, and the indemnified party shall be solely responsible for, all further defense of such Third Party Claim; (b) the maximum liability of the indemnifying party relating to such Third Party Claim shall be the amount of the proposed settlement if the amount thereafter recovered from the indemnified party on such Third Party Claim is greater than the amount of the proposed settlement; and (c) the indemnified party shall pay all attorneys' fees and legal costs and expenses incurred after rejection of such settlement by the indemnified party.

12.4   Termination of Indemnification.

(a)   As to Buyer. The right of Buyer to be indemnified under this Section 12 shall survive:

(i)   as to matters described in Section 12.01(a), 12.01(b), 12.01(c), 12.01(f) and 12.01(h), except as to matters arising from Third Party Claims covered by subsection (iii) below, until the second anniversary of the Closing Date;

(ii)   as to matters relating to Taxes, until the termination of the applicable statute of limitations (including any waivers or extensions thereof agreed to by Buyer);

(iii)   as to matters arising from Third Party Claims, except as to matters covered by subsection (iv), until the termination of the applicable statute of limitations on such claims (including any tolling thereof); and

(iv)   as to the matters described in Section 12.01(d), 12.01(e), and 12.01(g), whether or not arising from Third Party Claims, without limitation;

provided however that Buyer shall not be entitled to indemnification from Seller or Stockholders as to any Losses unless the aggregate amount of such Losses exceeds $[_____] and then only to the extent of the amount of such excess. The limitation provided by foregoing sentence shall not apply to Losses arising out of or resulting from Section 12.1(d), 12.1(e) or 12.1(g).

(b)   As to Seller. The right of Seller to be indemnified under this Section 12 shall survive until the second anniversary of the Closing Date.

(c)   Exceptions. Notwithstanding subsections (a) and (b) hereof:

(i)   any indemnity claim based on fraudulent misrepresentations or fraudulent material omission or fraudulent breach of warranty shall survive without any time limitations; and

(ii)   any indemnity claim based on any matter which has been described in a notice to an indemnifying party pursuant to Section 12.03 of this Agreement prior to the expiration of the applicable time limitation set forth in subsections (a) and (b) above shall survive until the claim is finally resolved.

12.5   Set Off. Buyer may and is hereby authorized at any time and from time to time to set off and apply against any sum which is due and payable to Seller by Buyer under this Section 11 any sum, liability or other obligation which may be owed to Buyer by Seller under this Agreement, pending final determination of such matters. The rights under this Section 12.05 are in addition to any other rights and remedies which Buyer may otherwise have.

SECTION 13. TERMINATION AND AMENDMENT

13.1   Termination. This Agreement may be terminated at any time prior to the Closing Date:

(a)   by mutual written agreement of the Buyer and the Seller;

(b)   by Buyer if at any time it determines that the conditions precedent to its obligations hereunder in Section 8 hereof will not be satisfied prior to _____ ____, 20____.

(c)   by Seller if at any time it determines that the conditions precedent to its obligations hereunder in Section 9 hereof will not be satisfied prior to _____ ____, 20____.

(d)   by Buyer if the transactions contemplated hereby have not been consummated, through no fault or failure of the Buyer, on or before _____ ____, 20____; or

(e)   by Seller if such transactions have not been consummated, through no fault or failure of Seller, on or before _____ ____, 20____.

13.2   Effect of Termination. If either Buyer or Seller terminates this Agreement pursuant to Section 13.01, this Agreement, except for the provisions of Section 14, shall become void and have no effect. Notwithstanding the foregoing, nothing in this Section 13.2 shall relieve any party to this Agreement for breach of any provision of this Agreement. Notwithstanding any other provision in this Agreement, if it is judicially determined that termination of this Agreement was the result of any intentional breach of this Agreement, then, in addition to other remedies at law or in equity for breach of this Agreement, the party so found to have intentionally breached this Agreement shall indemnify and hold harmless the other party for their respective costs, fees and expenses of counsel, accountants, financial advisors or other experts and advisors as well as fees and expenses incident to negotiation, preparation and execution of this Agreement and related documentation.

13.3   Amendment. No amendment of any provision of this Agreement shall be valid unless the same shall be in writing and signed by Buyer and Seller. No waiver by any party of any default, misrepresentation or breach of a warranty or covenant hereunder, whether intentional or not, shall be deemed to extend to any prior or subsequent default, misrepresentation or breach of a warranty or covenant hereunder or effect in any way any rights arising by virtue of any prior or subsequent to such occurrence.

SECTION 14. GENERAL

14.1   Costs and Expenses. Each of the parties hereto shall pay, without right of reimbursement from the other, all costs incurred by it incident to the preparation, execution and delivery of this Agreement and the performance of its obligations hereunder, whether or not the transactions contemplated by this Agreement shall be consummated, including, without limitation, fees and disbursements of legal counsel, accountants, and consultants employed by the respective parties hereto in connection with the transactions contemplated by this Agreement.

14.2   Parties in Interest; Assignment.

(a)   This Agreement shall be binding upon, and inure to the benefit of, the parties hereto and their respective successors and permitted assigns. Except as otherwise expressly provided in this Agreement, this Agreement is not made for the benefit of any Person not a party hereto, and nothing in this Agreement will be construed as giving any Person, other than the parties hereto and their respective successors and permitted assigns, any right, remedy, or claim under or in respect of this Agreement, or any provision hereof.

(b)   This Agreement shall not be assigned by Buyer or Seller without the prior written consent of the other party; provided, that Buyer shall have the right to assign all or any portion of its rights and obligations under this Agreement to an Affiliate of Buyer without the Seller's consent (including the right to receive title to any portion of the Purchased Assets). Any such assignment shall not release Buyer from its obligations herein, including its obligations with respect to the Assumed Liabilities.

14.3   Confidentiality. Each party to this Agreement shall take all reasonable precautions to maintain the confidentiality of the negotiation or existence of this Agreement, the identity of the parties hereto and any nonpublic information concerning the other parties or their Subsidiaries or Affiliates provided to or discovered by any of them or their respective represent¬atives and shall not disclose any of the above information to anyone other than (a) those people directly involved in the investigation and negotiations pertaining to the transactions contemplated by this Agreement, including without limitation, attorneys, accountants and similar representa¬tives, (b) such lenders or investors as may be necessary to finance the transactions contemplated hereby, and (c) such Persons or Governmental Authorities whose consents or approvals may be necessary or to whom notice needs to be given to permit consummation of the transactions contemplated hereby.

14.4   Public Statements. Neither party to this Agreement shall, without the prior written consent of the other party hereto, make or cause to be made any press release or other public statement or announcement that directly or indirectly discloses the transactions contem¬plated by this Agreement; provided, however, that Buyer and Seller may make any public disclosure which either of them is advised by independent counsel it is required to make by applicable law or any listing or trading agreement concerning its securities.

14.5   Choice of Law. This Agreement shall be governed by, construed, interpreted and the rights of the parties determined in accordance with the laws, including equitable principles but without regard to principles of conflict of laws, of the State of [_____].

14.6   Mediation. In the event of a dispute arising out of or related to this Agreement (other than with respect to the determination of the Final Closing Net Book Value), the parties shall, prior to initiating litigation, first submit the dispute to non binding mediation under the commercial mediation rules of the American Arbitration Association at its [_____], [_____] offices. The parties hereby acknowledge and agree that such mediation shall be deemed to be in the nature of settlement discussions and that neither the fact that such discussions took place, nor any statement or conduct of any participant in such discussions shall be admissible into evidence in any subsequent litigation or in any arbitration or other dispute resolution proceeding involving the parties. It is further understood and agreed that any disclosure in any form, including oral, by any Person participating in such mediation shall not operate as a waiver of any privilege, including work product or attorney client privilege, applicable to the subject matter thereof.

14.7   Notices. Any notice, request, consent, waiver or other communication required or permitted to be given hereunder shall be effective only if in writing and shall be deemed sufficiently given only if delivered in person or sent by telecopy, by a nationally¬ recognized overnight courier or by certified or registered mail, postage prepaid, return receipt requested, addressed as follows:

If to Seller and the [_____]:

[_____]
[_____]
[_____]
[_____]

[_____]
[_____]
[_____]
[_____]

with a copy in either instance to:

[_____]
[_____]
[_____]
[_____]

If to Buyer:

[_____]
[_____]
[_____]
[_____]

with a copy to:

[_____]
[_____]
[_____]
[_____]

or to such other Person or address as either such party may have specified in a notice duly given by the sender as provided herein. Such notice or communication shall be deemed to have been given as of the date so personally delivered, on the business day following delivery by sender to such an overnight courier, three business days after mailing or when receipt is confirmed if delivered by telecopy.

14.8   Entire Agreement. This Agreement (including the Schedules and Exhibits attached hereto) and the documents referred to herein as having been entered into by any of the parties hereto or delivered by a party hereto to another party hereto constitute the entire agreement and understanding of the parties relating to the subject matter hereof and supersede all prior and contemporaneous agreements and understandings, representations and warranties, whether oral or written, relating to the subject matter hereof.

14.9   Cumulative Remedies. The rights and remedies provided in this Agreement are cumulative and are not exclusive of any rights or remedies a party may otherwise have at law or in equity.

14.10   Waiver. Any failure of Seller or Buyer to comply with any obligation, covenant, agreement or condition contained herein may be expressly waived in writing by Buyer in the case of any such failure by Seller or by Seller in the case of any such failure by Buyer, but such waiver or failure to insist upon strict compliance shall not operate as a waiver of, or estoppel with respect to, any subsequent or other failure. Whenever this Agreement requires or permits consent by or on behalf of any party hereto, such consent shall be given in writing in a manner consistent with the requirements for a waiver of compliance as set forth in this Section 14.10.

14.11   Severability. The unenforceability or invalidity of any Section or subsection or provision of this Agreement shall not affect the enforceability or validity of the balance of this Agreement. If any provision of this Agreement is so broad as to be unenforceable, such provision shall be interpreted to be only as broad as is enforceable.

14.12   Headings. The headings of the Sections and subsections contained in this Agreement are for reference purposes only and shall not in any way affect the meaning, interpretation, enforceability or validity of this Agreement.

14.13   Counterparts. This Agreement may be executed in any number of counterparts, each of which so executed will be deemed to be an original, but all of which together will constitute one and the same agreement.

14.14   Facsimiles. Any facsimile signature of any party hereto or to any other agreement executed in connection herewith shall constitute a legal, valid and binding execution hereof by such party.

14.15   Construction. The Seller and the Buyer hereby agree that any rule of law or any legal decision that would require interpretation of any claimed ambiguities in this Agreement against the party that drafted it has no application and is expressly waived. Within this Agreement, the singular shall include the plural and the plural shall include the singular, and any gender shall include all other genders, all as the meaning and the context of this Agreement shall require. Section, Exhibit and Schedule references contained in this Agreement refer to those contained in or attached to this Agreement unless otherwise specified.

[Signatures appear on next page]

IN WITNESS WHEREOF, the parties hereto have caused this Agreement to be executed as of the date first above written.

[_____]

By: _____

Title: _____

[_____]

By: _____

Title: _____

Schedule 1 – Definitions

"Assumed Liabilities" means the liabilities and obligations of Seller assumed by Buyer under Section 2.06 of the Agreement, but not including the Excluded Liabilities

"CERCLA" means the Comprehensive Environmental Response, Compensation and Liability Act, as amended.

"Closing" means the act or acts by which the transactions contemplated by the Agreement are accomplished.

"Closing Date" means the date on which the Closing occurs. Unless the parties otherwise agree, any references to "after the Closing Date" means any time after the normal close of business of Seller on the Closing Date.

"Contamination" means the uncontained presence of Hazardous Substances at any property, or arising from any property, which may require remediation or otherwise give rise to liability under any applicable law whether or not present at levels exceeding the criteria set forth in the Connecticut Remediation Standard Regulation R.C.S.A §§133K-1 et seq.

"Environmental Investigation" means the investigation commissioned by Buyer of Seller's compliance with the Environmental Laws, the presence of Hazardous Substances or other toxic or hazardous materials on properties owned, leased or operated by Seller and the uses and condition of disposal sites for waste generated in connection with the operations of Seller.

"Environmental Laws" means all environmental or health and safety statutes, ordinances, regulations, orders, directives, decrees, permits, governmental approvals, contractual requirements and requirements of common law concerning (i) activities relating to the Business, (ii) the Purchased Assets or any other properties or assets owned, leased or operated by Seller in connection with the Business, (iii) repairs or construction of any improvements, (iv) handling of any materials, (v) discharges into the air, soil, surface, water or ground water, and (vi) storage, treatment or disposal of any waste at or connected with any activity at such properties.

"Excluded Assets" means the assets of Seller specifically excluded from the proposed transaction pursuant to Section 2.02 of the Agreement.

"Excluded Liabilities" means the liabilities and obligations of Seller relating to the Business, the Excluded Assets or Seller under Section 2.07 of the Agreement.

"Governmental Authority" means the government of the United States, any state or political subdivision thereof, any foreign country and any entity exercising executive, legislative, regulatory or administrative functions of or pertaining to government.

"Hazardous Substances" means "hazardous substances" or "pollutants or contaminants" as defined pursuant to CERCLA, "regulated substances" within the meaning of Subtitle I of the Resource Conservation and Liability Act, as amended, hazardous substances as defined under any applicable state or local Environmental Laws, petroleum or petroleum products, and any other substance considered toxic, hazardous or a potential threat to human health or the environment, or otherwise regulated under any applicable Environmental Law, the presence of which has resulted or may result in (i) an Environmental Lien, or (ii) a party incurring costs or liabilities, or (iii) a party being ordered or directed to investigate, remediate or otherwise respond to a potential environmental threat posed by such substances.

"Leased Real Property" means parcels of land, together with all rights, interests and appurtenances therein or thereto, and the buildings, structures, installations, fixtures and other improvements thereon, leased by Seller and used in the Business, as described in Schedule 4.12(b).

"Leases" means leases of Equipment and other tangible personal property, leases of Leased Real Property and other leases of Tangible Purchased Assets or intangible personal property, in each case whether classified as a capital or operating lease for accounting purposes.

"Liabilities and Obligations" means any direct or indirect indebtedness, lease obligation, guaranty, endorsement, claim, loss, damage, deficiency, cost expense, obligation or responsibility, fixed or unfixed, known or unknown, asserted or unasserted, choate or inchoate, liquidated or unliquidated, secured or unsecured, whether arising in contract, tort or otherwise, whether now existing or hereafter arising.

"Losses" means all claims, damages, losses, liabilities, costs and expenses (including attorneys' fees and disbursements and any other legal costs) suffered or incurred by a party.

"Permits" means all governmental permits, licenses, registrations, orders and approvals relating to the Business, all of which are listed in Schedule 2.01(m).

"Person" shall mean an individual, partnership, corporation, business trust, joint stock company, trust, unincorporated association, joint venture, limited liability company, or any other entity of whatever nature.

"Purchase Price" means the consideration payable for the Purchased Assets under Section 2.03 of the Agreement.

"Real Property" means the land, and the improvements thereon, owned by Seller and located in the Town of [_____], State of [_____], and known as [_____].

Courtesy of Pamela K. Elkow, Robinson & Cole LLP

APPENDIX G

SALE AND PURCHASE AGREEMENT FOR COMPANY ASSETS (HEAVILY NEGOTIATED, SELLER-FRIENDLY)

This Sale and Purchase Agreement for _____ Assets ("Agreement") is entered into as of [_____], 200__ ("Effective Date") by and between _____, a _____ corporation having a principal place of business in _____, _____ ("Seller"), and _____, a _____ corporation having a principal place of business in _____, _____ ("Purchaser").

Preliminary Statement

Seller is engaged in the [DESCRIPTION OF BUSINESS] ("COMPANY"). Purchaser desires and agrees to purchase substantially all of the property and assets of COMPANY, and Seller desires and agrees to sell to Purchaser such property and assets, on the terms and conditions set forth herein.

The execution and delivery of this Agreement by Purchaser and Seller shall constitute a binding and irrevocable agreement to purchase and sell the Assets, subject to and upon the terms and conditions set forth in this Agreement.

NOW THEREFORE, in consideration of the matters set forth in the Preliminary Statement, and the mutual promises and covenants herein set forth, and subject to the terms and conditions of this Agreement, the parties hereby agree as follows:

ARTICLE 1
DEFINITIONS

1.1   The following terms shall have the meanings set forth below for all purposes of this Agreement:

"Affiliate" means, with respect to a party, any individual or legal business entity that, directly or indirectly, controls, is controlled by or is under common control with, such party. The term "control" (including the terms "controlled by" and "under common control with") as used in the preceding sentence means the possession, directly or indirectly, of the power to direct or cause the direction of management and policies.

"Agreement" means this Sale and Purchase Agreement for _____.

"Assets" has the meaning specified in Section 2.1.1.

"CERCLA" has the meaning specified in Section 10.1.

"Environment" means soil, land surface or subsurface strata, surface waters (including navigable waters, ocean water, streams, ponds drainage basins and inland wetlands and water courses), groundwaters, drinking water supply, stream sediments, ambient air (including indoor air), plant and animal life, and any other environmental medium or natural resource. Environment also includes building materials.

"Environmental Condition" means the existence of Hazardous Materials or Petroleum Product at the Real Property, including in or on the soil, surface water, groundwater at, on or under the Real Property, or migrating from the Real Property to other property to the extent the levels of any such Hazardous Materials or Petroleum Product.

"Environmental Costs" means any actual costs or expenses, including reasonable and appropriate fees and disbursements for outside attorneys, engineers, health, safety, environmental and other outside consultants and investigators; provided, however, Environmental Costs shall not include costs or expenses for services performed by Purchaser's or its Affiliates' employees. For purposes of this Agreement, Environmental Costs shall be incurred when the relevant services are performed and the costs and expenses associated therewith are paid.

"Environmental Information" has the meaning set forth in Section 10.1.

"Environmental Laws" means all applicable federal, state, and local laws, statutes, ordinances, regulations, policies, common law, standards, prohibitions, restrictions, directives, interpretations, orders, decrees, notices, demands, requests for information, guidelines, permits, licenses, approvals, judicial decisions, treaties and entitlements that relate to the protection of human health, public or worker safety, natural resources, wildlife or the Environment or that create rights or obligations in connection with the presence, storage or transportation or Release of Hazardous Materials or Petroleum Products, including any future laws or amendments related thereto and any record keeping, notification, disclosure and reporting requirements respecting any of the foregoing.

"Environmental Liability" means any Liability arising out of or related to Environmental Laws, including, without limitation, any (i) natural resource damage claims and claims for Remediation, (ii) obligation to investigate, monitor, test, report to Governmental Authorities or other third parties, remediate or perform Remediation in connection with any onsite or offsite presence or Release of Hazardous Materials or Petroleum Products or any Environmental Condition, (iii) request, notice, administrative, regulatory or judicial action, enforcement order, compliance order, consent order, cleanup and abatement order, cease-and-desist order, directive, claim or lien, (iv) circumstances forming the basis of any violation or alleged violation of any Environmental Law, (v) all claims (including but not limited to property damage and personal injury) by any third party resulting from the presence or Release of any Hazardous Materials or Petroleum Products, any Environmental Condition or violations of any Environmental Law; (v) any Environmental Condition, or any other health or safety matters or conditions (including occupational safety and health matters and regulation of chemical substances or products), (vi) fines, penalties, judgments, awards, settlements, legal or administrative proceedings, damages, fees, losses, claims, investigative, remedial, or inspection costs and expenses arising under any Environmental Law; (vii) financial responsibility under any Environmental Law for cleanup costs or corrective action, including any investigation, cleanup, removal, containment, or other remediation or response actions required by applicable Environmental Law (whether or not such cleanup ha been required or requested by any Governmental Authority or any third party); or (viii) any other compliance, corrective, investigative, or remedial measures required under any Environmental Law.

"Environmental Notice" means any summons, citation, directive, notice, order, claim, pleading, proceeding, judgment, request for information, letter or any other written communication from the United States Environmental Protection Agency ("USEPA"), or any other Governmental Authority, or any third person, concerning any intentional or unintentional act or omission which has resulted in or which may reasonably be expected to result in (i) any Environmental Liability, (ii) the Release of any Hazardous Materials or Petroleum Products into the Environment, or (iii) a violation, or alleged or threatened violation of any Environmental Laws.

"Environmental Permit" means any and all Permits required under any Environmental Law in connection with the Real Property or the activities conducted thereon at any time prior to the Closing Date.

"Expert" shall mean one or more nationally recognized firms mutually selected by Seller and Purchaser or selected by the procedures set forth in Section 10.8.

"Governmental Authority" means any federal, state, local or foreign governmental authority, agency, board, commission, judicial body or other body having jurisdiction over the matter and/or any individual's or association's actions under the citizen suit provisions of any Environmental Law.

"Hazardous Materials" means any substance which is listed, regulated or defined as a hazardous substance, hazardous material, toxic substance, hazardous waste, hazardous chemical, hazardous air pollutant, contaminant or pollutant under any Environmental Laws, including, without limitation, (i) radioactive substances, (ii) asbestos or asbestos-containing material, (iii) radon, (iv) mercury, (v) lead-based paint, (vi) coal tar residue, and (vii) polychlorinated biphenyls ("PCBs"), but excluding Petroleum Products.

"Liability" means any known, unknown, contingent or non-contingent loss, claim (including, without limitation, tort claims, toxic tort claims, claims for personal injury, claims for property damage, natural resource damages, claims for diminution in property value and claims for injunctive relief), action, proceeding, charge, directive, demand, request for information or notice of non-compliance or violation, suit, judgment, decree, order, liability, obligation (civil, criminal or other), damage (including, without limitation, consequential damages and, in the case of third party claims, punitive damages), expense (including, without limitation, reasonable attorney and consultant fees and costs for investigation and defense), capital expenditure, operating expense, cost, fee, lien, fine or penalty. "Liability" shall include without limitation Environmental Liabilities and, in each instance, shall include without limitation all reasonable costs of investigating and defending any claim.

"Minimum Remediation Cost" shall mean the minimum cost necessary to implement the Minimum Remediation Method.

"Minimum Remediation Method" shall mean the minimum method of Remediation allowable under, and which satisfies the requirements of, Environmental Laws in effect at the time of such Remediation, as such may be modified on a case-by-case basis by the appropriate Governmental Authority to achieve the least stringent Remediation standard or cleanup criteria for the type of property affected consistent with its use as a _____ [CURRENT USE], which Remediation method utilizes demonstrated and proven technology or methods, and is in fact allowed by the applicable Governmental Authority.

"Order" means any judgment, order, writ, injunction or decree of any Governmental Authority having jurisdiction over the matter.

"Permits" means the permits, licenses, registrations, certificates, consents, orders, notices, approvals or similar rights from any Governmental Authority that are held by Seller in connection with the Assets, the Real Property or any activities conducted thereon.

"Permit Assessments" means any assessment issued by a Governmental Authority after the Closing in connection with any Permit regardless of whether such assessment is based on operating levels at the Real Property prior to, at or after the Closing.

"Petroleum Product" means petroleum hydrocarbons or petroleum based derivatives, including crude oil and any fraction thereof, and any product made from petroleum hydrocarbons, together with any additives to such products, including, without limitation, methyl tertiary-butyl ether

("MTBE"), ethyl tertiary-butyl ether ("ETBE") or tertiary-amyl methyl ether ("TAME").

"Purchaser's Assumed Environmental Liabilities" has the meaning specified in Section 10.4.

"Purchaser's Knowledge" means the actual knowledge of any of the employees of Purchaser listed on Schedule 1-P as of the date a particular representation or warranty is made, without any review of files or other due diligence on the part of such employees.

"RCRA" means the Resource Conservation and Recovery Act of 1976, as amended.

"Release" means any emission, spill, seepage, leak, escape, leaching, discharge, injection, pumping, pouring, emptying, dumping, disposing or release of Hazardous Materials or Petroleum Products into or upon the Environment.

"Remediation" means any investigation, sampling, analysis, monitoring, abatement, removal, decontamination, remediation, cleanup, management, treatment, storage or disposal related to the presence or Release of Hazardous Materials or Petroleum Products.

"Seller's Retained Environmental Liabilities" has the meaning specified in Section 10.2.

ARTICLE 2
SALE AND PURCHASE OF ASSETS

2.1   **Assets.**

    2.1.1   Sale. On the terms and subject to the conditions of this Agreement and for the consideration stated herein, at the Closing, Purchaser shall purchase and acquire from Seller, and Seller shall sell and deliver to Purchaser, all of Seller's right, title and interest in and to the following properties and assets (together with the property and assets listed in Section 2.1.2, the "Assets"):

* * *

2.2   Excluded Assets. Notwithstanding anything else in this Agreement, the Assets (and any defined term for any property included in the Assets) exclude the following (collectively, the "Excluded Assets"):

* * *

ARTICLE 3
PURCHASE PRICE

3.1   Purchase Price. In consideration of the Assets, Purchaser shall pay to Seller the total of the following:

> **3.1.1**   For the transfer, sale and assignment by Seller of the Assets other than those Assets listed elsewhere in this Section 3.1, $[_____] as adjusted pursuant to Sections ____ and ____, if applicable;

* * *

The aggregate amount payable pursuant to this Section 3.1 is referred to as the "Purchase Price."

3.2   Payment. The portion of the Purchase Price payable at Closing shall be as follows:

* * *

3.3   Earnest Money Deposit. Simultaneously herewith, Purchaser is delivering to Seller a deposit in the amount of $1,500,000 (the "Earnest Money Deposit") as consideration for Seller's entry into this Agreement. In the event the Closing occurs, the Earnest Money Deposit, together with interest or earnings thereon, shall be credited against the Cash Purchase Price. In the event the Closing does not occur by the Outside Closing Date and the failure to close is not the result of Purchaser's Default hereunder, then the Earnest Money Deposit, together with any interest or earnings thereon, shall be paid to Purchaser on the third business day following the

Outside Closing Date. If the Closing does not occur by the Outside Closing Date and the failure to close is the result of Purchaser's Default hereunder, then the Earnest Money Deposit shall be retained by Seller in accordance with Article 13.

3.4   Valuation. The parties agree that any property valuations established by the parties for the Assets are for purposes of (a) establishing an insured amount for the Title Commitments and title policies; (b) preparing the Closing statements and escrow instructions; (c) preparing affidavits of value and transfer tax returns; and (d) calculating recording fees and transfer taxes, if applicable. Such property valuations are not established necessarily for tax purposes or for financial or accounting ("book") purposes. Neither party shall have any liability to the other party with respect to such valuations.

3.5   Allocation of Purchase Price. Purchaser and Seller shall make their own allocations of the Purchase Price for tax and accounting purposes. Neither party shall be bound by any allocations of the Purchase Price by the other party.

ARTICLE 4
SELLER'S RETAINED LIABILITIES;
PURCHASER'S ASSUMED LIABILITIES

4.1   Seller's Retained Liabilities. Seller shall retain all liabilities not expressly included in the assumed Liabilities, including but not limited to following Liabilities (collectively, "Seller's Retained Liabilities"):

* * *

4.1.1   except as specifically set forth above in this Section 4.1, any other Liability (but specifically excluding any Environmental Liabilities) related to the ownership or operation of the Assets prior to Closing;

4.1.2   any Liability arising out of or relating to any of the Excluded Assets; and

4.1.3   except as limited in Article 10, any Seller's Environmental Liabilities.

The Retained Liabilities shall in no way be limited or reduced by any information contained in this Agreement, including the Schedules hereto.

4.2   Purchaser's Assumed Liabilities. In consideration of the transfer of the Assets, and subject to Seller's retention of the Seller's Retained Liabilities, Purchaser shall assume, and shall pay, perform and discharge when due, and shall indemnify and defend Seller and its Indemnitees against and shall hold them harmless from the following Liabilities (collectively, "Purchaser's Assumed Liabilities"):

* * *

4.3   Interpretation with Article 10. Notwithstanding the foregoing, this Article 4 is subject to the parties' obligations set forth in Article 10, and in the event of any conflict or ambiguity in the language of this Article 4 and Article 10, the language of Article 10 shall be controlling.

* * *

ARTICLE 5
RELATED AGREEMENTS

* * *

ARTICLE 6
CLOSING

6.1   Time and Place. Subject to satisfaction of the conditions set forth in _____, the closing of the transaction contemplated hereby (the "Closing") shall be held at Seller's offices in San Antonio, Texas or such other location as may be mutually agreed to by the parties on the date three business days after the conditions to Closing set forth in Sections 7.1 and 7.2 have been satisfied, but in no event after the Outside Closing Date, or at such other time or place or in such other manner, including by mail or facsimile, as Seller and Purchaser may mutually agree in writing; provided, however, if only the conditions to Closing set forth in Sections 7.1.4 and/or 7.2.4 have not been satisfied by the Outside Closing Date for any reason other than an act or omission of the applicable party, then the Outside Closing Date shall, unless the parties agree otherwise in writing, be automatically extended for an additional three month period.

* * *

6.2   Condition of Assets. EXCEPT AS EXPRESSLY PROVIDED IN THIS AGREEMENT, ALL ASSETS AND RIGHTS (INCLUDING, WITHOUT LIMITATION, THE REAL PROPERTY, PERSONAL PROPERTY, IMPROVEMENTS, PETROLEUM INVENTORY, NON-PETROLEUM INVENTORY, BOOKS AND RECORDS, CONTRACTS, MISCELLANEOUS ASSETS AND PERMITS) TO BE CONVEYED OR LICENSED HEREUNDER WILL BE CONVEYED OR LICENSED ON AN "AS IS," "WHERE IS," AND "WITH ALL FAULTS" BASIS AT THE CLOSING. EXCEPT AS EXPRESSLY PROVIDED HEREIN, SELLER MAKES NO WARRANTIES, EXPRESS OR IMPLIED, CONCERNING THE PHYSICAL CONDITION, UTILITY, FITNESS OR OPERABILITY OF ANY OF SUCH ASSETS AND RIGHTS, INCLUDING, WITHOUT LIMITATION, ANY WARRANTY OF MERCHANTABILITY OR OF FITNESS FOR PARTICULAR OR ORDINARY USES OR PURPOSES. PURCHASER HEREBY WAIVES THE UNIFORM COMMERCIAL CODE WARRANTIES OF MERCHANTABILITY AND FITNESS FOR A PARTICULAR PURPOSE AND ALL OTHER IMPLIED WARRANTIES WITH RESPECT TO THE ASSETS. PURCHASER HAS COMPLETED ALL DUE DILIGENCE PRIOR TO THE EFFECTIVE DATE, AND PURCHASER'S OBLIGATIONS HEREUNDER ARE NOT CONDITIONED ON ITS SATISFACTION WITH THE RESULTS OF ANY FURTHER INSPECTION, INVESTIGATION, REVIEW OR OTHER DUE DILIGENCE.

ARTICLE 7
CONDITIONS PRECEDENT TO CLOSING

7.1   Conditions to Purchaser's Obligations. The obligations of Purchaser at the Closing are subject to the following conditions:

7.1.1   Seller shall have performed in all material respects all covenants required by this Agreement to be performed by it at or prior to the Closing;

7.1.2   Seller shall have delivered to Purchaser all agreements, instruments, certificates and documents required to be delivered under this Agreement, including, without limitation, those listed in Section 6.2;

7.1.3   there shall not be in effect any Order barring the consummation of the transactions contemplated by this Agreement and neither party shall have received a written communication from any Governmental Authority challenging the legality of the transactions contemplated hereby;

7.1.4   Both parties shall have obtained the applicable approvals, if any, of the FTC and the Attorneys General of the State of _____ to the consummation of the transactions contemplated by this Agreement, in each case to the extent required by such agency or entity;

7.1.5   Seller shall have obtained all Consents as set forth on Schedule 8.3.

* * *

7.2   Conditions to Seller's Obligations. The obligations of Seller at the Closing are subject to the following conditions:

7.2.1   Purchaser shall have performed in all material respects all covenants required by this Agreement to be performed by it at or prior to the Closing;

7.2.2   Purchaser shall have delivered to Seller all agreements, instruments, certificates and documents required to be so delivered under this Agreement or such other agreements or instruments, including, without limitation, those listed in Section 6.3;

7.2.3   there shall not be in effect any Order barring the consummation of the transactions contemplated by this Agreement and neither party shall have received a written communication from any Governmental Authority challenging the legality of the transactions contemplated hereby; and

7.2.4   Both parties shall have obtained the applicable approvals, if any, of the FTC and the Attorneys General of the State of _____ to the consummation of the transactions contemplated by this Agreement, in each case to the extent required by such agency or entity.

7.3   Cooperation. From the Effective Date hereof until the Closing, Seller and Purchaser shall work together in the spirit of continuing cooperation to (a) cause the conditions to Closing set forth in this Article 7 to be satisfied as quickly as is reasonably possible, and (b) obtain any Consent required by Seller or Purchaser to consummate the transactions contemplated by this Agreement or otherwise in connection with Purchaser's ownership of the Assets or its proposed business operations relating thereto.

ARTICLE 8
SELLER'S REPRESENTATIONS AND WARRANTIES

In order to induce Purchaser to enter into this Agreement, Seller hereby represents and warrants to Purchaser as follows; provided, however that no representations or warranties as to Environmental Liabilities are given by Seller pursuant to this Article 8, which Environmental Liabilities are provided for in Article 10:

* * *

ARTICLE 9
PURCHASER'S REPRESENTATIONS AND WARRANTIES

In order to induce Seller to enter into this Agreement, Purchaser hereby warrants and represents to Seller that:

9.1   Organization. Purchaser is a limited partnership duly organized, validly existing and in good standing under the laws of the State of _____, and is duly qualified as a foreign corporation in the States of _____, _____, and _____.

9.2   Authority; Enforceability. Purchaser has the power and authority under applicable partnership law (a) to execute and deliver this Agreement and each agreement and instrument delivered or to be delivered by Purchaser pursuant to this Agreement, and to carry out its obligations hereunder and thereunder and (b) to own or lease and operate the Assets and to conduct its business thereon. The execution, delivery and performance of this Agreement and each agreement and instrument delivered or to be delivered pursuant to this Agreement by Purchaser, and the consummation of the transactions provided for hereby and thereby, have been duly authorized and approved by all requisite corporate action of Purchaser, and no other corporate act or proceeding on the part of Purchaser or its Affiliates or equity owners is necessary to authorize the execution, delivery or performance of this Agreement or of such other agreements and instruments, or of the transactions contemplated hereby or thereby. Each of this Agreement and such agreements and instruments is, or upon its execution and delivery will be, legal, valid, binding and enforceable against Purchaser in accordance with its respective terms, subject to the effects of bankruptcy, insolvency, reorganization, moratorium, fraudulent transfers, preferential transfers and other laws of general application relating to creditors' rights and equitable remedies.

9.3   Consents. Except as set forth on Schedule 9.3, to Purchaser's Knowledge, no material Consent of or by, or material filing with, any other person is required with respect to Purchaser or any of its Affiliates in connection with (a) the execution, delivery or enforceability of this Agreement or any agreement or instrument delivered or to be delivered pursuant to this Agreement by Purchaser, or (b) the consummation of any of the transactions provided in this Agreement and the other documents specified in clause (a).

9.4   No Breach. Except as set forth on Schedule 9.4, the execution and delivery of this Agreement and each agreement and instrument delivered or to be delivered pursuant to this Agreement by Purchaser, and the consummation of the transactions provided for hereby and thereby and the compliance by Purchaser with any of the provisions hereof or thereof does not and will not (a) violate, or conflict with, or result in a breach of any provisions of, or constitute a default (or an event which, with notice or lapse of time or both, would constitute a default) under, or result in the termination of, or accelerate the performance required under, any of the terms, conditions or provisions of (i) the Certificate of Organization or Agreement of Limited Partnership of Purchaser or (ii) to Purchaser's Knowledge, any agreement, instrument or obligation to which Purchaser is a party or by which a material part of its assets or operations otherwise are bound, or (b) to Purchaser's Knowledge, violate any order, injunction, statute, rule or regulation, or (c) to Purchaser's Knowledge, trigger any rights of purchase, or any buy/sell or similar rights.

9.5   Actions and Proceedings. To Purchaser's Knowledge, except as set forth on Schedule 9.5, no action, suit, proceeding or claim is pending or threatened seeking to restrain or prohibit this Agreement.

9.6   Brokers. All negotiations relating to this Agreement, the agreements and instruments delivered or to be delivered pursuant to this Agreement and the transactions contemplated hereby and thereby have been carried on without the intervention of any person acting on behalf of Purchaser or its Affiliates in such manner as to give rise to any valid claim against Seller for any broker's or finder's fee or similar compensation in connection with the transactions contemplated hereby or thereby. Purchaser shall indemnify and defend Seller and its Affiliates against, and shall hold them harmless from, any Liability arising out of claims by any person alleging a right to a broker's or finder's fee based upon any actions of Purchaser or its Affiliates.

9.7   Solvency; Funds. Purchaser is solvent and is not in the hands of a receiver. No application of receivership pending, and no proceedings are pending by or against it for bankruptcy or reorganization in any state or federal court. Purchaser has sufficient funds to deliver the Purchase Price at the Closing as contemplated in this Agreement without recourse to any debt or equity financing other than any which is irrevocably and unconditionally committed as of the Effective Date.

9.8   Independent Decision. Purchaser has made its own independent analysis and judgment of the commercial potential and usefulness of the Assets, and is not relying upon any projections from Seller regarding prospective operations of the Assets.

ARTICLE 10
ENVIRONMENTAL LIABILITIES

10.1   Allocation of Environmental Liabilities. The provisions of this Article 10 are the result of mutual compromise and an allocation of responsibility and risk for Environmental Liabilities arising out of or related to the Assets or the operation of the Assets as between Purchaser and Seller. Each party has given weight to these matters in entering into the Agreement and setting the Purchase Price. Purchaser and Seller intend that the allocations of risk and responsibility for Environmental Liabilities as set forth in this Article 10 and the other applicable provisions of this Agreement shall be given full effect and that the rights and remedies in this Article 10 and the other applicable provisions of this Agreement shall be the exclusive rights and remedies available to the parties. The parties acknowledge that they expressly waive and relinquish all other rights and remedies with respect to Environmental Liabilities, whether based on statute, regulation, common law or otherwise, including, without limitation, claims under the Comprehensive Environmental Response, Compensation and Liability Act of 1980, as amended ("CERCLA"). Additionally, Purchaser acknowledges that it has been given full access to environmental information related to the Assets (the "Environmental Information") as provided in the Montreal data room.

10.2   Seller's Retained Environmental Liabilities. Seller shall be solely responsible for, and shall indemnify and defend and hold harmless Purchaser and its Indemnitees against, and hold them harmless from, all Environmental Liabilities arising out of or related to the operation of the Assets, the Real Property or the operations conducted thereon, or the conduct of Seller's business prior to Closing without regard to the continuing nature of any Release, including the acts or omissions of any predecessors of Seller, and whether a claim is asserted by a Governmental Authority or third party, or represents an initiative of the Purchaser (voluntary or otherwise) to comply with Environmental Laws, whether or not a third party claim is made and regardless of whether such condition has been discovered or manifested itself prior to Closing ("Seller's Retained Environmental Liabilities"), as further described below:

10.2.1   Seller shall be solely responsible for, and shall indemnify and defend and hold harmless Purchaser and its Indemnitees against, and hold them harmless from, any Environmental Costs related to or associated with (i) the Remediation of any Environmental Condition identified in the Environmental Information or (ii) correcting or addressing any Environmental Compliance Liability identified in the Environmental Information.

10.2.2   Seller shall be solely responsible for, and shall indemnify and defend and hold harmless Purchaser and its Indemnitees against, and hold them harmless from, any Environmental Costs related to or associated with (i) the Remediation of any Environmental Condition not identified in the Environmental Information or (ii) correcting or addressing any Environmental Compliance Liability not identified in the Environmental Information; provided however, that Seller shall have no indemnification or defense obligation for any such Environmental Cost unless and until the aggregate Environmental Costs for such Remediation or for correcting or addressing such Environmental Compliance Liability exceeds _____ Dollars ($_____) in the aggregate, in which event Seller shall be responsible   only   for   the   excess   over _____ ($_____).   Purchaser shall be liable for, indemnify and defend Seller from and against each and every of the foregoing Environmental Costs represented by the foregoing aggregate threshold amounts; and

10.2.3   Seller shall have no indemnification or defense obligation for any Environmental Cost described in Sections 10.2.1 or 10.2.2 that exceeds the Minimum Remediation Cost.

10.2.4   Seller shall be solely responsible for, and shall indemnify and defend and hold harmless Purchaser and its Indemnitees against, and hold them harmless from any Environmental

Liabilities related to or arising from claims for personal injury, property damage, and/or natural resource damages and arising out of or related to the operation of the Assets, the Real Property or the operations conducted thereon, or the conduct of Seller's business prior to Closing, regardless of whether or not such claim is made and regardless of whether the condition or activity on which such claim is based has been discovered or manifested itself prior to Closing; provided however that Seller shall have no indemnification or defense obligation for any such Environmental Liability unless and until the Environmental Costs for any one such claim exceeds _____ Dollars ($_____) or the aggregate Environmental Costs for all such claims exceeds _____ Dollars ($_____) in the aggregate. Purchaser shall be liable for, indemnify and defend Seller from and against each and every of the foregoing Environmental Costs represented by the foregoing threshold amounts.

10.2.5   Seller shall be solely responsible for, and shall indemnify and defend and hold harmless Purchaser and its Indemnitees against, and hold them harmless from, any Environmental Liabilities related to or associated with (i) real property interests in land and buildings previously owned or occupied by Seller, any prior owner or operator of the Assets or Seller's business, or any related party whose liability Seller has retained or assumed either contractually or by operation of law, and (ii) the off-site disposal of waste or materials, including but not limited to Hazardous Materials and Petroleum Products by Seller, any prior owner or operator of the Assets or Seller's business, or any related party whose liability Seller has retained or assumed either contractually or by operation of law, prior to Closing.

10.3   Seller's Environmental Representations and Warranties. Except as set forth in Schedules 10.3.1 to 10.3.__ attached hereto, Seller represents and warrants:

10.3.1   Seller has provided to Purchaser true and complete copies of all material assessments, reports, data, results of investigations or audits and other information that is in the possession of or reasonably available to Seller regarding environmental matters pertaining to any Environmental Liability related to the Assets and Seller's business or other compliance (or noncompliance) by Seller with respect to any Environmental Laws or to any other Person whose conduct Seller may be held responsible under any Environmental Law.

10.3.2   There is no pending or threatened Proceeding requesting information or alleging potential liability (including, without limitation, potential liability for investigation costs, cleanup costs, governmental response costs, natural resources damages, property damages, personal injuries or penalties) arising out of, based on or resulting from (i) the potential presence or Release into the Environment of any Hazardous Materials or Petroleum Products at any of the Real Property owned or operated by the Seller or (ii) circumstances forming the basis of any violation, or alleged violation, of any Environmental Law in connection with the Assets that in either case is pending or threatened against Seller, any prior owner or operator of the Assets or Seller's business, or any related party whose liability Seller has retained or assumed either contractually or by operation of law.

10.3.3   There are no and, to the Knowledge of the Seller, have not been any actions, activities, circumstances, conditions, events or incidents, including, without limitation, the Release, emission, discharge, presence or disposal of any Hazardous Materials or Petroleum Products at any location owned or operated by the Seller with respect to the Assets, or Seller's business that would reasonably be expected to result in Environmental Liability or form the basis of any Proceeding against Seller, any prior owner or operator of the Assets or any related party whose liability Seller has retained or assumed either contractually or by operation of law.

10.3.4   Without in any way limiting the generality of the foregoing, (i) all on-site and off-site locations where the Seller has stored, disposed or arranged for the disposal of Hazardous Materials or Petroleum Products are identified in Schedule 10.3.4; (ii) all above ground and underground storage tanks, and the capacity and contents of such tanks, presently or formerly located on any of the Real Property are identified in Schedule 10.3.4; (iii) except as set forth in Schedule 10.3.4, there is no, and have been no asbestos or asbestos-containing materials present at the Real Property; and (iv) except as set forth in Schedule 10.3.4, no PCBs or PCB-containing items are or have been used or stored at the Real Property.

10.3.5   Seller has not received any Environmental Notice with respect to the Assets, the Real Property or Seller's operation thereof. Neither the Real Property nor any property used in the operation of the Assets formerly owned, operated or leased by Seller is on any federal, state or local list of hazardous sites, such as the USEPA's Comprehensive Response, Compensation and Liability Information System List (CERCLIS).

10.3.6   No lien under any Environmental Law has been filed against any of the Assets, and Seller does not have Knowledge of any circumstances that may reasonably be expected to give rise to such lien. Seller is not subject to any Environmental Laws requiring (i) the performance of a site assessment for Hazardous Materials or Petroleum Products or an audit for any potential Environmental Liability, (ii) the removal of remediation of Hazardous Materials or Petroleum Products, (iii) the giving of notice to or receiving the approval of any Governmental Authority, (iv) the recording or delivery of any disclosure document or statement pertaining to Environmental matters, each of the foregoing by virtue of the contemplated transaction, or (v) corrective or other remedial measures pursuant to Environmental Laws.

10.3.7   There are no Environmental Liabilities pending or threatened (i) against Seller, or (ii) against any of the Assets.

10.4   Purchaser's Assumption of Environmental Liabilities. Except to the extent the Environmental Liability is a Seller's Retained Environmental Liability, Purchaser shall assume and be solely responsible for, and shall indemnify and defend and hold harmless Seller and its Indemnitees from and against all Environmental Liabilities relating to or arising out of the operation of the Assets, the Real Property or the operations conducted thereon, or the conduct of Purchaser's business following Closing (collectively, "Purchaser's Assumed Environmental Liabilities").

* * *

10.5   Disclaimer of Representations and Warranties. EXCEPT AS OTHERWISE PROVIDED HEREIN, SELLER MAKES NO REPRESENTATIONS WITH REGARD TO ENVIRONMENTAL LAWS OR ENVIRONMENTAL LIABILITIES RELATING TO OR ARISING OUT OF THE ASSETS OR THE OPERATION OF THE ASSETS, WHETHER EXISTING OR ASSERTED BEFORE OR AFTER THE CLOSING DATE, WHETHER BASED ON PAST, PRESENT OR FUTURE CONDITIONS OR EVENTS, WHETHER OR NOT KNOWN TO PURCHASER ON THE CLOSING DATE AND WHEREVER LOCATED. SELLER EXPRESSLY REPUDIATES ANY IMPLIED REPRESENTATION OR WARRANTY REGARDING ENVIRONMENTAL LAWS OR ENVIRONMENTAL LIABILITIES.

ARTICLE 11
TITLE MATTERS

* * *

ARTICLE 12
RISK OF LOSS

* * *

ARTICLE 13
DEFAULT; REMEDIES

13.1   Purchaser's Default. In the event that all of the conditions precedent to the Purchaser's obligation to close have been satisfied as provided herein but Purchaser fails to consummate this Agreement (a "Purchaser Default"), then Seller may, at its sole option, take any of the following courses of action:

13.1.1 terminate this Agreement and collect liquidated damages, as follows:

IF THE PURCHASER DEFAULTS IN ITS OBLIGATION TO PURCHASE THE ASSETS ON OR BEFORE THE OUTSIDE CLOSING DATE, THEN PURCHASER AGREES THAT THE SELLER WILL INCUR DAMAGES BY REASON OF SUCH DEFAULT WHICH ARE IMPRACTICAL AND DIFFICULT TO ASCERTAIN OR QUANTIFY. PURCHASER AND SELLER, IN A REASONABLE EFFORT TO ASCERTAIN THE SELLER'S DAMAGES, HAVE AGREED THAT AN AMOUNT EQUAL TO THE EARNEST MONEY DEPOSIT IN CASH SHALL BE DEEMED TO CONSTITUTE A REASONABLE ESTIMATE OF THE SELLER'S DAMAGES. ACCORDINGLY, IF PURCHASER DEFAULTS IN ITS OBLIGATION TO PURCHASE THE ASSETS, SELLER SHALL HAVE THE RIGHT TO RETAIN THE EARNEST MONEY DEPOSIT AS LIQUIDATED DAMAGES (the "LIQUIDATED DAMAGES AMOUNT").

or

13.1.2 enforce specific performance of this Agreement and the transaction provided for herein according to the terms hereof by all means available at law or in equity.

13.2   Election of Remedies. In the event Seller elects first to enforce this Agreement by specific performance and at any time during pursuit of enforcement elects not to pursue specific performance, then Seller shall be entitled to pursue its remedies under this Article 13 as if it had elected to do so as above set forth, and such subsequent election to pursue its courses of action under this Article 13 shall be deemed to be an election of remedies at that time and not before.

13.3   Seller's Default. In the event of non-performance, default or breach of this Agreement by Seller that results in the failure to consummate this Agreement (a "Seller Default"), then Purchaser may, at its sole option, as its exclusive remedy, enforce specific performance of this Agreement and the transaction provided for herein according to the terms hereof by all means available at law or in equity.

ARTICLE 14
CHANGES IN REPRESENTATIONS AND WARRANTIES

If either Seller or Purchaser discovers on or before the Closing that any representation or warranty made by it or the other party was or becomes not true and correct in any material respect, it shall so notify the other party in writing. The representations and warranties made in this Agreement shall be deemed to be modified by any matter contained in such notice. In the case of any such change in the representations or warranties by Seller, if the cumulative changes so made would adversely affect the fair market value of the Assets by 5% or more of the Cash Purchase Price, Purchaser may object thereto by written notice to Seller within ten days after receipt of the notice. If such objection notice is not given within the ten day period, or the cumulative changes do not have such adverse effect, then the Closing shall take place without prejudice to Purchaser's right to seek indemnification under Article 10. If such objection notice is timely given and the effect of the cumulative changes on the fair market value of the Assets exceeds such amount, and Seller determines that it cannot cure such adverse effect prior to the Closing by using commercially reasonable efforts, then the parties shall negotiate in good faith a reduction of the Purchase Price to fairly reflect the impact of the change on the fair market value of the Assets. In the event that the parties are unable to agree on a reduction of the Purchase Price prior to the Closing, then the parties agree to submit the matter to binding arbitration pursuant under Article 28 for resolution after the Closing.

ARTICLE 15
INDEMNIFICATION

15.1 Indemnification Liabilities. Seller and Purchaser ("Indemnitors") each shall indemnify and defend the other and the other's officers, directors, employees, subsidiaries (in each case including those of their Affiliates) and their successors and assigns ("Indemnitees") against, and shall hold them harmless from, each and every Liability which results from, arises out of or is attributable in any way to any of the following:

15.1.1   Liabilities expressly assumed or retained by the Indemnitor pursuant to this Agreement; provided, however, that any claim which is subject to indemnification pursuant to Article 10 shall not be subject to indemnification pursuant to this Article 15.

* * *

ARTICLE 16
RECORDS

* * *

ARTICLE 17
SELLER'S ACCESS AFTER CLOSING

17.1   Access to Assets. Purchaser shall afford Seller and its duly authorized representatives reasonable access to the Assets with respect to any legal, technical or operational matter relating to Seller's obligations under this Agreement or Seller's operations of the Assets before the Closing, including, without limitation, removal of any Excluded Assets from the Assets, provided that Seller gives Purchaser reasonable prior notice, and provided further that Seller's access does not unreasonably interfere with Purchaser's normal operations. The rights granted to Seller hereunder include the right to duplicate at Seller's expense the books and records included in the Assets related to the Excluded Assets, Seller's operation of the Assets, and to Seller's Employees. It is understood and agreed that Seller shall remove all Excluded Assets from the Assets prior to the Closing, or, if necessary, as soon as practicable thereafter.

17.2   Access to Employees. Purchaser shall, following Closing, cooperate with Seller for purposes of assisting Seller in its involvement in any claims, demands, suits, proceedings or actions arising in connection with any Seller's Retained Liabilities pursuant to Section 4.1, and for such purpose shall, at no cost to Seller other than reasonable out-of-pocket travel and similar costs incurred by Employees, provide Seller with access to the Employees and procure such Employees' time and assistance to allow Seller and its counsel to fully participate in and/or defend any such claims, demands, suits, proceedings or actions.

ARTICLE 18
PURCHASER'S INSPECTIONS

18.1 Access. At times mutually agreed by the parties, but in any event during normal operating hours, Purchaser may inspect the Real Property, personally or through agents, employees, contractors, or subcontractors, at Purchaser's expense.

18.2 Purchaser's Entry Shall be at Purchaser's Sole Risk. Each entry by Purchaser or its representatives onto the Real Property shall be at Purchaser's sole risk, and Purchaser shall indemnify and defend Seller and its Affiliates against, and shall hold them harmless from all Liabilities arising from or in connection with such entry. If Purchaser conducts any tests or causes any such tests to be conducted at any of the Assets, Purchaser agrees to restore each such Asset to the condition existing immediately prior to such tests. Purchaser shall promptly provide Seller, at no cost to Seller, with copies of the results or reports of any inspection, review or test conducted with regard to the Assets by, or at the request of, Purchaser. Notwithstanding anything contained herein to the contrary, Purchaser shall not perform any physical test of any Asset without first obtaining Seller's prior written consent, which consent shall not be unreasonably withheld.

18.3 NO RELIANCE. NOTWITHSTANDING THE FOREGOING, PURCHASER AGREES THAT IT CANNOT AND WILL NOT RELY ON ANY FACT, CONDITION, OR STATEMENT MADE DURING ITS ACTIVITIES CONDUCTED PURSUANT TO THIS SECTION UNLESS SUCH FACT, CONDITION, OR STATEMENT IS REDUCED TO WRITING AND INCORPORATED IN THIS AGREEMENT BY AMENDMENT.

ARTICLE 19
COVENANTS

19.1 General. Except as contemplated in, or provided for by, this Agreement or as required by any applicable law, from the Effective Date until the Closing Date, Seller agrees and covenants that (a) the business operations of the Assets shall be conducted only in the ordinary course of business, and (b) without limiting the foregoing, Seller shall not (i) sell, mortgage, or otherwise transfer or convey any material portion of the Assets, (ii) except in the ordinary course and consistent with past practice in the conduct of the business operations of the Assets, amend, modify, terminate or suspend any of such operations (except in immaterial respects); (iii) except in the ordinary course and consistent with past practice in the conduct of such operations, enter into any new Contract or waive or relinquish any right (except in immaterial respects) under any Contract, Permit or applicable law, or (iv) increase or agree to increase the compensation or benefits of any employee.

19.2   Operation Pending Closing. Seller will use reasonable commercial efforts to maintain the current operations on, and the repair and maintenance of, the Real Property between the Effective Date and the Closing Date.

19.3   Assistance Regarding Transfers of Rights. Seller shall provide such assistance as Purchaser may reasonably request in Purchaser's efforts to obtain consents to the assignment of any Contracts and Permits which Seller is unable to obtain prior to the Closing; provided that Seller shall have no liability to Purchaser for the failure to obtain such agreements or consents.

ARTICLE 20
PUBLICITY; CONFIDENTIALITY

20.1   Public Statements. At no time prior to the Closing will either party make any press release or other public statement concerning this Agreement or the transactions contemplated hereby, or disclose the terms hereof or thereof to any third party, except with the other party's prior consent, or as required by law or regulation, or in connection with any Permit application in furtherance of this Agreement.

20.2   Confidentiality. The parties acknowledge that they are and continue to be bound by the terms of the Confidentiality Agreement dated [Insert Date] between Seller and Purchaser. In addition, Seller and Purchaser agree that they will, unless otherwise mutually agreed to in writing, keep confidential and not disclose to a third party any of the terms or provisions of this Agreement for a period of two years after the Closing Date, except for disclosure of information that:

20.2.1 is or becomes publicly available by other than unauthorized disclosure;

20.2.2 is made pursuant to the requirement or request of a Governmental Authority of competent jurisdiction to the extent such disclosure is required by a valid law or Order, and sufficient notice is given by the disclosing party to the other party to permit the other party to seek an appropriate protective order or exemption from such requirement or request, if it so desires. If such protective order or other remedy is not obtained, or if the other party waives compliance with the provisions of this Section 20.2 for this purpose, the disclosing party shall furnish only that portion of the information that is legally required and will exercise commercially reasonable efforts to obtain reliable assurance that confidential treatment will be accorded the information by the Governmental Authority.

ARTICLE 21
EMPLOYEES AND BENEFITS

* * *

ARTICLE 22
TRANSFER OF PERMITS AND
ASSIGNMENT OF CONTRACTS

22.1 Transfer of Permits. It shall be Purchaser's responsibility to obtain the issuance or transfer of all environmental and other Permits; provided, however, that Seller shall cooperate with any efforts of Purchaser to complete the actions required in connection with transferring or obtaining the issuance of all such Permits. All Permits, including Environmental Permits, currently held by Seller and related to or arising out the Assets, the Real Property, or Seller's operations thereon are identified on Schedule _____.

22.2   Delays in Transfer of Permits or Assignment of Contracts. If there are prohibitions against, or conditions to, the conveyance of any Contracts or Permits, without the prior written consent of third parties, then any provision contained in this Agreement to the contrary withstanding, the transfer of title to, or assignment of, such Contracts or Permits pursuant to this Agreement shall not become effective unless and until such consent requirement is satisfied, waived or no longer applies. When and if such consent requirement is so satisfied, waived or no longer applies, to the extent permitted by applicable law, the assignment of such Contracts or Permits shall become effective automatically as of the Closing Date, without further action on the part of Seller or Purchaser and without payment of further consideration. Each of Seller and Purchaser agrees to use its commercially reasonable efforts to obtain satisfaction of any consent requirement on a timely basis; provided that Seller shall not be obligated to expend any moneys in connection with satisfying any such consent requirement. To the extent that any consent requirement for any Contracts or Permits cannot be obtained, Seller will, upon request of Purchaser, use its commercially reasonable efforts (without infringing upon the legal rights of any outside party or violating any applicable law) to provide Purchaser with the benefits of such Contracts or Permits or equivalent contracts or permits effective as of the Closing Date, provided Purchaser assumes all responsibilities and liabilities under any such Contracts or Permits with respect to the period after the Closing.

ARTICLE 23
CERTAIN TAX MATTERS

* * *

ARTICLE 24
BULK SALES

* * *

ARTICLE 25
ASSIGNMENT

25.1   Limitation on Assignment. Subject to Section 25.2 hereof, this Agreement may not be assigned by either party, in whole or in part without the prior written consent of the other party, which consent shall not be unreasonably withheld. Notwithstanding the foregoing, Purchaser may not assign the benefit of Seller's representations and warranties without Seller's prior written consent, which consent Seller may grant or withhold in its sole discretion.

25.2   Assignability to Affiliates. Seller and Purchaser may each assign this Agreement, in whole or in part, to one or more of their respective Affiliates, upon prior notice to the non-assigning party; provided, that the non-assigning party may require as a condition of such assignment that the assigning party reasonably demonstrate and/or assure the assignee's financial and technical capability to perform its proposed obligations hereunder. Any attempted assignment of this Agreement in violation of this Article 25 shall be null and void.

25.3   Scope of Permitted Assignments. This Agreement shall inure to the benefit of the parties and their respective heirs, legal representatives, successors and permitted assigns. This Agreement shall be binding upon the parties and their respective heirs, legal representatives, successors and assigns, except that any such assignment shall not relieve the assigning party of its obligations hereunder. This Agreement is not intended to, and does not create, any rights in any third parties.

ARTICLE 26
LIKE-KIND EXCHANGE

* * *

ARTICLE 27
PAYMENTS

* * *

ARTICLE 28
ARBITRATION

28.1   Negotiation of Disputes and Disagreements. In the event of any controversy or claim ("Claim"), whether based on contract, tort, statute or other legal or equitable theory (including but not limited to any claim of fraud, misrepresentation or fraudulent inducement or any question of validity or effect of this Agreement including this section) arising out of or related to this Agreement (including any amendments or extensions and any documents delivered or to be delivered pursuant hereto), or the breach or termination thereof, which the parties have been unable to settle or agree upon within a period of 30 days after the dispute or disagreement arises, each party shall nominate a senior officer of its management to meet at a mutually agreed time and place not later than 45 days after the dispute or disagreement has arisen to attempt to resolve such dispute or disagreement. Should a resolution of such dispute or disagreement not be obtained within 15 days after nomination of senior officers for such purpose, either party may then, by notice to the other, submit the dispute to arbitration in accordance with the provisions of Section 28.2.

* * *

ARTICLE 29
AMENDMENTS

This Agreement cannot be altered, amended, changed or modified in any respect or particular unless each such alteration, amendment, change or modification shall have been agreed to by each of the parties and reduced to writing in its entirety and signed and delivered by each party.

ARTICLE 30
SURVIVAL OF REPRESENTATIONS AND WARRANTIES

All representations and warranties of the parties contained in this Agreement shall survive for a period of one year following the Closing Date. No claim, for indemnity or otherwise, with respect to any representation or warranty shall be brought unless written notice of such claim is given to the party making such representation or warranty on or before the end of such survival period. It is the parties' intent that such surviving representations and warranties shall not merge in the Closing or in the conveyancing instruments delivered at the Closing.

ARTICLE 31
POST-CLOSING FINANCIAL STATEMENTS

* * *

ARTICLE 32
GENERAL; ADDITIONAL COVENANTS

32.1   Entire Agreement. This Agreement, including all of the Attachments, Exhibits and Schedules, constitutes the entire understanding between the parties with respect to the subject matter contained herein and supersedes any prior understandings, negotiations or agreements, whether written or oral, between them respecting such subject matter. There are no representations and warranties except as expressly set forth in this Agreement.

32.2   Construction. Words of any gender used in this Agreement shall be construed to include any other gender, and words in the singular number shall include the plural, and vice versa, unless the context requires otherwise. The words "include" and "including" are to be construed without limitation.

32.3   Captions. The captions used in connection with the Articles and Sections of this Agreement are for convenience only and shall not be deemed to enlarge, limit or otherwise modify the meaning or interpretation of the language of this Agreement. Any references to "Articles," "Sections," "Attachments," "Exhibits," and Schedules" are to Articles, Sections, Attachments, Exhibits, and Schedules of this Agreement.

32.4   Attachments, Exhibits and Schedules. Each Attachment, Exhibit, and Schedule referred to herein is incorporated into this Agreement by such reference; provided that to the extent of any conflict or inconsistency between any of the Attachments, Exhibits or Schedules and this Agreement, this Agreement will prevail.

32.5   Severability. If any provision of this Agreement is held to be illegal, invalid, or unenforceable under any present or future laws, such provision shall be fully severable; this Agreement shall be construed and enforced as if such illegal, invalid or unenforceable provision had never comprised a part of this Agreement; and the remaining provisions of this Agreement shall remain in full force and effect, unaffected by the illegal, invalid or unenforceable provision or by its severance from this Agreement. In lieu of such illegal, invalid, or unenforceable provision, there shall be added automatically as a part of this Agreement a provision as similar in terms to such illegal, invalid or unenforceable provision as may be possible and be legal, valid and enforceable.

32.6   No Waiver. The failure of any party to insist upon strict performance of any of the terms or conditions of this Agreement will not constitute a waiver of any of its rights hereunder.

32.7   Governing Law; Choice of Forum. This Agreement shall be governed by and construed in accordance with the laws of the State of _____ applicable to agreements made and to be performed entirely in the State of _____. Notwithstanding the foregoing sentence, matters relating to real estate law and local and state environmental law shall be construed and enforced in accordance with the laws of the States of _____, _____, and _____, as applicable. The parties irrevocably submit to the exclusive jurisdiction of the United States District Court for the Southern District of _____ for the purposes of this Agreement, except for those matters over which that Court does not have subject matter jurisdiction.

32.8   Notices. All notices or other communications required hereunder shall be in writing, shall be addressed as specified below and shall be deemed to have been given: (a) at the time of delivery when delivered personally; (b) upon receipt when sent by Federal Express, or similar overnight service, or (c) upon completion of successful transmission when sent by facsimile (unless transmission is completed outside recipient's normal working hours, in which case such notice shall be deemed given at the start of recipient's next business day), immediately followed by U.S. posting, postage prepaid.

Seller:

_____

_____

_____

Facsimile:
Phone:

Purchaser:

_____

_____

_____

Facsimile:
Phone:

Either Party may change its address or facsimile number by providing written notice to the other at least ten days prior to the effective date of such change.

32.9   Commercially Reasonable Efforts; Time of Essence. Except as otherwise specifically provided herein, Purchaser and Seller shall each use commercially reasonable efforts to satisfy the conditions to Closing and otherwise consummate the transactions contemplated by this Agreement as promptly as practical.

* * *

32.10   Counterparts. This Agreement may be executed in any number of counterparts and any party may execute any such counterpart, each of which when executed by both parties and delivered shall be deemed to be an original. It shall not be necessary in making proof of this Agreement or any counterparts hereof to produce or account for any of the other counterparts.

32.11   Extensions of Time; Waiver. It is agreed that any party to this Agreement may extend time for performance by any other party or waive the performance of any obligation of any other party or waive any inaccuracies in the representations and warranties of any other party, but any such waiver shall be in writing, and shall not constitute or be construed as a waiver of any other obligation, condition, representation or warranty under this Agreement.

32.12   Further Assurances. Purchaser and Seller shall take such additional action, and shall cooperate with one another, as may be reasonably necessary to effectuate the terms of this Agreement and any agreement or instrument delivered pursuant to this Agreement.

32.13   No Presumption Against Drafter. Purchaser and Seller have each fully participated in the negotiation and drafting of this Agreement. If an ambiguity, question of intent or question of interpretation arises, this Agreement must be construed as if drafted jointly, and there must not be any presumption, inference or conclusion drawn against either party by virtue of the fact that its representative has authored this Agreement or any of its terms.

32.14   Expenses. Except as otherwise specifically provided in this Agreement, each party to this Agreement shall bear its own expenses in connection with this Agreement and the transactions contemplated hereby, including, without limitation, attorneys' fees and expenses.

[Signature page follows.]

IN WITNESS WHEREOF, the parties have executed this Agreement on the day and year first written above.

[Seller]

[_____]

By: _____

Title: _____

[Purchaser]

[_____]

By: _____

Title: _____

EXHIBITS

Exhibit A   Form of Assignment and Assumption of Permits and Contracts

Exhibit B   Form of Brand License Agreement

Exhibit C   Transition Services Agreement

Exhibit D   Form of Supply Agreement

Exhibit E   Forms of Limited Warranty Deed

Exhibit F   Form of Bill of Sale

Exhibit G   Form of Assignment and Assumption of Lease Agreement

Exhibit H   Title Commitments

Courtesy of Pamela K. Elkow, Robinson & Cole LLP

APPENDIX H

INDEMNIFICATION AND RELEASE AGREEMENT

THIS INDEMNIFICATION AND RELEASE AGREEMENT ("Indemnification Agreement") is made effective as of this _____ day of _____, by and between Seller, and Buyer.

Recitals

A.   Buyer and Seller are parties to that certain Amended and Restated Purchase and Sale Agreement dated _____ (the "Purchase Agreement") related to the sale by Seller to Buyer of the properties described in the Purchase Agreement collectively as the Property.

B.   Pursuant to the terms of the Purchase Agreement, Buyer and Seller enter into this Indemnification Agreement. All capitalized terms not otherwise defined herein shall have the meaning given them in the Purchase Agreement.

Agreement

NOW, THEREFORE, in consideration of the foregoing recitals, the terms and conditions of this Indemnification Agreement and other consideration the sufficiency of which is hereby acknowledged, Buyer and Seller agree as follows:

1. Definition of Terms. The following capitalized terms shall have the following meanings for purposes of this Indemnification Agreement:

> 1.1. The term "Hazardous Material" means any substance, material or waste, or combination thereof, the presence of which is regulated under any federal, state or local laws, ordinances or regulations, or under any existing or future reported decision of a state, local or federal court, including, but not limited to: (i) substances, materials and wastes that are now or become listed in the United States Department of Transportation Hazardous Materials Table (49 CFR 172.101) or by the Environmental

Protection Agency (40 CFR Part 302), and amendments thereto, as hazardous substances; (ii) substances, materials and wastes designated as a "hazardous substance" pursuant to Section 311 of the Clean Water Act, 33 U.S.C. § 1251 et seq. (33 U.S.C. § 1321) or listed pursuant to Section 307 of the Clean Water Act (33 U.S.C. § 1317); (iii) substances, materials and wastes defined as a "hazardous waste" pursuant to Section 1004 of the Resource Conservation and Recovery Act, 42 U.S.C. § 6903); (iv) substances, materials and wastes defined as a "hazardous substance" pursuant to Section 101 of the Comprehensive Environmental Response, Compensation, and Liability Act, 42 U.S.C. § 9601, et seq. (42 U.S.C. § 9601); (v) substances, materials and wastes defined as a "hazardous substance," "hazardous waste" or "dangerous waste" under the laws of the State; (vi) petroleum and petroleum products; (vii) asbestos; (viii) poly-chlorinated biphenyls; and (ix) any substances, materials and wastes that are or become defined as a toxic or hazardous substance, material, pollutant or contaminant under any existing or future federal, state or local laws, ordinances or regulations, or under any existing or future reported decision of a state, local or federal court, or (x) any substances, materials and wastes, the presence of which requires or may require investigation or remediation under any existing or future statutory or common law theory, all as amended, replaced, or succeeded.

1.2. The term "Environmental Contamination" means the presence, disposal or release of any Hazardous Material at, on, above, under, within, or from the Property or any portion thereof, whether past, present or future, including without limitation the presence or release of Hazardous Material in or into the air, soil, groundwater, or surface water at, on, above, under, within or from the Property, or any portion thereof, and Hazardous Material that is transported or migrates from the Property to other property. Without limiting the generality of the foregoing, the term Environmental Contamination shall include, without limitation, any and all Hazardous Material that is present at the Property or in the air, soil, groundwater, or surface water at, on, above, under, or within the Property, or any portion thereof, before, on, or after the date of this Agreement and that migrates, flows, percolates, diffuses, or in any way moves onto, into, or under the air, soil, groundwater or surface water at, on, above, under, or within other property, or any portion thereof, before, on, or after the date of this Agreement, irrespective of whether such Environmental Contamination shall be present or suspected to be present on or at the Property or in the air, soil, groundwater, or surface water at, on, about, above, under, or within the Property or other property, or any portion thereof, as a result of any release, discharge, disposal, dumping, spilling, or leaking (accidental or otherwise) onto the Property, or any portion thereof, occurring before, on, or after the date of this Agreement or caused by any person or entity.

2. Indemnification. Buyer shall be responsible for and shall indemnify, protect, defend and hold harmless Seller and Seller's affiliates, directors, officers, shareholders, employees, trustees, beneficiaries, agents, attorneys, representatives and contractors, and their successors and assigns (collectively with Seller, the "Seller Parties"), from and against any and all claims (including without limitation claims by: (i) any third-party alleging claims for contribution, personal injury or real or personal property damage or by any other third-party or parties, including adjacent or nonadjacent property owners; (ii) any governmental authority (including, but not limited to, the State or the United States Environmental Protection Agency, and any successor agencies)) or actions (including without limitation any citation, directive, order or investigation), administrative proceedings (including without limitation both formal and informal proceedings), judgments, damages, punitive damages, penalties, fines (including without limitation reasonable attorneys' fees and expenses, consultant fees, and expert fees), liabilities (including without limitation sums paid in settlements of claims), damages or losses, together with all other costs and expenses of any kind or nature (including without limitation the cost of any environmental investigation or remediation required under any federal, state or local laws, ordinances or regulations, or under any existing or future reported decision of a state, local or federal court (collectively, the "Costs") that arise directly or indirectly from, out of, or in connection with any actual, alleged or suspected Environmental Contamination (the "Environmental Indemnification").

2.1. Without limiting the generality of the foregoing, the Environmental Indemnification shall specifically apply to and include: Costs arising under existing or future federal, state or local laws, ordinances or regulations, or under any existing or future reported decision of a state, local or federal court, all as amended, replaced or succeeded; Costs related to any substances, materials and wastes imposing liability for cleanup or response costs or expenses on any person or entity under any existing or future statutory or common law theory, all as amended replaced or succeeded; Costs for releases, seepages, migrations, discharges or spills of any Hazardous Material on or around the Property; Costs for claims brought by or on behalf of any past or present tenants, occupants, or other users of the Property; Costs relating to past, present or future actual, alleged or suspected Environmental Contamination; Costs arising from Seller's failure to perform any environmental operations or maintenance required by any federal, state or other governmental entity or to comply with any permit relating to Environmental Contamination; Costs for any investigatory, assessment, cleanup, containment, remedial, removal, oversight or restoration work required or performed by any federal, state, or local governmental agency or political subdivision or performed by any nongovernmental entity or person because of actual, alleged or suspected Environmental Contamination; and any claims of third parties for contribution, loss or damage due to such actual, alleged or suspected Environmental Contamination. In the event Seller shall suffer or incur any such Costs, Buyer shall pay to Seller the total of all such Costs suffered or incurred by Seller upon written demand therefore by Seller.

2.2. Notwithstanding the foregoing, the Environmental Indemnification shall not apply to any of the following claims (collectively "Excluded Claims"): (i) the presence of Hazardous Material on property other than the Property (off-site), but only to the extent such Hazardous Material did not migrate off-site from the Property; (ii) worker health claims (including but not limited to claims or damages for workers' compensation, personal injury, disease or death) arising or resulting from pre-Closing injury or exposure; (iii) third party personal injury claims of any nature arising or resulting from pre-Closing injury or exposure; and (iv) all liabilities or obligations, including all liabilities or obligations related to Hazardous Material or Environmental Contamination, of Seller that, under the Bankruptcy Code, are discharged pursuant to confirmation by the Bankruptcy Court of a plan of reorganization in Seller's Chapter 11 case. Seller agrees to seek discharge of environmental liabilities to the maximum extent permitted under the Bankruptcy Code, including an obligation to appeal any Bankruptcy Court order that does not provide such discharge. Notwithstanding the foregoing and without limiting any other provisions in this Agreement, the following claims shall not be Excluded Claims: (i) claims arising from activities or exposure on the Property after Closing; and/or (ii) claims arising from, relating to or that are triggered by Hazardous Material disturbed or altered by Buyer or its successors or assigns.

2.3. Buyer shall indemnify and hold the Seller Parties harmless from and against any and all obligations, liabilities, losses, damages, demands and costs to the extent incurred by the Seller Parties as a result of any statements or representations made by Buyer in the Purchase Agreement.

3. Assignment and Assumption of Permits and Contracts. Seller hereby transfers and assigns to Buyer, subject to approval of such transfer and assignment by the parties thereto if required, all of Seller's right, title and interest in and to the permits, licenses, approvals, contracts, decrees and orders ("Permits and Contracts") listed in Exhibit A, which Exhibit shall be completed and attached hereto on or before the Closing Date, and Buyer hereby assumes and agrees to perform, discharge, fulfill and observe all of the obligations, terms, covenants, provisions and conditions under the Permits and Contracts. Buyer also agrees to execute all applicable documents and cooperate with Seller to take all other action necessary to effect the transfer, assignment and assumption of Permits and Contracts.

4. Release. Buyer, for itself and its affiliates, directors, officers, shareholders, members, managers, employees, trustees, beneficiaries, agents, attorneys, representatives and contractors, and their successors and assigns, does hereby completely and irrevocably release and forever discharge the

Seller Parties and their successors and assigns from any and all past, current, future and contingent Costs, excepting only the Excluded Claims, of any and every kind and nature, whether currently known or unknown including without limitation, any claims sounding in tort, negligence, contract, environmental or statutory liability or otherwise, relating to (i) any statements or representations of the Seller Parties made in the Purchase Agreement (provided that the release in this subsection (i) shall be of no force or effect in the event any Seller Party disclaims its statements in the Purchase Agreement) or (ii) actual, alleged or suspected Environmental Contamination, including without limitation, Costs resulting from or by reason of any conduct, cause or course of action whatsoever which has been done or omitted by Seller. The foregoing release includes all known, unknown, unforeseen, unanticipated and unexpected Costs and the consequences thereof, as well as any now in existence.

5. Performance of Buyer Obligations. Performance of the Buyer's obligation to indemnify Seller shall be in conformance with all applicable federal, state and local laws, regulations, judicial orders, and all agreements affecting the Property. In the event Buyer shall fail to timely commence, cause to be commenced, or fail to diligently prosecute to completion its obligations under this Agreement, Seller may, but shall not be required to, cause such obligations to be performed for the account of Buyer, and all Costs thereof, or incurred in connection therewith, shall be covered as part of the Environmental Indemnification and paid by Buyer. All such Costs shall be due and payable by Buyer upon demand therefore by Seller.

6. Request for Information. Buyer shall timely respond to Seller's reasonable requests for information regarding its obligations under this Agreement.

7. Miscellaneous.

> **7.1. Subrogation of Rights.** If Buyer fails to perform its obligations under this Indemnification Agreement, Seller shall be subrogated to any rights Buyer may have against any present, future or former owners, tenants, occupants, or other users of the Property (or any portion thereof), relating to the matters covered by this Indemnification Agreement.

7.2. Independent Obligations; Survival. The obligations of Buyer under this Indemnification Agreement shall survive the Closing of the Purchase Agreement. The obligations of Buyer under this Indemnification Agreement are separate and distinct from the obligations of Buyer under the Purchase Agreement and other documents referenced therein and executed in connection therewith. This Indemnification Agreement may be enforced by Seller without regard to any other rights and remedies Seller may have against Buyer under the Purchase Agreement and other documents referenced therein and executed in connection therewith and without regard to any limitations on Seller's recourse as may be provided in the Purchase Agreement and other documents referenced therein and executed in connection therewith.

7.3. Default Interest. Any Costs and other payments required to be paid by Buyer to Seller under this Indemnification Agreement that are not paid on demand therefore shall thereupon be considered delinquent. In addition to all other rights and remedies of Seller against Buyer as provided herein, or under applicable law, Buyer shall pay to Seller, immediately upon demand therefor, interest on any such payments that are or have become delinquent at a rate that is the lesser of nine percent (9%) or the highest rate allowed under applicable laws. The interest shall be paid by Buyer from the date such payment becomes delinquent through and including the date of payment of such delinquent sums.

7.4. Time. Time is of the essence of every provision contained in this Indemnification Agreement. If the time for performance of any obligation hereunder shall fall on a Saturday, Sunday or holiday (national or in the states in which the Properties are located), the time for performance shall be extended to the next day which is not a Saturday, Sunday or holiday.

7.5. Further Assurances. Each of the parties shall execute and deliver any and all additional papers, documents and other assurances, and shall do any and all acts and things reasonably necessary in connection with the performance of its obligations hereunder in good faith to carry out the intent of the parties herein so long as such are consistent with the terms of this Indemnification Agreement and impose no greater duties on the party.

7.6. Attorneys' Fees. In the event suit or action is instituted to interpret or enforce the terms of this Indemnification Agreement, or in connection with any arbitration or mediation of any dispute, the prevailing party shall be entitled to recover from the other party (as between Seller and Buyer) such sum as the court, arbitrator or mediator may adjudge reasonable as such party's costs and attorney's fees, including such costs and fees as are incurred in any trial, on any appeal, in any bankruptcy proceeding (including the adjudication of issues peculiar to bankruptcy law) and in any petition for review.

7.7. Construction. Buyer and Seller each acknowledge that: (a) they have been represented by independent counsel in connection with this Indemnification Agreement; (b) they have executed this Indemnification Agreement with the advice of such counsel; and (c) this Indemnification Agreement is the result of negotiations between Seller and Buyer and the advice and assistance of their respective counsel. Any uncertainty or ambiguity in this Indemnification Agreement shall not be construed against the party that drafted the agreement because that party's counsel prepared this Indemnification Agreement. The section headings contained in this Indemnification Agreement are for convenience only and shall in no way enlarge or limit the scope or meaning of the various and several sections hereof. In the event of a conflict in the terms and conditions of this Indemnification Agreement and the Purchase Agreement, the terms and conditions of this Indemnification Agreement shall govern and control.

7.8. No Joint Venture; Benefit. This Indemnification Agreement is for the benefit of the parties thereto, and except for the Seller Parties and their successors and assigns, no other person or entity will be entitled to rely on this Indemnification Agreement, receive any benefit from it or enforce any provisions of it against Buyer or

Seller. Neither this Indemnification Agreement nor anything contained in this Indemnification Agreement shall create, or be deemed to create, a partnership, joint venture or other joint or equity type agreement between Buyer and Seller.

7.9. Governing Law. This Indemnification Agreement shall be construed and interpreted in accordance with and shall be governed and enforced in all respects according to the laws of the State without regard to conflict of law principles.

7.10. Counterparts. This Indemnification Agreement may be executed in one or more counterparts. All counterparts so executed shall constitute one contract, binding on all parties, even though all parties are not signatory to the same counterpart.

7.11. No Waiver. No covenant, term or condition of this Indemnification Agreement, other than as expressly set forth herein, shall be deemed to have been waived by any party hereto unless such waiver is in writing and executed by such party.

7.12. Successors and Assigns. Buyer shall not assign this Indemnification Agreement without Seller's prior written consent, which consent Seller may withhold in its sole discretion. Subject to the previous sentence, this Indemnification Agreement shall inure to the benefit of and be binding upon and enforceable against the parties hereto and their respective successors and assigns. No assignment hereunder, whether consented to or not, shall be deemed to relieve Buyer from any liability or obligation under this Indemnification Agreement. The giving of consent to any assignment hereunder shall not release Buyer from obtaining consent to any other assignment hereunder.

7.13. Notices. All notices, demands, deliveries and communications under this Indemnification Agreement shall be in writing and shall be sent by (i) first class, registered or certified U.S. mail, postage prepaid, return receipt requested, (ii) nationally recognized overnight carrier, (iii) facsimile (provided the original notice is also sent via a nationally recognized overnight carrier on the next business day and received within three business days from deposit with the carrier), or (iv) personal delivery. All notices shall be deemed to have been given: three (3) business days following deposit of first class, registered or certified U.S. mail, one (1) business day following deposit with a nationally recognized overnight carrier, or upon receipt by facsimile or personal delivery, whichever occurs first. All notices shall be addressed to the party at the address below or to such other address as either party may designate by notice pursuant to this Section:

To Seller:

_____

_____

_____

To Buyer:

_____

_____

_____

7.14. Entire Agreement. This Indemnification Agreement contains the entire agreement of the parties with respect to the subject matter hereof and supersedes any and all other written or oral understanding or agreement with regard to the subject matter hereof. No amendment, change or modification of this Indemnification Agreement shall be valid, unless in writing and signed by Buyer and Seller.

7.15. Authority. Buyer represents and warrants that it has the power and authority to enter into this Indemnification Agreement and consummate the transactions contemplated herein, and the signatory hereto is duly authorized to execute and deliver this Indemnification Agreement and perform all of such party's obligations hereunder. By executing and delivering this Indemnification Agreement, Buyer represents and warrants that no further approval, authorization, or order of (or filing with) any court is required in connection with such party's execution and delivery of this Indemnification Agreement and no consent, approval, or order of any other body, entity or third party is required in connection with such party's execution and delivery of this Indemnification Agreement. Further, Buyer acknowledges that it has voluntarily executed this Indemnification Agreement upon its own behalf, with opportunity for advice of counsel of its own choosing, for the purpose of making a full and final compromise, adjustment and settlement of all claims and matters described above, and for the express purpose of forever precluding any controversy, litigation or expense relating thereto or arising therefrom. Buyer WARRANTS THAT IT HAS COMPLETELY READ THIS INDEMNIFICATION, AND SPECIFICALLY THE RELEASE, ASSUMPTION OF RISK AND LIABILITIES AND INDEMNIFICATION PROVISIONS, AND FULLY UNDERSTANDS IT.

[End of text. Signatures appear on next page.]

IN WITNESS WHEREOF, Seller and Buyer have executed this Indemnification Agreement as of the day and year first written above.

BUYER:

By: _____

Its: _____

Date: _____

SELLER:

By: _____

Name: _____

Title: _____

Courtesy of David H. Quigley, Akin Gump Strauss Hauer & Feld LLP

APPENDIX I

ENVIRONMENTAL CONTRACTUAL PROVISIONS FOR REAL ESTATE TRANSACTION

I. DEFINITIONS

A.   "Environmental Claim" means any investigation, notice, violation, demand, allegation, action, suit, injunction, judgment, order, consent decree, penalty, fine, lien, proceeding, or claim (whether administrative, judicial, quasi-judicial or private in nature) arising (a) pursuant to or in connection with any actual or alleged violation of any Environmental Law, or (b) in connection with any Hazardous Material, from any abatement, removal, remedial, corrective, or other response action in connection with a Hazardous Material, Environmental Law, or from any actual or alleged damage, injury, threat, or harm to health, safety, natural resources, or the environment, regardless of whether such matter is now known or unknown, or how or when such matter occurred or is discovered.

B.   "Environmental Law" means (a) any present or future federal, state or local law or regulation relating to the handling, use, control, management, treatment, storage, disposal, release or threat of release of any Hazardous Material, including without limitation, the federal Comprehensive Environmental Response, Compensation, and Liability Act ("CERCLA"), 42 U.S.C. §§9601 et seq., the federal Resource Conservation and Recovery Act ("RCRA"), 42 U.S.C. §§ 6901 et seq., the federal Water Pollution Control Act ("CWA"), 33 U.S.C. §§1251 et seq., the federal Clean Air Act ("CAA"), 42 U.S.C. §§ 7401 et seq., the Toxic Substances Control Act ("TSCA"), 7 U.S.C. §§ 136 et seq., the Safe Drinking Water Act ("SDWA"), 42 U.S.C. §§ 300f et seq., the Occupation Safety and Health Act of 1970 (the "OSH Act"), 29 U.S.C. §§ 651 et seq., and any similar state or local laws, rules or regulations, and (b) any and all requirements arising under applicable present and future federal, state or local laws, statutes, rules, ordinances, codes, orders, licenses, permits, approvals, plans, authorizations, concessions, or the like, and all applicable judicial, administrative, and regulatory decrees, judgments, and orders, relating to the protection of human health or the environment, including without limitation: (i) any and all requirements pertaining to reporting, licensing, authorizing, approving, permitting, investigating, and remediating emissions, discharges, releases, or threat of releases of any Hazardous Materials into the indoor or outdoor air, surface water, groundwater, or land, or otherwise into the environment, or relating to the manufacture, operation, processing, distribution, use, treatment, storage, disposal, transport, handling or management of any Hazardous Material; and (ii) any and all requirements pertaining to the protection of the health and safety of employees or the public and/or the environment.

C.   "Hazardous Material" means any substance or material: (a) the presence of which requires investigation or remediation under any Environmental Law, (b) which is or becomes regulated by any federal, state or local governmental authority, including without limitation, any substance or waste material which is defined or listed as a "hazardous waste," "extremely hazardous waste," "restricted hazardous waste," "industrial waste," "hazardous substance," "solid waste," "hazardous material," "pollutant" or "contaminant" under any Environmental Law; (c) which contains gasoline, diesel fuel or other petroleum hydrocarbons or a petroleum derivative; (d) which contains polychlorinated biphenyls ("PCBs"), asbestos or urea formaldehyde; (e) which is explosive, corrosive, flammable, infectious, radioactive or toxic; or (f) which poses an unreasonable risk of injury to human health or the environment.

D.   "Release" shall mean any spilling, leaking, seeping, pumping, pouring, emitting, emptying, discharging, injecting, escaping, leaching, dumping, placement, burying or disposing in or upon or under any land or water or air, or otherwise into the indoor or outdoor environment, including, without limitation, the abandonment or discarding of barrels, drums, containers, tanks, and other receptacles containing or previously containing any Hazardous Material.

E.   "Property" shall mean [_____].

II.   REPRESENTATIONS AND WARRANTIES OF SELLER

Except as set forth in Schedule [_____] (the "Scheduled Conditions"), Seller represents and warrants as of the closing date that:

A.   the Seller and the Property comply with all applicable Environmental Laws;

B.   the Seller has obtained all permits, registrations, licenses, approvals and authorizations (collectively, "Permits") required for the Property by any applicable Environmental Law, and is currently in compliance, and has been in compliance at all times in the past, with all of the terms, conditions and requirements of such Permits, a complete list of which is set forth in Schedule __, and there are no pending or threatened proceedings seeking to revoke, cancel or suspend any such Permit;

C.   neither the Seller and nor any other person has caused, and the Property is not adversely affected by, any Release, threatened Release, or disposal of any Hazardous Material at the Property or originating or emanating from any other property;

D.   there are no Hazardous Materials on, in or under the Property, whether contained in barrels, tanks, equipment (moveable or fixed) or other containers, deposited or located in land, waters, sumps or in any other part of the site, incorporated into any structure on the site, or otherwise existing thereon;

E.   the Property does not contain and has not contained any: (a) underground storage tank, (b) asbestos-containing building material, (c) any landfills or dumps, (d) hazardous waste management facility as defined pursuant to RCRA or any comparable state law, or (e) site designated for any removal or cleanup activity pursuant to CERCLA or any comparable state law;

F.   neither the Seller nor any other person has used any Hazardous Materials, nor conducted any activities involving the use, handling, treatment, storage, transportation or disposal of any Hazardous Material, at the Property, including but not limited to activities involving any sort of: (i) manufacturing, processing or refining; (ii) cleaning or degreasing of equipment, machinery, part or component; (iii) sale, storage or transport of Hazardous Materials, (iv) services which utilize Hazardous Materials; (v) drilling, mining or production of oil, gas, minerals or other naturally occurring products; or (vi) agricultural activities involving the use and storage of fertilizers or pesticides;

G.   the Seller has no pending or contingent liability, and has received no notice, relating to any Environmental Claim concerning the Property, and there are no conditions or occurrences at the Property which could form the basis for an Environmental Claim against the Seller or the Property;

H.   the Seller has not submitted to any governmental agency or other person any notice, and is not required to give any such notice, regarding any Release on, under, or from the Property;

I.   the Property is not subject to, and the Seller has no knowledge of, any restriction on the ownership, occupancy, use, or transferability of the Property in connection with any (a) Environmental Law or (b) Release, threatened Release, or disposal of a Hazardous Material;

J.   there are no Environmental Claims against any person whose liabilities for environmental matters, or any violation of Environmental Laws, the Seller has or may have retained or assumed contractually or by operation of law;

K.   there are no conditions or circumstances at the Property which pose an unreasonable risk to the environment or the health or safety of persons in connection with any Hazardous Material; and,

L.   the Seller has provided or otherwise made available to Buyer all environmental audits, reports, and assessments concerning the Seller and Property which Seller possesses or reasonably could have obtained.

The foregoing representations and warranties shall survive the effective date of this agreement and shall and shall accrue to the benefit of Buyer and its successors and assigns.

III.   ASSUMPTION, INDEMNIFICATION, AND WAIVER

A.   Notwithstanding any other assumption and exclusion of liabilities or obligations in this agreement, Seller assumes and agrees to pay, and to perform all necessary investigatory and/or remedial activities to Buyer's satisfaction relating to, all demands, claims, liabilities, fines, penalties, or costs ("Damages") in connection with the Property to the extent they arise from: (a) any Scheduled Condition; (b) any matter, activity, omission, event, circumstance, occurrence, Release, threatened Release, or condition that occurred or was in existence at the Property on or before the closing date, whether known or unknown; or, (c) the operation of Seller's business at the Property on or before the closing date (collectively, the "Pre-closing Conditions").

B.   Seller shall indemnify, hold harmless, defend, and hereby waives any claim for contribution against, Buyer, its partners, officers, directors, trustees, employees, and agents, and any successors to Buyer's interests in the chain of title to the Property, their partners, directors, officers, trustees, employees, and agents, for any Damages related in any way to:

1.   a Pre-closing Condition arising from:

a.   any Release, threatened Release, or disposal of any Hazardous Material at the Property, regardless of when or how discovered;

b.   the operation or violation of any Environmental Law at the Property; or,

c.   any Environmental Claim in connection with the Property; or,

2.   the inaccuracy or breach of any representation, warranty or covenant by Seller in this section of this agreement.

C.   This assumption, indemnification, and waiver shall survive the effective date of this agreement and shall be binding upon successors and assigns of Seller and shall accrue to the benefit of Buyer and its directors, officers, employees and agents, and their successors and assigns.

D.   With respect to Seller's defense obligations set forth in this paragraph, Buyer shall have the right to participate in the defense of, or at its option to assume the defense of, any action, suit, proceeding, demand, assessment or judgment brought by any party against Seller, its representatives, agents, or affiliated companies, and all of its directors, officers, employees, agents, representatives, successors or assigns.

Courtesy of Steven Humphreys, Kelley Drye & Warren LLP

APPENDIX J

ENVIRONMENTAL CONTRACTUAL PROVISIONS FOR CORPORATE TRANSACTION

Definitions

(a)   As used herein, the term "Group Company's Environmental Costs" shall mean all Environmental Costs, whether direct or indirect, known or unknown, joint or several, whenever arising (including after closing), based on, arising out of or otherwise in respect of the Group Company's assets, the Business, or property currently or formerly owned, operated, used or leased by the Group Company or its predecessors (including off-site locations) and arising out of: (i) any Environmental Conditions at, in on, under or near any such property on or prior to the closing date; (ii) the operation of the Business by the Group Company or its predecessors on or prior to the closing date; or (iii) the Group Company's alleged or actual non-compliance on or prior to the closing date with any requirements of Environmental Laws.

(b)   As used herein, the term "Environment" shall include, but is not limited to, air, land, surface water or groundwater, and any building, building interior, fixture or equipment.

(c)   As used herein, "Environmental Condition" shall mean any condition (including, without limitation, any Hazardous Substances Contamination) with respect to the Environment, whether or not yet discovered, as a result of which any person (i) could incur or has incurred, or which results in any damage, loss, cost, expense, claim, or liability to any person or property (including, without limitation, any government authority), or (ii) could or has become subject to any order or demand to remediate such condition, including, without limitation, any condition resulting from the operation of the Business or the operation of the business of any other property owner or operator in the vicinity of any leased premises or any other real property used in the operation of the Business.

(d)   As used herein, the term "Environmental Costs" shall mean all charges, damages, dues, penalties, fines, costs, amounts paid in settlement, liabilities, obligations, taxes, liens, losses, expenses and fees, including all reasonable attorneys', experts' and consultants' fees and court costs, arising under or related in any way to Environmental Laws, or relating to the protection of health, safety, or the Environment, including, without limitation, any costs and expenses relating to (i) non-compliance with Environmental Laws; (ii) assessment of environmental damage and preparation of cleanup plans and engineering and feasibility studies; (iii) remediation of the Environment and treatment or disposal of Hazardous Substances; (iv) construction of facilities to prevent the spread of, or decrease the amount of concentration of any Release of, Hazardous Substances into the surrounding Environment; (v) investigations, actions and lawsuits instituted by private parties or governmental agencies in respect of any such matter; (vi) business disruption, relocation of equipment or place of business, and lost profits resulting from the performance of environmental investigation and/or remediation activities; and/or (vii) damage caused by, and the restoration of any improvement affected by, any implementation, entry, performance, inspection, treatment, disposal, excavation, operation, or maintenance activity undertaken in order to comply with any Environmental Law.

(e)   Definition of "Environmental Law(s)": As used in this Agreement, the term "Environmental Laws" shall mean any and all present and subsequently enacted laws, common law, statutes, codes, rules, or regulations, ordinances, treaties, conventions, permits, policy statements, guidance documents and judicial decisions applicable to, affecting or relating to the protection, preservation or remediation of the environment enacted or promulgated, published, decided or required by any federal, state, provincial, county or municipal legislative, executive, judicial or regulatory authority, as the case may be, including: (1) the Comprehensive Environmental Response, Compensation, and Liability Act of 1980, as amended by the Superfund Amendments and Reauthorization Act of 1986, 42 USCA 9601 et seq., (2) Solid Waste Disposal Act, as amended by the Resource Conservation and Recovery Act of 1976, as amended by the Hazardous and Solid Waste Amendments of 1984, 42 USCA 6901 et seq., (3) Federal Water Pollution Control Act of 1972, as amended by the Clean Water Act of 1977, as amended, 33 USCA 1251 et seq., (4) Toxic

Substances Control Act of 1976, as amended, 15 USCA 2601 et seq., (5) Emergency Planning and Community Right-To-Know Act of 1986, 42 USCA 11001 et seq., (6) Clean Air Act of 1966, as amended by the Clean Air Act Amendments of 1990, 42 USCA 7401 et seq., (7) National Environmental Policy Act of 1970, as amended, 42 USCA 4321 et seq., (8) Rivers and Harbors Act of 1899, as amended, 33 USCA 401 et seq., (9) Endangered Species Act of 1973, as amended, 16 USCA 1531 et seq., (10) Occupational Safety and Health Act of 1970, as amended, 29 USCA 651 et seq., (11) Safe Drinking Water Act of 1974, as amended, 42 USCA 300 (f) et seq., (12) Pollution Prevention Act of 1990, 42 USCA 13101 et seq., (13) Oil Pollution Act of 1990, 33 USCA 2701 et seq., (14) the Atomic Energy Act of 1954 (42 U.S.C.A. 2011, et. seq.), and any rules, regulations, ordinances, permits, policy statements, guidance documents and judicial decisions enacted, issued, or promulgated, published, decided or required by or under the laws referred to in Section 2.24(a) (1)-(14) above, as well as any similar state, county or municipal statutes, codes, rules or regulations ordinances, permits, policy statements, guidance documents, and judicial decisions as the case may be.

(f)   Definition of "Environmental Permits": As used in this Agreement, the term "Environmental Permits" shall mean any and all permits, licenses, approvals, authorizations, consents or registrations required by any Environmental Laws in connection with the ownership, construction, equipping, use and/or operation of the Business or the Properties, for the storage, treatment, generation, transportation, processing, handling, production or disposal of Hazardous Substances or the sale, transfer or conveyance of the Properties.

(g)   Definition of "Hazardous Substance": As used in this Agreement, the term "Hazardous Substance" shall mean, without limitation, any flammable, explosive or radioactive materials (including without limitation any source, byproduct, or special nuclear material), radon, asbestos, urea formaldehyde foam insulation polychlorinated biphenyls, petroleum, petroleum constituents, petroleum products, methane, hazardous materials, hazardous wastes, hazardous or toxic substances or related materials, pollutants, and toxic pollutants, as defined in or which is otherwise the subject of any requirement pursuant to any Environmental Law, other than de minimis quantities of ordinary lubricating and janitorial fluids used for their intended purpose.

(h)   As used herein, "Hazardous Substances Contamination" shall mean, with respect to any premises, building or facilities, or the Environment, contamination by a Release or the presence of Hazardous Substances.

(i)   Definition of "Release": As used in this Agreement, the term "Release" shall include any "release" and/or "threat of release" as those terms are defined under any Environmental Law, including without limitation the Comprehensive Environmental Response, Compensation and Liability Act of 1980, as amended (42 USCA Section 9601, et seq.), and the regulations promulgated there under.

Representations and Warranties

Except as otherwise disclosed in Schedule _____ hereto:

(i)   Each Group Company has been and is currently in compliance with, and not subject to any potential or actual liability pursuant to, Environmental Laws and any contractual obligation relating to any Hazardous Substances or structure containing Hazardous Substances and, to the best of each Group Company's and Principal Vendor's knowledge, there are no conditions or circumstances that would either prevent the continued and uninterrupted operation of the Business in full compliance with Environmental Laws after the Closing or require additional capital expenditures in order to maintain the continued and uninterrupted operation of the business in full compliance with Environmental Laws after the Closing.

(ii)   None of the Group Companies has entered into any lease, contract, or other agreement of any type whatsoever, obligating it at any time to investigate, remove and/or remediate (or pay for the cost of investigating, removing and/or remediating) any Hazardous Substances stored, treated, generated, transported, processed, handled, produced or disposed of, by any third party on, under, near or originating from the Properties, whether the presence of such Hazardous Substances is currently known or unknown and regardless of when or how any such Hazardous Substances are discovered.

(iii)   There has been no Release, storage or treatment of any Hazardous Substance on, at, in or from the Properties or, to the best of the Group Company's knowledge, any property adjacent to or within the immediate vicinity of the Properties which through soil, subsoil, bedrock, surface water, groundwater or airborne migration could come to be located on, at, in or under the Properties.

(iv)   None of the Properties been affected by any Hazardous Materials Contamination or Environmental Condition.

(v)   There are no Hazardous Substances at, on, in or under any of the Properties contained in barrels, sumps, tanks, equipment (moveable or fixed) or other containers incorporated into any structure on the Properties, or otherwise existing thereon.

(vi)   To the Group Company's knowledge, none of the Properties is the subject of any form of notice or inquiry from any federal, state, provincial or local governmental agency or authority, any prior owner, operator, tenant, subtenant, licensee or occupant of the Properties or any owner or operator of property adjacent to or within the immediate vicinity of the Properties or any property adjacent to or within the immediate vicinity of the Property relating to any potential liability and/or compliance requirements under any Environmental Law.

(vii)   None of the Group Companies has transported or arranged for the disposal or treatment of any Hazardous Substances to or at any off-site property that is not authorized to receive such Hazardous Substances for disposal or treatment under applicable Environmental Laws or any off-site property that is designated for investigation and/or cleanup on the National Priorities List or any other similar local, provincial, state or federal list.

(viii)   All Environmental Permits necessary for the construction, equipping, ownership, use and uninterrupted operation of the Business or the Properties have been obtained and are in full force and effect and each Group Company is in compliance therewith.

(ix)   All Environmental Permits that are required to be transferred to the Purchaser's Group in order to allow the Purchaser's Group to continue to operate the Business uninterrupted after the Closing have been assigned by each Group Company to the Purchaser's Group.

(x)   To the best of any of the Group Companies' or Principal Vendor's knowledge, no event has occurred with respect to the Business or the Properties which, with the passage of time or the giving of notice, or the failure to give notice, would constitute a violation of or non-compliance with, any applicable Environmental Laws or Environmental Permits.

(xi)   There are no agreements, consent orders, decrees, judgments, license or permit conditions or other orders or directives or any federal, state, provincial or local court, or governmental entity relating to the past, present or future construction, equipping, ownership, use, operation, sale, transfer or conveyance of the Business or the Properties which require any change in the present condition of the Business or the Properties or any work, repairs, construction, containment, cleanup, investigations, studies, removal or remedial action or capital expenditures in order for the Business or the Properties to be in compliance with any Environmental Laws or Environmental Permits.

(xii)   None of the Group Companies has received written notice of any Environmental Claim against the Company nor written notice from any governmental authority nor any other person related to any actual or threatened Release or the presence of any Environmental Condition at, in, on, under or about the Properties, and no Environmental Claims are pending against any of the Group Companies;

(xiii)   None of the Group Companies has any pending or contingent liability to any Governmental Authority or other person relating to any Environmental Condition or any Hazardous Materials Contamination or violation of Environmental Laws and there are no conditions or occurrences at the Leased Premises or any off-site properties which could form the basis for any Environmental Claim against any Group Company.

(xiv)   Adequate reserves have been established on each Group Company's balance sheet to cover all of each Group Company's Environmental Costs;

(xv)   All equipment needed for the continued and uninterrupted operation of the Business without any Release of Hazardous Substances in excess of permitted or regulatory limits is in good working order and is not in need of repair other than for routine maintenance.

(xvi)   To the best of each Group Company's and the Principal Vendor's knowledge, there are no proposed or pending changes in Environmental Laws or in the Group Company's Environmental Permits that would increase the present costs of operating the Business as a result of compliance with such laws, or change any methods of operation of the Business.

(xvii)   Other than as allowed by any Environmental Permits which have been obtained by each Group Company and are in full force and effect, the operation of the Business, as presently conducted, does not involve the Release of any Hazardous Material into the air, soil, or into any stream, creek, river, lake, pond, or other body of water, or into groundwater, or into any sewer system or storm water drainage system at concentrations in excess of permitted or regulatory limits.

(xviii)   Each Group Company has made all filings with governmental authorities required by Environmental Laws in connection with the Business and there have been no failures by any Group Company to file in a timely manner any report required under Environmental Laws in connection with the Business.

(xix)   Each Group Company has disclosed and made available to the Purchaser's Group all information, including all studies, analyses and test results, in the possession, custody or control of each Group Company and its respective affiliates relating to (i) any Environmental Conditions on, under or about the Properties, and (ii) Hazardous Substances used, managed, handled, transported, treated, generated, stored or Released by the Group Company or any other Person at any time on any Properties, or otherwise in connection with the use or operation of the properties or assets used in or held for use in connection with the Business.

(xx)   The following is a complete and accurate list of all Environmental Permits required for the operation of the Business, correct and complete copies of which have been delivered to the Purchaser's Group:

Courtesy of Steven Humphreys, Kelley Drye & Warren LLP

APPENDIX K

PRO-BUYER ENVIRONMENTAL TRANSACTION AGREEMENT PROVISIONS

I.   Example Environmental Definitions

"Environmental Law" shall mean all federal, state, local and foreign statutes, regulations, ordinances and similar provisions having the force or effect of law, all judicial and administrative orders and determinations, all contractual obligations and all common law concerning public health and safety, worker health and safety, or pollution or protection of the environment, including without limitation all those relating to the presence, use, production, generation, handling, transportation, treatment, storage, disposal, distribution, labeling, testing, processing, discharge, release, threatened release, control, or cleanup of any hazardous materials, substances or wastes, chemical substances or mixtures, pesticides, pollutants, contaminants, toxic chemicals, petroleum products or byproducts, asbestos, polychlorinated biphenyls, noise or radiation, as such of the foregoing are enacted or in effect, prior to, on, or after the Closing Date.

"Hazardous Substance" means any pollutants, contaminants or chemicals, and any industrial, toxic or otherwise hazardous materials, substances or wastes with respect to which liability or standards of conduct are imposed under any Environmental Laws, including without limitation, noise, odors, radiation, petroleum and petroleum-related substances, products, by-products and wastes, asbestos, urea formaldehyde and lead-based paint.

II.   Example Environmental Representation

[Section X.x]   Environmental and Safety Matters.
Except as disclosed on [Schedule X]:

(a)   The [Company and all of its Subsidiaries][1] [is/are] in compliance and [has/have] at all times complied with all Environmental Laws.

---

[1] Terms in brackets should be conformed to meet the relevant defined terms in the particular Agreement.

(b)   The [Company and all of its Subsidiaries] [has/have] obtained, maintains and [has/have] at all times complied with, and [is/are] in compliance with, all permits, licenses and other authorizations that may be required pursuant to Environmental Laws for the occupation of [its/their] facility[ies] and the operation of the [Business], and no proceedings or other actions are pending, or to the knowledge of the [Company], threatened to revoke, cancel, limit, terminate, challenge, amend or modify any such permits, licenses or other authorizations.

(c)   The [Company and all of its Subsidiaries] [has/have] not received any written or oral notice, report or other information regarding any actual or alleged violation of Environmental Laws, or any liabilities or potential liabilities, including any investigatory, remedial or corrective obligations, arising under any Environmental Laws and relating to [it or its/any of them or their] past or present facilities or operations.

(d)   [To the Knowledge of the Seller,] none of the following exists at any property or facility owned or operated by the [Company or any of its Subsidiaries]: (i) underground storage tanks; (ii) asbestos containing material in any form or condition; (iii) materials or equipment containing polychlorinated biphenyls; or (iv) landfills, surface impoundments, or other disposal areas.

(e)   None of the Partnership or the Facility or any of their respective predecessors or Affiliates has (i) treated, stored, disposed of, arranged for or permitted the disposal of, transported, handled, or Released any Hazardous Substance so as to give rise to any material liabilities or any material investigative, corrective or remedial obligations under any Environmental Law, or (ii) either expressly or by operation of law, assumed or undertaken any material liability, including without limitation any material obligation for corrective or remedial action, of any other Person under any Environmental Laws.

[(f)   Neither this Agreement nor the consummation of the transaction that is the subject of this Agreement will result in any obligations for site investigation or cleanup, or notification to or consent of government agencies or third parties, pursuant to any "transaction triggered" or "responsible property transfer" Environmental Laws.][2]

---

[2] Use only if the Target has facilities or operations in Connecticut or New Jersey.

(g) [Neither [the Company, any of its Subsidiaries] nor any of [its/their] respective predecessors or Affiliates has manufactured, sold, marketed, installed or distributed products containing asbestos, and with respect to such entities, no basis in law or fact exists to support an assertion of any claim, action or obligation with respect to the presence or alleged presence of asbestos or asbestos-containing in any product or at or upon any property or facility.][3]

(h) The [Seller/Company] has furnished to [Buyer] all environmental audits, reports and other material environmental documents relating to the past or current properties, facilities or operations [of the Company, any of its Subsidiaries or any of [its/their] respective predecessors or Affiliates] that are in its possession or under its reasonable control.

III. **Example Retained/Excluded Environmental Liability Definition** [4]

"Excluded Environmental Liabilities" means any [Liability] or investigatory, corrective or remedial obligation, whenever arising or occurring, arising under or relating to Environmental Laws with respect to [Seller/Company], [any of their Subsidiaries] or any of their predecessor(s) or Affiliate(s), the [Acquired Assets] or any current or former properties, facilities or operations of any Seller, any of their Subsidiaries or any of their predecessors or Affiliates (including without limitation any arising from the on-site or off-site Release, threatened Release, treatment, storage, disposal, or arrangement for disposal of Hazardous Substances) whether or not constituting a breach of any representation or warranty herein and whether or not set forth on any disclosure schedule attached hereto, except to the extent, and in the proportion, that the facts or circumstances underlying such [Liability] or obligation are first created by the operation of the [Business] by Purchaser after the Closing Date.

Courtesy of Lewis T. Putman, Milbank, Tweed, Hadley & McCloy LLP

---

[3] Use only if the Target is believed to have asbestos product or premises liability.

[4] Typically used to define the scope of excluded pre-closing environmental liabilities in a asset purchase/sale transaction, but can also be modified and used to define the scope of indemnified environmental liabilities under a straight indemnity in a stock purchase/sale.

APPENDIX L

SPECIAL ENVIRONMENTAL PROCEDURES ANALYSIS

A.   Typical Buyer/Seller Positions on Special Environmental Procedures

Topic	Typical Buyer Position	Typical Seller Position
Control over corrective action	Buyer Controls	Seller Controls
"No Dig"	No	Yes
No communication with authorities	No	Yes
Incidental/consequential damages	Covered as damages	Not covered as damages
No material effect on operations	Yes	No
Consent to Institutional Controls/Engineered Barriers	Yes	No
Endpoint	No further Remediation ("NFR") Letter	Consultant sign-off

B.   Typical Resolution of Disputes Over Special Environmental Procedures

- Cost sharing/sliding scale indemnification for environmental matters—Buyer has "skin in game" so it has a financial disincentive to seek out problems subject to indemnification by Seller.

- Party not controlling gets substantial right of participation (ability to comment on reports and work plans—reasonable comments to be accepted, attend meetings, consent to material actions).

- End point = NFR, or if not available, consultant sign-off.

- No dig provision, but with exceptions for legal requirements, emergencies or future due diligence.

Courtesy of Lewis T. Putman, Milbank, Tweed, Hadley & McCloy LLP

APPENDIX M

SPECIAL ENVIRONMENTAL PROCEDURE PROVISIONS

I.   Example Special Environmental Procedure Provisions

[Section X.x]   Special Environmental Procedures.

(a)   Notwithstanding any other provisions contained in [this Agreement],[5] [Buyer][6] shall have the right to direct, manage and control, and take such actions in connection with, any Remedial Action or defense or other resolution (collectively, the "Primary Control Rights") of any claim, event or condition subject to indemnification under [the Sections relating to environmental indemnification from [Seller] under this Agreement]. In the event [Buyer] does not elect to assume Primary Control Rights, [Seller] shall have the right to assume the Primary Control Rights over the claim, event or condition. In the event that [Seller] assumes primary control rights under this [Section X.x], upon advance written notice by [Seller] to [Buyer], [Buyer] shall provide [Seller] with access to the [Real Property] reasonably necessary for [Seller] to exercise its Primary Control Rights under this [Section X.x]. [Seller] shall notify and consult with [Buyer] with respect to such matters prior to taking action and, to the extent any claim, event or condition subject to indemnification involves or requires work to be performed at the [Real Property], [Seller] shall in all material respects:

(i)   comply with all Applicable Laws (including, without limitation, Environmental Laws) and all leases related to the [Real Property];

(ii)   use the [Real Property] and perform Remedial Action in a manner that will not unreasonably interfere with or unreasonably interrupt the operations or business thereon or unreasonably

---

[5] Terms in brackets should be conformed to meet the relevant defined terms in the particular agreement.

[6] This provision places primary control over remedial activities with Buyer, which is what a Buyer will want for acquired properties. Obviously the issue of primary control is subject to negotiation between the parties, and often an indemnifying Seller retains control, subject to Buyer participation and other protections.

compromise the safety of the [Real Property] or the business or operations thereon; and

(iii)   promptly, upon completion of any phase of Remedial Action, restore any adversely affected portion of the [Real Property] to its pre-disturbed condition to the extent practicable, such that [Buyer] can continue its operations in the manner in which such operations were conducted prior to the commencement of the Remedial Action.

(b)   The Party with the Primary Control Rights shall indemnify and hold the other party and its Affiliates harmless from any Losses[7] arising from any negligent act or omission or willful misconduct in performing Remedial Action.

(c)   [Buyer] shall not conduct nor allow any other party under the control of [Buyer] to conduct any Phase II or other intrusive environmental testing and/or sampling during the [survival period of the [Seller]'s environmental indemnity], and [Seller] shall not be required to provide indemnification under [the Sections relating to environmental indemnification from [Seller] under this Agreement] with respect to environmental conditions first identified by such testing or sampling, unless such testing or sampling is (i) required by a demand, complaint, order, directive or similar enforceable request of a [Governmental Authority] directed to [Buyer] acting within the scope of its jurisdiction or authority; (ii) reasonably necessary to comply with Environmental Law; (iii) required to respond to or correct an imminent and substantial threat of a material risk to human health or the environment, provided [Buyer] uses reasonable best efforts to notify [Seller] in advance of such situation posing such imminent and substantial threat; (iv) necessary for construction specifically required to comply with "Current Good Manufacturing Practices" (as defined in 21 CFR Part 111) ("cGMP Construction"), maintenance or repair activities on the [Real Property], which construction, maintenance or repair is performed for a bona fide business purpose; (v) necessary for construction activities which are not cGMP Construction activities on the

---

[7] Losses in this context should be defined to include any consequential, incidental or special damages, including damages for lost profits or business interruptions.

[Real Property], which construction is performed for a bona fide business purpose; or (vi) necessary to respond to any reasonable due diligence request in connection with any bona fide existing or future issuance of bonds or any other bona fide financing transaction by [Buyer] or future sale of all or substantially all of the assets and business of [Buyer].[8]

(d)   With respect to any Remedial Action or other defense or other resolution of any claim, event or condition subject to indemnification or reimbursement, the party with the Primary Control Rights shall provide the party without the Primary Control Rights with a right to observe and, to the extent set forth below, participate in such matters, including a right for the party without Primary Control Rights to (i) receive, review and comment on copies of written proposals with respect to any proposed Remedial Action and the results of any sampling and analysis (including any status reports of work in progress or other submissions) or reports required to be submitted to any Governmental Authority in connection with conducting the Remedial Actions prior to submission to any Governmental Authority and/or implementation by the party with the Primary Control Rights (and the party with Primary Control Rights shall incorporate any reasonable comments of the other party with respect to the same); and (ii) attend [as an observer, but not participate in,][9] meetings with Governmental Authorities or other Persons; and in any event [Buyer], if not the Party with Primary Control Rights shall be given the right to consent to any activity that would reasonably be expected to have a material adverse impact on any [Real Property] or the operation of the Business.[10]

(e)   Each Party agrees that it shall not, and shall use its commercially reasonable efforts to ensure that each of its Affiliates shall not, directly or indirectly, communicate orally or in writing with any Governmental Authority relating to any actual or potential Environmental Liabilities for which the other Party might be responsible under this Agreement; provided that in the event [Buyer] or [Seller] believes in good faith that such communication is either (i) required by any Applicable Law (including any Environmental Law), or (ii) is otherwise required in the ordinary course of business in an emergency or exigent situation, [Buyer] or [Seller] shall be

---

[8] Typical "no dig" provision, with carve outs.

[9] Subject to negotiation.

[10] Typical mutual participation/cooperation covenant.

entitled to make such communication subject to the provisions of this [Section X.x(e)]. With respect to communication under clause (i) above, [Buyer] or [Seller], as the case may be, shall notify the potentially Indemnifying Party in advance of making such communication and shall give such other party a reasonable period of time to either make such communication itself (but in no event exceeding any timeframes for such reporting under any Applicable Law, including any Environmental Law) or to provide a written opinion of independent counsel that such communication is not legally mandated, in which event, the party providing such opinion shall agree, in writing, to indemnify, defend and hold harmless the requesting party for the failure to so communicate.[11]

(f)   Each party's obligations to conduct any Remedial Action pursuant to their obligations shall be deemed satisfied so long as the remedy (i) complies with the minimum standards enforceable under applicable Environmental Laws in effect at the time of the performance of the Remedial Action, (ii) is approved or authorized by Governmental Authorities with jurisdiction over such matters if such approval or authorization is required by applicable Environmental Laws, (iii) complies with the minimum standards set forth in the applicable leased [Real Property] lease, if any, (iv) complies with any enforceable order of a Governmental Authority, or (v) is necessary to respond to any third party claim (the "Remediation Standard"). The Indemnifying Party may use the most cost effective method of achieving the Remediation Standard including, without limitation, the use of commercial, industrial and/or other forms of non-residential cleanup criteria and the use of environmental land use restrictions or similar institutional controls to the extent that such criteria, restrictions and controls (i) are appropriate given the use of the subject property as such property was used on the Closing Date by [Seller] and (ii) do not unreasonably and materially interfere with [Buyer's] operation of the [Business] as such [Business] was operated by [Seller] on the Closing Date. The parties agree that, subject to the preceding sentence, if such environmental land use restrictions or similar institutional controls are approved or authorized by Governmental Authorities or Environmental Laws, as applicable, for use on or affecting any [Real Property], [Seller] shall obtain the prior written consent of [Buyer] (such consent not to be

---

[11] Typical provision limiting indemnitee's ability to trigger governmental action by reports to Governmental Authorities.

unreasonably withheld or delayed) for any such restrictions or similar controls, and if [Buyer] provides such consent, [Buyer] will execute any required documents and will cooperate with [Seller] in (i) obtaining any other signatures or consents required and (ii) the recording, on the applicable land records, of such environmental land use restrictions or similar controls.[12]

(g)   Without limiting any other provisions of this Agreement, [Seller's] obligation to [Buyer] under [the Sections relating to environmental indemnification from [Seller] under this Agreement] to conduct any Remedial Action shall be deemed satisfied upon the issuance of a NFA or similar sign-off issued for the benefit of [Buyer] and its successors and assigns by the Governmental Authority with jurisdiction over such matters where such governmental sign-off is required and available under Environmental Laws to document compliance with the Remediation Standard.[13]

II.   Related Definitions

"Remedial Action" shall mean all actions required to (a) investigate, clean up, remove or treat Hazardous Substances that are present or have been Released; (b) restore or reclaim the environment or natural resources with respect to such presence or Release(s) of Hazardous Substances; (c) perform remedial investigations, feasibility studies, corrective actions, closures and post-remedial or post-closure studies, investigations, operations and maintenance and monitoring with respect to such presence or a Release; and (d) prepare and submit any reports or other submissions or other responses required to be provided to or filed with any Governmental Authority in connection with any such activities and, to the extent necessary or appropriate, respond to any comments from any Governmental Authority in connection therewith; in each case to the extent any of the foregoing are necessary to achieve the Remediation Standard.

"Release" shall mean any release, spill, emission, leaking, pumping, injection, deposit, disposal, discharge, dispersal, migration or leaching of Hazardous Substances.

Courtesy of Lewis T. Putman, Milbank, Tweed, Hadley & McCloy LLP

---

[12] Typical remediation standard provision.
[13] Typical "end point" provision.